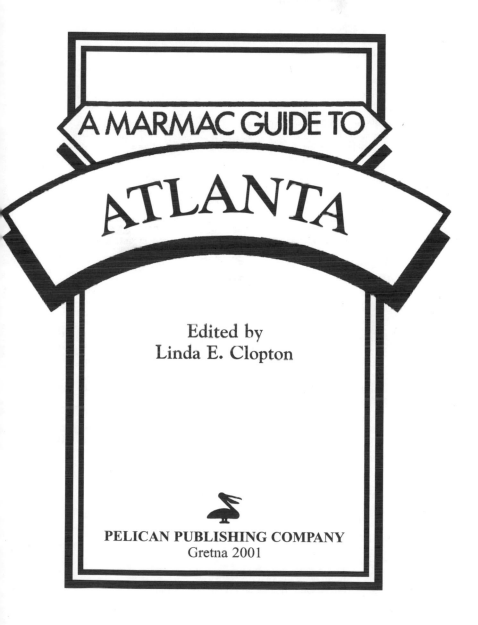

A MARMAC GUIDE TO

ATLANTA

Edited by
Linda E. Clopton

PELICAN PUBLISHING COMPANY
Gretna 2001

---

*The word "Pelican" and the depiction of a pelican are trademarks
of Pelican Publishing Company, Inc., and are registered
in the U.S. Patent and Trademark Office.*

LCN: 84-644543
ISBN: 1-56554-817-5

The Marmac Guidebook series was created by Marge McDonald of Atlanta, Georgia. As owner of a convention and sightseeing service in Atlanta for fourteen years, she learned from visitors and those relocating to Atlanta what information was important to them. She also served as president and CEO of the Georgia Hospitality and Travel Association for four years and in 1978 was named Woman of the Year in Travel by the Travel Industry Association of America.

Information in this guidebook is based on authoritative data available at the time of printing. Prices and hours of operation of businesses listed are subject to change without notice. Readers are asked to take this into account when consulting this guide.

Printed in Canada
Published by Pelican Publishing Company, Inc.
1000 Burmaster Street, Gretna, Louisiana 70053

IN LOVE
AND IN LAUGHTER

A PORTRAIT OF
ROBERT MACKIE

A MARMAC GUIDE TO

ATLANTA

CONTENTS

Foreword 7
Atlanta Past 15
Atlanta Today 19
Matters of Fact 27
Transportation 31
Lodging 40
Dining 59
Performing Arts 92
Nightlife 99
Sights 105
Visual Arts 120
Shopping 127
Sports 157
Special Events 174
Self-Guided City Tours 183
One-Day Excursions 199
New Residents 207
Special People 236
Bits and Pieces 255
Index 259

MAPS

Metropolitan Atlanta 8-9
Downtown Atlanta 10-11
MARTA Rail Stations 38
Downtown Walking Tour 184
One-Day Excursions 200
Atlanta Region Counties 225
Georgia in the USA 236

KEY TO LETTER CODE

E	Expensive	CH	Entrance Charge
M	Moderately Expensive	NCH	No Charge
I	Inexpensive		

FOREWORD

The Marmac guidebooks are designed for the resident and traveler who seek comprehensive information in an easy-to-use format and who have a zest for the best in each city and area mentioned in this national series.

We have chosen to include only what we can recommend to you on the basis of our own research, experience, and judgment. Our inclusions are our reputation.

We first escort you into the city or area, introducing you to a new or perhaps former acquaintance, and we relate the history and folklore that is indigenous to this particular locale. Second, we assist you in learning the ropes—the essentials of the community, necessary matters of fact, transportation systems, lodging and restaurants, nightlife, attractions, and the visual and performing arts. Third, we point you toward available activities—sightseeing, museums and galleries, shopping, sports, and excursions into the heart of the city and to its environs. And last, we salute the special needs of special people—the new resident, the international traveler, students, children, senior citizens, and persons with disabilities.

A key area map is placed at the opening of each book, always at your fingertips for quick reference. The margin index, keyed 1-6 and A-F, provides the location code to each listing in the book. Subsidiary maps include a downtown street map keyed 7-12 and G-L, and intown and out-of-town touring maps. A comprehensive index at the back of the book makes the Marmac guidebook a breeze to use. Please write to us with your comments and suggestions at Pelican Publishing Company, P.O. Box 3110, Gretna, LA 70054-3110. We will always be glad to hear from you.

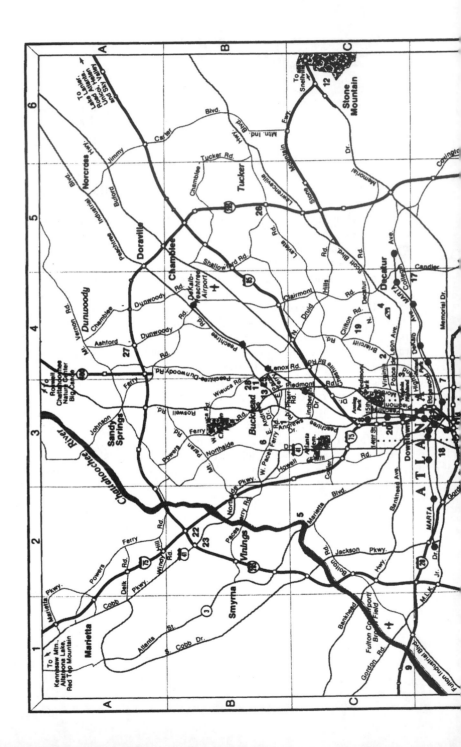

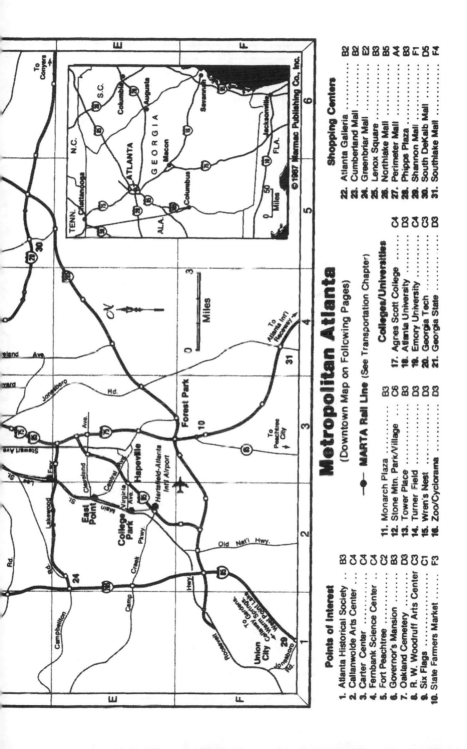

Metropolitan Atlanta

(Downtown Map on Following Pages)

━●━ MARTA Rail Line (See Transportation Chapter)

© 1987 Marmac Publishing Co., Inc.

Points of Interest

1. Atlanta Historical Society	B3
2. Callanwolde Arts Center	C4
3. Carter Center	C4
4. Fernbank Science Center	C4
5. Fort Peachtree	C2
6. Governor's Mansion	B3
7. Oakland Cemetery	D3
8. R. W. Woodruff Arts Center	C3
9. Six Flags	C1
10. State Farmers Market	F3
11. Monarch Plaza	B3
12. Stone Mtn. Park/Village	C6
13. Tower Place	B3
14. Turner Field	D3
15. Wren's Nest	D3
16. Zoo/Cyclorama	D3

Colleges/Universities

17. Agnes Scott College	C4
18. Atlanta University	D3
19. Emory University	C4
20. Georgia Tech	C3
21. Georgia State	D3

Shopping Centers

22. Atlanta Galleria	B2
23. Cumberland Mall	B2
24. Greenbriar Mall	E2
25. Lenox Square	B3
26. Northlake Mall	B5
27. Perimeter Mall	A4
28. Phipps Plaza	B3
29. Shannon Mall	F1
30. South DeKalb Mall	D5
31. Southlake Mall	F4

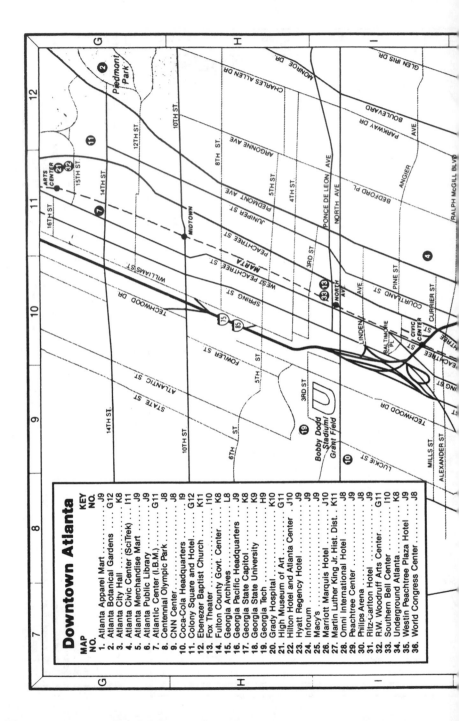

Downtown Atlanta

	KEY NO.
MAP NO.	
1. Atlanta Apparel Mart	J9
2. Atlanta Botanical Gardens	G12
3. Atlanta City Hall	K8
4. Atlanta Civic Center (SciTrek)	I11
5. Atlanta Merchandise Mart	J9
6. Atlanta Public Library	J9
7. Atlantic Center (I.B.M.)	G11
8. Centennial Olympic Park	J8
9. CNN Center	J8
10. Coca-Cola Headquarters	I9
11. Colony Square and Hotel	G12
12. Ebenezer Baptist Church	K11
13. Fox Theater	I10
14. Fulton County Govt. Center	K8
15. Georgia Archives	L8
16. Georgia Pacific Headquarters	J9
17. Georgia State Capitol	K8
18. Georgia State University	K9
19. Georgia Tech	H9
20. Grady Hospital	K10
21. High Museum of Art	G11
22. Hilton Hotel and Atlanta Center	J10
23. Hyatt Regency Hotel	J9
24. Inforum	J9
25. Macy's	J9
26. Marriott Marquis Hotel	J10
27. Martin Luther King Jr. Hist. Dist.	K11
28. Omni International Hotel	J8
29. Peachtree Center	J9
30. Phillips Arena	J8
31. Ritz-Carlton Hotel	J9
32. R.W. Woodruff Arts Center	G11
33. Southern Bell Center	I10
34. Underground Atlanta	K8
35. Westin Peachtree Plaza Hotel	J9
36. World Congress Center	J8

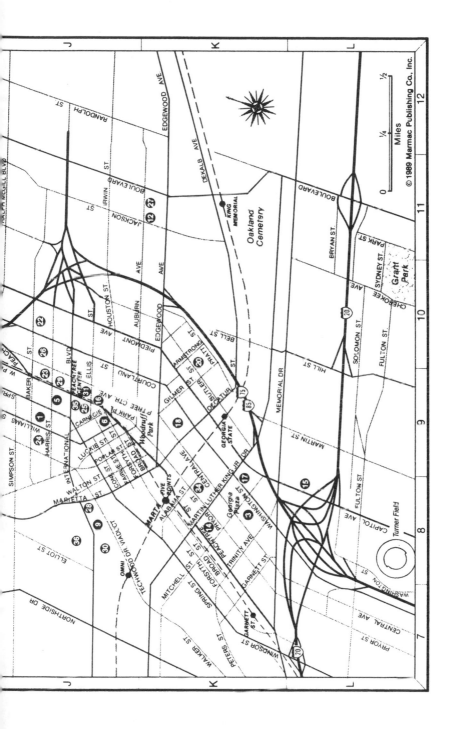

© 1989 Marmac Publishing Co., Inc.

A MARMAC GUIDE TO

ATLANTA

Atlanta Skyline

Courtesy Atlanta Convention and Visitors Bureau

ATLANTA PAST

Native American Origins

When Georgia ratified the U.S. Constitution in 1788, four-fifths of the new state was Indian territory. The Creek and Cherokee tribes were both in the Atlanta area establishing trade relationships with the first English traders from Charleston, who were selling cloth goods, hardware, and guns. Present Atlanta occupies the former site of the Indian village called Standing Peachtree, at the confluence of the Chattahoochee River and Peachtree Creek, where there was a natural fording area across the river due to the sandbar at that point. Settlements were made on the high banks of the Chattahoochee, which provided protection from flooding. The sandy flood plain was ideal for hoe agriculture, springs were abundant, the land was rich for growing corn and grain, and the river was the natural mode of transportation to other settlements. This village was on the Indian trail circuit, the Hightower Trail, which ran from Augusta, Georgia, through Madison, past Stone Mountain and just north of Dunwoody, crossing the river at Roswell, continuing to the Cherokee town of New Echota, and into northern Alabama.

Thus, the first period of Atlanta's prominence as a major crossroad and transportation center began where Indian trails and the Chattahoochee River converged.

In 1813 a Federal Militia outpost, Fort Gilmer, was established at the Standing Peachtree site to protect the state from the Creeks, who were sympathetic to the British during the War of 1812. In 1837 the Western and Atlantic Railroad extended its tracks from Tennessee into Georgia and drove a stake into the heart of a new white settlement, Terminus—Atlanta's first name, meaning "the end of the line." Just as the natural terrain had influenced the course of the Indian trails and the Indian trails had influenced the direction of the county roads and the county roads had influenced the railroad right-of-way, the railroad also helped to determine the physical configuration of streets in what, in 1850, was commercial antebellum Atlanta and is today the heart of

15

the Central Business District. Even Atlanta's new rapid transit system is determined by the city's most permanent feature, the original street pattern, and Atlanta's transportation patterns have consistently followed original environmental patterns from the pre-industrial Indians to today. Although the Creek Indians were removed from Georgia before 1830 and the Cherokees were relocated to Oklahoma in the infamous "Trail of Tears" forced march of 1835, their names and patterns of movement have been absorbed into the civilization called Atlanta, whose main street is still Peachtree Street.

The land rush for former Indian territory in the Atlanta area was stimulated even further by the rapid development of the railroad system which linked Terminus first to Tennessee in 1837, then to Marietta in 1842, and to Augusta, Georgia, three years later. In 1843 Terminus was renamed Marthasville after a daughter of Georgia's governor Wilson Lumpkin. Then, in 1845, Marthasville became Atlanta, a name associated with the town's first railroad, the Western and Atlantic. From this time to the outbreak of the Civil War, Atlanta thrived—building churches, banks, hotels, a city government, newspapers, fire departments, more railroads, new businesses and courthouses; installing gaslights; and compiling city directories. By 1862, with a population over 9,000, Atlanta was a major Confederate military post, supply hub, and hospital and relief center.

Atlanta Burns

And then the city fell. The Battle of Atlanta in the Civil War was a turning point for both the Union and the Confederacy. Atlanta had to be taken by the Federal forces because of its strategic location for the Confederacy. General William Tecumseh Sherman's Federal army of 100,000 fought its way from Tennessee to Atlanta in May 1864 following the route of the Western and Atlantic railroad. The city had prepared for siege with a 12-mile circle of formidable trenches. But Federal troops broke through from all directions, cutting the major railroad lines to Atlanta. The mayor surrendered in September and ordered civilian evacuation. General Sherman burned the city to the ground and set out on his march to the sea to take Gen. Robert E. Lee's rebel forces from their own southern flank. Atlanta, the dynamo of the Confederacy, was silenced.

But Atlantans came back undaunted to build together a New South from the ashes of destruction, a new social, economic, and political fabric. As the building process began again, out of it grew a public school system; hotels; railed streetcars; uniformed police; yet more railroads; public water works; telephones; colleges for blacks and whites, men and women; a soft drink called Coca-Cola; a public-health hospital; an opera house; three international cotton expositions; and in 1901 the first Atlanta automobile.

A New South Arises

The 20th century opened a progressive era of continued enterprise.

In the 1920s, Metro Atlanta's population soared to more than 200,000; radio stations were established; a municipal airport was begun; the Historical Society and the High Museum of Art initiated their programs; air mail was introduced; the Fox Theater, Atlanta's new movie palace resembling something from the Arabian Nights, was completed; and the present city hall was built the year the stock market crashed.

Atlanta not only survived the Depression of the 1930s—she challenged it. In 1930 Atlanta's own Bobby Jones won the grand slam of golf, and both Delta and Eastern airlines began scheduled passenger service from the city. President Franklin D. Roosevelt dedicated the first public housing in the nation next to Georgia Tech. In 1936 *Gone with the Wind*, Margaret Mitchell's best-seller during these trying times, flooded bookstores, reminding the nation of its ability to persevere by depicting earlier trauma in its history, the Civil War, and by projecting the image of Atlanta in the character of the upstart but "can-do" Scarlett O'Hara. The "burning of Atlanta" scene in the movie three years later left an indelible symbol in the national memory of a city that survived its trial by fire.

World War II was followed by the TV age. Channel 8 (now Channel 2) signed on the air in September 1948 broadcasting pro football, church services, spelling bees and other shows. In 1954 it introduced the first network in the South with Camel News Caravan. Atlanta's population had grown from 2,500 in 1850 to 331,000 a century later.

The sixties were a time of building resurgence along with social reordering. The crest of Peachtree Street was crowned with the first new building of Peachtree Center, the Merchandise Mart, and about the same time Marriott opened the first new downtown hotel in many years.

The building pace exploded in the 1970s and 1980s, driven by the metro area's unprecedented economic growth. Hotels, office towers, megastructures, and suburban malls settled on the modern urban landscape. The city's newly enlarged Hartsfield International Airport became the nation's largest—and one of its busiest. Paying homage to her past, Atlanta began lending an ear and funding to key historic preservation projects to insure that the city's history would remain a living and relevant part of her future. Her hosting of the Centennial

Olympic Games in 1996 spurred yet another flurry of building, restoration and growth, which catapulted her into the new millennium and shows no sign of stopping.

In 1868 Atlanta became the capital of the state of Georgia, only four years after the city had been leveled by Federal troops during the Civil War. Originally a backwoods Georgia trading post, first for Indians and then for colonists, Atlanta took over the leadership of the largest state east of the Mississippi. The city's official emblem is the phoenix. In Egyptian mythology it is a bird of great beauty said to live 500 years in the desert and then to consume itself by fire, rising from its ashes young and beautiful to live through another cycle. The city's governmental motto, "Resurgens," complements the phoenix symbol of renewing spirit.

ATLANTA TODAY

"This is Atlanta. This is an uncompleted city. This is the South. It is an uncompleted story."

With these words, Georgia governor Ellis Arnall predicted in 1949 Atlanta's central role in the destiny of what we now call "the Sunbelt." What even the visionary Arnall could not see in 1949 was Atlanta's eventual international status.

A Crossroads for the World

Atlanta has never seen herself as a completed city; she is constantly tempted by the future, willfully creating her own future, fascinated by what she can become. When New Hampshire surveyor Stephen Long, in 1837, drove a stake into the upland Georgia wilderness to mark the best spot for a railroad from Tennessee to link with Georgia branch lines, he pronounced the site good for "a tavern, a blacksmith's shop, a general store, and nothing else." The years have proven Long to be an excellent surveyor but an abysmal prophet. That site is now today's Atlanta, a city more than 3 million people call home.

Atlanta is unlike other Southern cities that rely on valuable natural raw resources, as does Birmingham, Alabama, with its steel industry. She is also unlike Southern port cities, such as Jacksonville, Florida, or Norfolk, Virginia. And finally, she is unlike Southern cities that exhibit the charm of colonial preservation, like Charleston, South Carolina, and Savannah, Georgia. Atlanta's uniqueness is predicated on her geographic position as the South's major crossroad, and as the marketplace of the South, the key warehousing and distribution center, the transportation hub, and the financial and communication command post for the region.

Over the years, Atlanta has invented herself so successfully, time after time, that her civic boosterism has taken on the mantle of prophecy. In 1847, when the city was no more than a scruffy, backwoods railroad town, local sawmill owner Jonathan Norcross petitioned to have the place named Georgia's state capital, a feat that made him a laughing stock—temporarily. Atlanta *was* named Georgia's capital a scant 21 years later, following the Civil War.

19

Atlanta has never been bashful about promoting herself to outsiders. As early as the 1880s the city boldly declared herself "the Gateway of the South." In 1925 the "Forward Atlanta" public relations campaign—Atlanta's voice in the roaring twenties—began to attract more business to the city. Throughout the 1960s and most of the 1970s, the Chamber of Commerce published one of the nation's earliest "city" magazines, *Atlanta*. And in the 1990s the "Vision 2020" project involved citizens in future speculation and plans for the "Big A" of the 21st century.

In 1987, Atlanta attorney, ex-football player and admitted dreamer Billy Payne launched a movement to bring the Olympic Summer Games to Atlanta, eventually. Three years later, the come-from-behind contender was awarded the 1996 Games—sooner than even Payne himself first thought possible.

In the early 1970s, the Atlanta Chamber of Commerce adopted the slogan "Atlanta—The World's Next International City." After the Olympics announcement, the slogan was quietly retired. One more prophecy had come true.

The Corporate Explosion

You are not coming to the sleepy South when you arrive in Atlanta. Although the air may be thick with the scent of magnolias and gardenias, you are coming to the regional headquarters for some 450 of the Fortune 500 companies. Delta Airlines and the Coca-Cola Company, two longtime Atlanta corporate giants, were joined in the mid-1980s by Georgia-Pacific. The 1990s added UPS and Holiday Inn Worldwide to their number when they, like Georgia-Pacific before them, relocated their national headquarters to this hospitable Southern address. The city is also becoming a magnet for national nonprofit agencies. The American Cancer Society, Boys and Girls Clubs of America, and CARE have their national offices in Atlanta.

Lockheed, one of the nation's major airplane manufacturers, is also one of Atlanta's main employers. The city is becoming a national center for communications and electronics. Scientific-Atlanta, one of the nation's leading makers of cable television equipment and earth stations, is based here. Two popular Internet service providers, Earthlink and Mindspring, merged in February 2000 and have headquarters in Atlanta. The city is also a regional hub for IBM and AT&T. Turner Broadcasting System continues its strong presence in the city. Turner's WTBS/TV reaches viewers in all 50 states, and his cable-news network (CNN), the nation's first 24-hour continuous news network, has become a major force in international journalism. The city is also a financial center for the region, as the headquarters of the Sixth District Federal Reserve Bank and the Fifth District Federal Home Loan Bank.

Identifying with Tourists

Atlanta has made a lasting commitment to another aspect of its Big Business: the convention and hospitality industry. The monuments to that commitment have literally changed the skyline of the city.

The Westin Peachtree Plaza, designed by renowned Atlanta architect John Portman, is a 73-story, mirrored cylinder with a seven-story atrium lobby, and is topped by a tri-level restaurant and lounge. The Marriott Marquis, also designed by Portman, is the city's largest hotel and one of the largest in the world. The pioneer in Atlanta's splurge of hotels is Portman's Hyatt Regency, with its full-height interior atrium and with a revolving restaurant capping the structure. The blue glass dome of the Hyatt Regency and the shining cylinder of the Peachtree Plaza are landmarks you can easily spot amid the new postmodern office towers as you enter the city. The Ritz-Carlton is a luxury hotel whose 25 stories of glass and marble grace Peachtree Street at Georgia-Pacific Plaza. (A second Ritz-Carlton has become an important center of activity in Atlanta's Buckhead area, along with Swissotel and the Grand Hyatt Atlanta.) The impressive Embassy Suites at Centennial Olympic Park gives visitors easy access to all major sports venues. Days Inn has its first downtown location next to the Apparel Mart. Add to these hotels the Hilton and Towers and the Omni in Downtown, plus Colony Square, Marriott Suites, the Wyndham, and the spectacular Four Seasons in midtown, and you will have a wide choice of hotel rooms in the core city. These hotels mark the first phase of allegiance to the visitor. Hotel and office complexes in the Buckhead area to the north and on the Perimeter encircling the city continue this development into the greater metro area.

Atlanta offers multiple options for accommodating visitors. You can find the small European-style hotel, the apartment-type hotel lodging, and suites for short-term leasing. You'll also find intimate bed and breakfast accommodations in small inns and private homes. We will see that you are aware of these special options for your special needs in the chapter on lodgings.

Atlanta's convention business is heavily dependent on four large trade facilities, as well as the meeting rooms and halls of the hotels themselves. The Georgia World Congress Center is one of the largest exhibit halls in the country. Atlanta's Merchandise Mart is the retail distribution center for the Southeast market, and the adjoining Atlanta Apparel Mart and the Atlanta Gift Mart place the city in active national competition as an apparel, fashion, and gift center. Inforum, a mart specializing in high-technology information-processing equipment, including computer, phone, and office automation systems, is also part of this complex, known as the Atlanta Market Center. All four marts were designed and developed by Portman, as was the recently expanded Atlanta Decorative Arts Center (ADAC) in Buckhead. These marts together bring hundreds of thousands of buyers and manufacturers to Atlanta each year.

In addition, the enormous Georgia Dome accommodates the largest shows and functions, along with sporting events such as Falcon football; the Atlanta Civic Center accommodates trade shows and concerts; and the Atlanta Braves play baseball at Turner Field. Next to the CNN Center, the new Philips Arena, with its state-of-the-art technology, hosts some 200 events per year, from wrestling to opera, and is home to the Atlanta Hawks (basketball) and the Atlanta Thrashers (ice hockey). Marts, hotels, restaurants, and exhibit halls, combined with professional sports and a spate of other attractions, all make Atlanta one of the major convention cities in the United States. On the outskirts, the Atlanta Exposition Center hosts the huge Don Scott Antiques Market 12 times yearly as well as the Southeastern Flower Show and other large events.

Government Center and Academic Forum

Atlanta is the locus of four systems of government: the regional center of the federal government, the capital of the state of Georgia, the seat of Fulton County and the municipality of Atlanta. One of the world's most respected medical research centers is located in Atlanta, the U.S. Public Health Service's Centers for Disease Control. South of the Central Business District you'll find Capitol Hill crowned by the gold-domed state house and the surrounding county and municipal structures. Capitol Hill is a delightful place to visit, with gardens, a state museum, restaurant, and outdoor park where you can enjoy your lunch in the arbored sunlight.

Former U.S. president Jimmy Carter maintains offices at the Carter Presidential Center, a fascinating tour less than two miles from the city's center.

Historically, Atlanta has been a thriving educational city, with more than 30 institutions granting undergraduate and graduate degrees. Atlanta University pioneered college education for blacks in the South immediately following the Civil War and is the largest consortium of

Georgia State Capitol, topped with 23-karat gold   *Courtesy Atlanta Convention and*
Visitors Bureau

predominantly black colleges and universities in the nation. Agnes Scott College began education of women in the 19th century. The Georgia Institute of Technology (Georgia Tech) opened its doors in 1888 and today attracts students from among the nation's best and brightest for programs in science and engineering. Emory University has educated a significant percentage of the South's doctors, lawyers, preachers, and teachers, and has grown in national stature with recent endowments. Georgia State University is now the second largest state university in Georgia with about 23,000 students. Oglethorpe University, Kennesaw State College, Clayton State College, and the Atlanta College of Art are among numerous other prominent Atlanta educational institutions. The city's colleges and universities keep it young and challenging. Check their musical programs, lecture schedules, and art museums for a taste of Atlanta's academic life.

Cultural Clusters

The universities and colleges contribute substantially to the total cultural environment in Atlanta through co-sponsorship of special events and joint educational endeavors. In addition, the cultural community has developed umbrella associations and centers for the visual and performing arts throughout the city to pool creative expression, financial support, and patronage. The dominant alliance is the Robert W. Woodruff Arts Center, originally erected in memory of 122 Atlanta art patrons killed in an airplane crash in Paris in 1962 and later named for the city's premier philanthropist and longtime leader of the Coca-Cola Company. The building is headquarters for the Atlanta Arts Alliance, which includes the Alliance Theatre, the Atlanta Children's Theatre, the Atlanta Symphony, and the Atlanta College of Art. The High Museum of Art building adjoins the Robert W. Woodruff Arts Center, a galaxy of cultural excitement and works.

Smaller arts centers in key neighborhoods provide access to both composite and specialized cultural activities. The Callanwolde Fine Arts Center in DeKalb County, Chastain Arts Center on the northwest side of town, King Plow Arts Center downtown, and the Arts Exchange on the near south side offer classes, performances, and exhibitions in a wide gamut of the visual and performing arts. Other arts centers, cultural programs, and organizations serve diverse groups and communities throughout the metro Atlanta area.

Transportation Hub

Atlanta's accessibility promotes education, culture, trade, and business. The city is the pivotal transportation point in the Southern region; the great railroad days which began in 1837 have been super-seded by the age of air travel. Atlanta's Hartsfield International Airport has the world's largest passenger terminal, capable of handling millions of passengers a year, with ease! A 225,000-square-foot renovation to the heart of the terminal, completed before the 1996 Summer Olympics, creates a dramatic four-story atrium, with seating areas, food court, meeting and conference space, offices, and baggage-handling area—all built over the existing airport rapid rail system.

MARTA (Metropolitan Atlanta Rapid Transit Authority) offers res-idents and visitors the South's first rapid-rail transit system. The east-west branches opened in 1979, and the first section of the north-south branch began service in late 1982. More than 50 miles were completed in the early 1990s, and it continues to expand. MARTA's rapid rail puts Atlanta's attractions within easy reach. Take a ride on the North line from Peachtree Center to the Arts Center where you can enjoy the the-ater, the museum, or the symphony. Or ride farther north to the Southeast's shopping hub—Lenox Square and Phipps Plaza. Or take a ride from Five Points station east to the historic yet cosmopolitan town of Decatur.

A Word on Climate and Dress

A temperate climate adds to Atlanta's appeal for visitors and for both family and corporate relocation. Atlanta's high altitude of 1,050 feet above sea level distinguishes it from most Southern cities which experience long summer heat and humidity. Atlanta's elevation allows for four distinct seasons, with spring and fall competing for the glory of climatic exuberance. Cold spells are short-lived, although Atlanta occasionally is surprised by an inch of snow or an ice storm in the win-ter. During the summer's hottest spells, the city averages less than three consecutive days above 90° F. You will find Atlanta informal in attire most of the year, but residents don black tie and flowing gowns for spe-cial social occasions. Coats and ties for men are the general rule, although casual dress is accepted now in most establishments. Spring and summer call for lightweight clothes, and a jacket to wear in the air-conditioned buildings. Autumn requires a light jacket or sweater out-doors. Carry a coat in winter. According to the former mayor Ivan Allen, one of Atlanta's best attractions is her "altitude." Atlanta's weather makes a pleasant course throughout the entire year.

The City's People

Who are Atlantans? The population of the metro area is more than 3 million. The local population continues to diversify. Southern accents, Midwestern drawls, and Northern twangs mix with foreign accents as newcomers move South because of job transfers, business opportunities, and personal preferences. Old Atlanta families have a tradition of community service and a refreshing open social acceptance of newcomers from other parts of the country and the world. The city is experiencing moderate, steady immigration, especially among Hispanics and Asians, and more recently from eastern Europe, but Atlanta is not characterized by the rigid ethnic neighborhood pattern prevalent in some large urban areas.

The Atlanta black community is today a powerful political and economic force in the city. Birthplace and burial place of civil rights leader Dr. Martin Luther King, Jr., Atlanta has always been on the forefront in attracting and respecting diversity in its population. With the city's openness to social change and the election of a string of strong black mayors starting in the 1970s, and with its concentration of the largest per dollar investment in black business in the South, Atlanta is an attractive home for new black residents.

Who are Atlantans? They are the residents of the New South. You will find Atlanta a fine city to visit and revisit. Southerners have traditionally "gone to Atlanta" to shop, to eat, to see the Braves or Hawks or Falcons play, to attend theater and symphony performances and other cultural events, to seek their business fortunes, to be entertained, to meet people from all over the world, and to find new expressions of Southern living. Now visitors from far beyond the South feel the lure of Atlanta, touchstone of the New South and a true international city.

MATTERS OF FACT

AAA—Auto Club South, travel information (800) 222-1134; north Buckhead office (404) 843-4500.

Ambulance Service—911; TTY call (404) 525-1122. Or check telephone Yellow Pages under "Ambulance."

Area Codes, telephone—404, 770, 678. You must dial the area code when making a local call in metro Atlanta, but do not dial 1 first except for 800, 877 and 888 toll-free numbers.

Babysitter—Check with your hotel desk.

Calendar of Events—*Atlanta* Magazine monthly, *Creative Loafing* weekly and the Weekend Saturday supplement of the *Atlanta Journal-Constitution* for local daily events.

Climate—Annual Averages

Rainfall: 47.14 inches (120 cm).

Snow or ice: 1.6 inches (4 cm).

Clear days: 220.

Days above 90° F (32° C): 21.

Days below 32° F (0° C): 60.

Driest month: October.

Rainiest month: March.

Coldest month: January.

Warmest month: July.

Wind: Northwest prevailing.

Dentist—Northern District Dental Society Referral Service, (770) 270-1635 (8:30 am-4:45 pm weekdays), or the Georgia Dental Assn., (404) 636-7553.

Doctor—Medical Association of Atlanta Information and Referral Service, (404) 881-1714 (9 am-12 noon Mon.-Fri.) or (800) 265-8624; or contact hotel doctor or visit nearest hospital—see below.

Emergency Mental Health Services—Fulton County, (404) 730-1600; DeKalb County, (404) 892-4646; Cobb and Douglas Counties, (770) 422-0202; Gwinnett County, (770) 985-2494; Clayton County, (770) 996-4357; TTY (all metro counties), (404) 525-1122.

Emergency Rooms—911. Or check telephone Yellow Pages under "Emergency Minor Medical Facilities and Services."

Fire—911.

Foreign Auto Service—Automotive Service and Repair (C4), 2099 Liddell Dr., (404) 881-9400. Or check telephone Yellow Pages under "Automobile Repair & Service."

Hospitals—Grady Memorial Hospital (K10), 80 Butler St., SE; (404) 616-4307. Atlanta Medical Center (I12), 303 Parkway Dr., NE; (404) 265-4000. Northside Hospital (B4), 1000 Johnson Ferry Rd., NE; (404) 851-8000. Piedmont Hospital (C3), 1968 Peachtree Rd., NW; (404) 605-5000. Or check telephone Yellow Pages for additional listings.

Lawyer—Atlanta Bar Association Referral Service, (404) 521-0777.

Legal Aid—(404) 524-5811.

Libraries, Public—Atlanta-Fulton County Central Branch (J9), 1 Margaret Mitchell Square, NE; (404) 730-1700. Other counties: Clayton, (770) 478-7120. Cobb, (770) 528-2320. DeKalb, (404) 370-3070. Gwinnett, (770) 822-5361. Paulding, (770) 445-5680. Rockdale, (770) 388-5040.

Local Liquor Laws—Liquor age requirements—must be 21, no sale of alcoholic beverages in stores, or before 12:30 pm in bars and restaurants, on Sunday.

MARTA bus and rail—Call 6 am-11 pm weekdays; 8 am-10 pm weekends for schedules; (404) 848-4711. Web site www.itsmarta.com

Newspapers—*The Atlanta Journal-Constitution, Atlanta Daily World, Clayton News-Daily, Creative Loafing* (weekly). Other weeklies include *Atlanta Business Chronicle* and *Atlanta Press.*

Pets—Atlanta Humane Society; (404) 875-5331. Leash Law in effect.

Pharmacy, 24-hour: CVS in Emory Village (C4), 1554 North Decatur Rd., (404) 373-9208.

Poison Control—(404) 616-9000; (404) 616-9287 (TTY).

Police—911 or (404) 525-1122.

Population—3.8 million.

Post Office—Downtown Branch (K8), 400 Pryor St.; 1-800-275-8777.

Radio Stations—

FM—

WABE (90.1) Classical/NPR.

WALR (104.7) Adult Contemporary/Oldies.

WAMJ (107.5) R&B Oldies.

WAZX (101.9) Regional Mexican Talk/Music.

WBTR (92.1) Country.

WCHK (100.1) Oldies.

WCKS (102.7) Hot Contemporary Adult.

WCLK (91.9) Jazz.

WEKS (92.5) Country.

WFOX (97.1) Rock and Roll Oldies.

WGST (105.7) News/Talk.

WHTA (97.5) Hip Hop.
WJZF (104.1) Jazz.
WKHX (101.5) Country.
WKLS (96.1) Album Rock.
WMJE (102.9) Hot Adult Contemporary.
WMKJ (96.7) Adult Contemporary.
WNNX (99.7) New Rock.
WPCH (94.9) Light Rock Favorites.
WREK (91.1) Alternative/Diverse.
WRFG (89.3) Listener Supported/Alternative.
WSB (98.5) Soft Rock.
WSTR (94.1) Contemporary Hits.
WVEE (103.3) Urban Music.
WVFJ (93.3) Christian.
WWEV (91.5) Adult Contemporary Christian.
WYAY (106.7) Young Country.
WZGC (92.9) Classic Rock and Roll.

AM—
WAEC (860) Contemporary Christian Talk/Urban Gospel.
WAFS (920) Christian.
WAOK (1380) Traditional Gospel.
WATB (1420) Multicultural Music/Talk.
WAZX (1550) Mexican Talk/Music.
WCHK (1290) Oldies.
WCNN (680) News.
WDWD (590) Disney: Children's Programs.
WDUN (550) News/Talk/Weather.
WGFS (1430) Oldies/Sports.
WGGA (1240) Adult Standard Music.
WGKA (1190) Christian Talk/Gospel.
WGST (640) News/Talk/Ga. News Network.
WGUN (1010) Information/Inspiration.
WKGE (1160) Classic Country.
WKHX (590) Country.
WLBA (1130) Spanish/Music.
WLTA (1400) Christian Talk.
WNIV (970) Christian Talk.
WPBS (1050) Christian.
WPLO (610) All Spanish 24-hour.
WQXI (790) Sports Talk.
WSB (750) News/Talk.
WSSA (1570) Talk.
WTJH (1260) Gospel.

WXLL (1310) Full Gospel.

WWWE (1100) Mexican Music/Talk/Sports/Christian.

WYZE (1480) Black Gospel.

Senior Citizens—American Association of Retired Persons, (404) 888-0077.

Social Services—United Way Information and Referral Service, (404) 527-7200.

State Patrol—(404) 624-6077.

Tickets—Ticketmaster, (404) 249-6400.

Time—(770) 455-7141.

Time Zone—Eastern Standard (Daylight Savings plus 1 hour from April through October).

Tourist Information—Atlanta Convention and Visitors Bureau, (404) 521-6688; Georgia Department of Industry, Trade and Tourism, (770) 535-5757.

Traffic Laws, State—Right turn allowed on red light, except where posted. Headlights must be switched on when it is raining.

Traveler's Aid—(404) 817-7070.

TV—ABC Channel 2; CBS Channel 46; NBC Channel 11; PBS Channels 8 and 30; TBS Channel 17; FOX Channel 5; Warner Brothers Channel 36.

Weather—(770) 455-7141.

TRANSPORTATION

Atlanta has been the hub of Southeastern transportation since its official founding in the railroad era. The city now stars as the air capital of the Southeast. The following information will assist you in traveling to Atlanta by air, highway, rail, and bus and in getting around the metro area.

TO ATLANTA

Air

Atlanta's Hartsfield International Airport (E3) boasts the world's largest passenger terminal and is one of the busiest airports in the world. The airport combines efficiency of land use in its relatively small site with both heightened fuel efficiency and maximum productivity, to handle more than 78 million passengers annually.

The airport is located ten miles south of the central city near the southern metro communities of College Park, East Point, Hapeville, and Forest Park. The airport site is in the convenient triangle formed by I-85, I-75, and I-285, with the airport exit on I-85.

The complex consists of the connected North and South terminals, five domestic concourses, an International Terminal and the spectacular "Concourse E" to handle international passengers, as well as an underground transit mall. Signs, color codes, audio instructions, and space design guide you to your destination point. Remember, the space in between the concourses accommodates two jumbo jets. Allow 15 to 20 minutes to proceed from gate to concourse to transit mall, then, via underground train or people-mover, to terminal and baggage claim. Concessions and amenities are located in the new atrium area on the main level, on the two connecting bridges of the terminals, and on each concourse. A full-service restaurant, open 24 hours, is located on the eastern bridge.

The new airport atrium, completed in time for the 1996 Olympics, revolutionized the appearance of the main terminal area. Its location, directly over MARTA's rapid rail surface transportation facility, is convenience itself. The four atrium levels include a food court, fine dining, auto rental and other amenities, as well as space for offices, meeting facilities, and baggage handling. The airport's general information number is (404) 530-6830. Contact individual airlines directly—see below.

Atlanta has nonstop air service to many international destinations, including Puerto Rico, Great Britain, Holland, Belgium, France, Germany, Italy, Japan, Korea, China, and Mexico. Nationally, airlines operating out of the Atlanta airport have flights to hundreds of cities, including Honolulu and Anchorage.

Airlines Serving Atlanta (with reservation and information telephone numbers)

Aeromexico www.aeromexico.com . . . . (800) 237-6639
Air ALM . . . . (800) 327-7230
Air Canada . . . . (800) 776-3000
Air Jamaica . . . . (800) 523-5585
Air Tran www.airtran.com . . . . (770) 994-8258
American Airlines www.aa.com . . . . (800) 433-7300
America West . . . . (800) 235-9292
ASA Atlantic Southeast Airlines . . . . (404) 765-2000
Austrian Airlines . . . . (800) 843-0002
British Airways www.britishairways.com . . . (800) 247-9297
Cayman Airways . . . . (800) 422-9626
Continental www.continental.com . . . . (800) 523-3273
Corporate Airlines . . . . (800) 555-6565
Delta Air Lines . . . . (404) 765-5000
Frontier www.frontierairlines.com . . . . (800) 432-1359
Korean Air . . . . (800) 438-5000
Lufthansa www.lufthansa-usa.com . . . . (800) 645-3880
Midway Airlines . . . . (800) 446-4392
Midwest Express www.midwestexpress.com . (800) 452-2022
Northwest Airlines/KLM www.nwa.com . . . (800) 225-2525
ProAir . . . . (800) 477-6247
Sabena . . . . (800) 955-2000
Swissair . . . . (800) 221-4750
TWA www.twa.com . . . . (800) 221-2000
United Airlines . . . . (800) 241-6522
USAirways . . . . (800) 428-4322
Vanguard Airlines . . . . (800) 826-4827

Ground Services To and From the Airport

Atlanta Airport Shuttle. At Airport South Terminal Ground

Transportation area. Leaves airport every 15-20 minutes to major downtown hotels, Buckhead, and Decatur. Cost: $12 to downtown, $18 to Buckhead and Decatur. Call (404) 525-2177. Leaves hourly for Cobb County (Windy Hill Rd.) and Roswell Station (Holcomb Bridge Rd. at Georgia 400). Cost: $22 to Cobb Co.; $24 to Roswell. Call (404) 524-3400.

MARTA Rail. The MARTA Airport rail station is located inside between the North and South terminals. Trains leave every 8 minutes for Downtown and other destinations on the MARTA line (every 10-15 minutes on Saturdays and Sundays). Departures begin about 4:30 am M-F, 4:45 Sat. and 5:12 Sun. Trains run until 1 am. Fare is $1.50. When taking a MARTA train to the airport, be sure the train is marked "Airport." Not all trains on the South Line go to the airport.

Taxi. Atlanta's taxis at the airport are a mixed bag of independent operators and name cabs. Cabs line up at the airport taxi stand. The approximate fare from the airport to Downtown is $18 plus tax plus additional per passenger.

Aircraft Rental and Charter

At DeKalb-Peachtree Airport (B4) in northeast Atlanta (770) 936-5440, call **Epps Aviation** (770) 458-9851; or **Helicopters, Inc.** (770) 454-6958.

At Gwinnett County Airport call **GeorgiaJet** (770) 603-2623.

At McCollum Field in Cobb County call **AvTech** (770) 422-2345.

At Fulton County Brown Field call **Raytheon Aircraft Services** (404) 699-9264.

Automobile

Five interstate highways intersect in Atlanta. Georgia interstates are maintained in excellent driving condition.

I-85 runs northeast to southwest from South Carolina to Alabama.

I-75 runs northwest to southeast from Tennessee to Florida.

I-20 runs east to west from South Carolina to Alabama.

The fourth interstate circles the city, is approximately 12 miles from the central city, and is designated I-285, "the Perimeter."

The fifth interstate, I-695, links I-75 near Stockbridge, south of Atlanta, to the eastern portion of I-285.

A sixth key transportation artery, GA 400, runs from the city's Buckhead area through the north Atlanta suburbs, past Lake Lanier and into the north Georgia mountains.

We recommend calling your hotel or destination point when you reach I-285 to ensure accurate exit directions from the interstates. Since Atlanta interstates have both right and left lane exits and compulsory lane exits, specific travel directions coming into the city are very helpful.

Bus ————————————————————————————————

Greyhound and Southeastern Stages have terminals in downtown Atlanta.

Greyhound (J9), 232 Forsyth St., (404) 584-1738. For Greyhound reservations call (800) 231-2222.

Southeastern Stages is at 226 Alexander St., NW, (404) 874-2741.

Rail ————————————————————————————————

AMTRAK (800) 872-7245. Brookwood Station (C3) is at 1688 Peachtree St., NW, three miles north of the central city. The AMTRAK-operated "Crescent" provides the only regularly scheduled passenger service through Atlanta, the evening train leaving for Washington and New York and the morning train departing for New Orleans. Check current schedules.

AROUND ATLANTA

Auto Rental ——————————————————————————

Rental cars are available by the day, week, or longer. Rental locations include the airport and most major hotels. Major credit cards expedite the procedure. An International Driver's License is usually valid for car rental in Atlanta. Ask when you call. As prices vary we suggest you call around to check rates that will suit your travel needs.

Armada Van Rental . . . . (770) 994-9929
Avis Rent-A-Car . . . . (800) 831-2847
Budget Rent-A-Car . . . . (404) 530-3000
Dollar Rent-A-Car . . . . (404) 766-0244
Enterprise Rent-A-Car . . . . (800) 736-8222
Hertz Rent-A-Car . . . . (800) 654-3131
National Car Rental . . . . (800) 227-7368
Thrifty Car Rental . . . . (800) 367-2277

For others see Yellow Pages under "Automobile Renting."

Chauffeured Limousine Service:
Carey Executive Limousine . . . . (404) 223-2000
Davis Limousine Service . . . . (404) 524-3413
Vintage City Limo Service, Inc. . . . . (404) 870-0746

Private Car

Atlanta's city streets follow the ecological, curving patterns of the early Indian trails and railroad routes. The hills and winding streets add to the beauty of this tree-lined garden city, but can also add confusion to the traveler or newcomer who anticipates a rigid rectangular layout of the city. Streets sometimes change names at intersections so advance directions are advised. Major north-south arteries are Peachtree Street and Piedmont Road. Major east-west corridors are Memorial Drive on the south side, North Avenue and 14th Street in Midtown, and West Paces Ferry Road on the northside. Most of these major streets have a comfortable volume and flow of traffic (even during rush hours), although traffic is extra heavy when the Atlanta Braves play a home game.

The interstates I-75, I-85, and I-20 intersect within the city and also with the Perimeter interstate I-285, making all quadrants of the city and outlying areas accessible to the visitor. The intersection of I-85 and I-285 is known to local commuters as "Spaghetti Junction," but is officially named the Thomas B. Moreland Interchange. This junction is one of the largest interstate intersections in the nation, with 15 bridges in one intersection.

During rush hours, 7-9 am and 4-6:30 pm, the interstate traffic moves slowly but steadily, in and out of the city. Trucks are not permitted on I-75 and I-85 inside the Perimeter except by special permit for deliveries. Because of the speed and convenience of "crossing town" on the expressways, Atlantans use them extensively. With our trusty map and an adventurous spirit you too can traverse metro Atlanta by either surface streets or interstate.

There is ample parking in downtown Atlanta, mainly in parking lots. Always carry sufficient change to cover maximum prepayment at some lots. Many downtown restaurants have complimentary parking with lunch and dinner, so be sure to inquire about this benefit. When necessary, have your parking ticket validated by the restaurant or store before you leave.

In case of emergencies or need for assistance:
AAA (Auto Club South) . . . . (800) 222-4357
Atlanta Police . . . . 911 or (404) 658-6666
State Patrol . . . . (404) 624-6077

Public Transportation

MARTA (Metropolitan Atlanta Rapid Transit Authority) is the city's public transit system. It operates 154 public bus lines throughout metro Atlanta and a rapid-rail system. If your destination is on a MARTA route, we recommend MARTA's reliable and swift service. MARTA has been named the safest bus system in North America (for a population area of one million) by the American Public Transit Association 15 times in the past 20 years.

Buses and trains sport a rainbow logo of blue, yellow, and orange. The rail system is an ever-expanding system, with new stations being added every year. The North/South Line includes stops at the airport, Peachtree Center, the Civic Center, Midtown, the Arts center, Lenox, Chamblee and Sandy Springs. The East/West Line includes stops at Avondale, Inman Park, Georgia State University, the CNN Center, and Hightower. The two lines intersect at Five Points in downtown Atlanta. A ride on the MARTA rail system will give you a panoramic view of the city.

On weekdays, trains run every 8 minutes during the day, every 10 minutes in the evenings, and shut down between 1 and 5 am. Maps are available in the stations. On Saturdays, the trains run every 10 minutes. On Sundays, trains run every 15 minutes, day or evening.

Each MARTA rail station offers unique space design and lively art. Like the airport, Atlanta's rapid-transit structures are sights to see in themselves.

Bus stops are marked with concrete pillars or MARTA signs. For schedules and maps of bus routes call MARTA information (404) 848-4711, 6 am to 11 pm weekdays, 8 am to 10 pm weekends and holidays, or click on www.itsmarta.com on the Internet.

Fare for both bus and rail is $1.50, payable by tokens or exact change (no pennies). Transfers are free. Tokens can be bought at MARTA stations or at all Ride Stores. The "Transcard" for unlimited rides on both bus and rail costs $12 per week, or $45 per month, valid from the first of the month, and is also available at Kroger and scores of other locations in Fulton and DeKalb counties. Half Fare Cards are available to Seniors (65+) or persons with disabilities. Out-of-towners in groups of 15 or more may order Visitor's Passes 15 business days in advance. Cost is $6 for 1-day pass, increasing $1 a day up to $12 for a 7-day pass.

Cobb Community Transit (CCT) runs buses that link suburban Cobb County to Atlanta's MARTA line. The buses run along the county's five major traffic corridors and connect at the Marietta Transfer Station. They deliver passengers to MARTA's Arts Center line. The fare on CCT buses is $1.25. Transfers between MARTA and CCT are free. CCT buses run Mondays through Saturdays. Times vary by route.

MARTA is Atlanta's bus and rapid rail system

For schedule information, call (770) 427-4444 from 6 am to 8 pm weekdays and 7 am to 8 pm Saturdays.

Taxi

Taxicabs line up at all major hotels. They are difficult to hail, so we suggest a phone call. Numerous taxi companies have listings in the telephone Yellow Pages. Several companies serve the entire metro area. Other companies specialize in specific neighborhoods or quadrants of Atlanta.

Cost is $2.90 plus $1.40 per mile, plus $1 each additional passenger, plus 7% sales tax.

Approximate fares
Airport—Downtown, $18-20
Lenox—Downtown, $12-15
I-285/Perimeter Mall—Downtown, $20

A few suggested cab companies:
Checker Cab (404) 351-1111
Buckhead Safety Cab (404) 233-1152
Yellow Cab (404) 521-0200

Tours

Several companies now offer daily sightseeing tours of the city and attractions near the city. Call for time and tours or check at your hotel. **American Sightseeing Atlanta**, (404) 233-9140; **Helicopters, Inc.**, (770) 454-6958; **Inshirah Horse Drawn Carriages**, (404) 523-3993.

For group tours only, we recommend **Atlanta Arrangements, Inc.**, an excellent special guide service available seven days a week, with multilingual guides available. Call (404) 262-7660 weekdays between 9 am and 5 pm.

Atlanta Preservation Center offers guided tours in Atlanta's historic districts. These are ongoing March through November with no reservation required but will be canceled in case of rain except for the Fox Theater tour. No tours on legal holidays. In addition to the Fox Theater, several historic neighborhoods are toured, including Ansley Park, Druid Hills (featured in *"Driving Miss Daisy"*), Inman Park, historic Downtown, and the Sweet Auburn/MLK District. Free for APC members, $5 for non-member adults, $4 for seniors and students. Group tours available by reservation. Call (404) 876-2041. Most walking tours last 1-1 1/2 hours.

Walking

The habitual walker who enjoys a few hours seeing the city on foot will find this a rewarding way to view many Atlanta attractions. We recommend the daylight hours for walking and taxi service during the evening. An excellent downtown starting point is Five Points at Woodruff Park. From there you can walk in all directions returning to the park or proceeding north to the Arts center in Midtown. A downtown walking tour is included in the SELF-GUIDED CITY TOURS chapter.

LODGING

The meeting center of the Southeast is also the prime innkeeper of the region. Atlanta's hotels, motels, and alternate accommodations are the contemporary resting places for both the first-timer and the repeat traveler to this busy city.

Atlanta has been a leader in new lodging concepts at both ends of the hospitality market. The city's unusual skyline is a remarkable testament to that fact. Architect John Portman revolutionized the look of large luxury hotels worldwide with his atrium and dramatic cylindrical hotel architecture, which he pioneered and perfected in Atlanta; the late Cecil Day founded the Days Inn economy motel chain in Atlanta offering clean, no-frills lodging for the budget-minded traveler; Ritz-Carlton with its downtown and Buckhead locations is an Atlanta-owned hotel company; and Holiday Inns Worldwide calls Atlanta its corporate home. Atlanta's hotel development continues unabated as Portman and other developers and chains add new hotels. Meanwhile, small hotels have sprung up and old ones have spruced up.

Most national and international hotel chains serve the Atlanta area in multiple locations, and there is a place for every visitor in every price range, offering a variety of services and facilities, including alternatives such as the increasingly popular bed-and-breakfast program, short-term leasing, living suite accommodations, home exchange, and a small selection of campgrounds in the metro area. To complete the picture, we list a selection of nearby resort hotels. Our selective listings will help you find the lodging of your choice.

Remember, the code letters directly after the name reference each hotel or motel to the maps at the beginning of the book, giving you the section location of the lodging within the city.

In most hotels, children under 12 stay free with parents. During weekends, holidays, and off-seasons, some hotels and resorts offer bargain package visits at greatly reduced rates. Many also give AAA, AARP, government/military and corporate discounts.

The following key is used to indicate pricing:
E   Expensive, more than $100 per double room per night
M   Moderate, $70 to $100
I   Inexpensive, less than $70

40

The listings are in three subsections: conventional lodgings—hotels and motels, alternative lodgings including campgrounds, and resorts.

HOTELS AND MOTELS

BEST WESTERN GRANADA SUITE HOTEL (H11), 1302 W. Peachtree St. NW, Atlanta 30309; (404) 876-6100. M to E. This lovely hotel was originally built as an apartment building in 1924. Completely renovated in 1988, this European-style hotel offers 103 apartments, suites, and rooms. Guests are served complimentary Continental breakfast each morning. A complimentary bar is available Mon-Thu from 5 to 7 pm. Guests have health club privileges at the Atlanta Athletic Club. A complimentary shuttle service expands the convenience of this wonderful location.

BEVERLY HILLS INN (C3), 65 Sheridan Dr., NE, Atlanta 30305; (404) 233-8520. E. A former apartment house in the Buckhead residential area has been transformed into a European-style bed-and-breakfast inn. The 18 units are decorated with period furniture and have natural wood floors and balconies. Breakfast is served in the Garden Room or on the patio. Fine restaurants are nearby.

CHESHIRE MOTOR INN (C4), 1865 Cheshire Bridge Rd., Atlanta 30309; (404) 872-9628. I. Modern, well-maintained motel between Downtown and Buckhead. Adjacent to popular *Colonnade Restaurant*.

COMFORT INN, M to E, offers moderately priced lodging at several Atlanta locations, including Atlanta Airport (E2), 4820 Massachusetts Blvd., College Park, (770) 996-0000; Buckhead (B3), 2115 Piedmont Rd., NE, (404) 876-4365; and Downtown (J8), 101 International Blvd., NE, (404) 267-0051. For information on other Comfort Inns in the metro area and worldwide, and for reservations, call (800) 228-5150.

COURTYARD BY MARRIOTT. M to E. The Courtyards are small hotels designed around a landscaped courtyard. Amenities include king-size beds, a hydro-therapy pool, meeting rooms, a restaurant, and lounge. A few locations are listed here. Call toll-free (800) 321-2211 for others.

Courtyard by Marriott—Atlanta Airport North (E2), 3399 Interstate Blvd., Hapeville; (404) 559-1043.

Courtyard by Marriott—Atlanta Airport South (E2), 2050 Sullivan Rd., College Park; (770) 997-2220.

Courtyard by Marriott—Cumberland Center (B2), 3000 Cumberland Cir., NW, Atlanta; (770) 952-2555.

Courtyard by Marriott—Executive Park (C4), 1236 Executive Park Dr., NE, Atlanta; (404) 728-0708.

Courtyard by Marriott—Medical Center (A4), 5601 Peachtree-Dunwoody Rd., NE, Atlanta; (404) 843-2300.

Courtyard by Marriott—Perimeter Center (A4), 6250 Peachtree-Dunwoody Rd., Atlanta; (404) 393-1000.

Crowne Plaza Ravinia (A4), 4355 Ashford-Dunwoody Rd., NE, Atlanta 30346; (770) 395-7700. 492 rooms and suites. Indoor pool, outdoor Jacuzzi, sauna, health club, two restaurants—*Cafe Ravinia* and *La Grotta*; Ivories lounge. This beautiful suburban hotel is in the heart of the thriving Perimeter Center commercial/retail/residential area of north DeKalb County. Executive services, including free faxing and photocopying, are available for business travelers. The Crowne Plaza Club Level, on the top floor, offers complimentary Continental breakfast and cocktail-hour hors d'oeuvres, along with free daily newspapers.

DAYS INN. Founded by the late Cecil Day of Atlanta, Days Inn hotels and lodges are designed for families and business travelers who seek quality accommodations at cost-effective rates.

Days Inn Downtown (J10), 300 Spring St., Atlanta 30303; (404) 523-1144. M *to* E. 267 rooms, across from the Merchandise Mart and Apparel Mart.

Days Inn Peachtree St. (I10), 683 Peachtree St., Atlanta 30308; (404) 874-9200. M *to* E. Across from the Fox Theatre, in the Midtown theatre/dining/entertainment area and the Midtown Historic District.

Days Inn Sandy Springs (A3), off I-285, 5750 Roswell Rd., Atlanta 30328; 252-5782. M. Modern, comfortable guest rooms in the busy corporate, retail, dining, and entertainment area of Sandy Springs.

Numerous other Days Inn facilities are located throughout the metro Atlanta area. In Atlanta, for reservations and information worldwide on Days Inns of America or Days Lodges, call (800) 325-2525.

DOUBLETREE GUEST SUITES ATLANTA GALLERIA (B2), 2780 Whitley Rd., NW, Atlanta 30339; (770) 980-1900. M *to* E. At the juncture of I-75/I-285 near Cumberland Mall in Cobb County. The ultra-modern Doubletree has 155 spacious guest rooms, first-class dining, and numerous other amenities.

DOUBLETREE SUITES ATLANTA (A4), 6120 Peachtree-Dunwoody Rd., NE, Atlanta 30328; (770) 668-0808. M *to* E. This pioneer in suite hotels continues to set standards with spacious suites, fine dining, and exceptional service. Visitors receive freshly baked chocolate chip cookies upon check-in.

EMBASSY SUITES HOTELS. Five metro area locations: (A2), Atlanta Galleria area, 2815 Akers Mill Rd., Cobb County, Atlanta 30339, (770) 984-9300; (A4), Perimeter Center, 1030 Crown Pointe Pkwy., Atlanta 30346, (770) 394-5454; (B3), Lenox Square, 3285 Peachtree Rd., Atlanta 30326, (404) 261-7733; (E2) Atlanta Airport, 4700 South Port Rd., College Park 30337, (404) 767-1988; (D3), Centennial Olympic Park, 267 Marietta St., Atlanta 30313, (404) 223-2300. *E*. All accommodations are deluxe two-room suites, with separate living room/dining room and kitchen.

EVERGREEN HOTEL AND CONFERENCE CENTER (C6), One Lakeview Dr., Stone Mountain 30086; (770) 879-9900. *M-E*. A 48-acre resort and conference center, Evergreen is nestled among the pines and hardwoods across the lake from Stone Mountain. Amenities include an excellent restaurant, two lounges, indoor and outdoor pools with Jacuzzis, tennis courts, and jogging trails. Hotel guests have access to all activities of Stone Mountain Park—golf, swimming, fishing, boating, bicycling, hiking, ice skating, and picnicking. The conference center offers 45,000 square feet of meeting space, including a complete business center. Located 30 miles from the airport, 16 miles from Downtown.

FAIRFIELD INNS BY MARRIOTT. In order to provide quality lodging at economical prices, Marriott has created Fairfield Inns, an excellent option for travelers who want clean, well-managed, no-frills lodging. Toll free (800) 228-2800. *M*.

(B5), Northlake, 2155 Ranchwood Dr., NE, Atlanta; (770) 491-7444.
(A1), 2191 Northwest Pkwy., SE, Marietta; (770) 952-9863.
(E2), 2451 Old National Pkwy., College Park; (404) 761-8371.
(A6), 3500 Venture Pkwy., Duluth; (770) 623-9300.

FOUR SEASONS HOTEL ATLANTA (G11), 75 Fourteenth St., NE, Atlanta 30309; (404) 881-9898. *Very E*. This is the place where Europe and the New South meet, in a European-concept megabuilding that is hotel, office tower, apartments, condominiums, and penthouses all in one. You will not find lodgings more opulently Continental than this hotel's 244 rooms and 18 suites. You will, of course, find a fully equipped health club and pool, business services, meeting rooms, and a spectacular grand ballroom. Seasonal New American cuisine is available in *Park 75*, and pets receive royal treatment, including homemade dog biscuits and beluga caviar on the Pet's Gourmet menu.

THE GEORGIAN TERRACE (C3), 659 Peachtree St., Atlanta 30308; (404) 897-1991. *Very E*. The only Atlanta hotel listed on the National Register of Historic Places, this elegant building stands directly across from the Fox Theater and just a few blocks from the Margaret Mitchell House and Museum and the Woodruff Arts Center. It has newly renovated one-, two-, and three-bedroom luxury suites, pool and two restaurants. Breakfast buffet.

GRAND HYATT ATLANTA (B3), 3300 Peachtree Road, Atlanta 30305; (404) 365-8100 or (800) 233-1234. *E.* You'll find 440 luxury guest rooms in this stunning post-modern high-rise that is one of Atlanta's newest luxury hotels. *Cassis* restaurant serves dishes influenced by the South of France, while *Kamogawa* presents authentic Japanese cuisine. Meeting facilities accommodate 10 to 2,000 and the Hyatt is a popular spot for local charity functions. Guests will find an executive business center, a health club, a sauna, and an outdoor pool.

HAMPTON INNS. An award-winning national chain serving budget-minded travelers features free local calls, free Continental breakfast, free in-room movies. Kids stay free with parents. Eight Atlanta locations. Call (800) 426-7866 for reservations in Atlanta and nationwide. *M.*

HAWTHORNE SUITES HOTEL (B2), 1500 Parkwood Cir. off Powers Ferry Rd., Atlanta 30339; (770) 952-9595. *E.* Offering roomy suites in a park like atmosphere, this hotel provides complimentary Continental breakfasts, whirlpool and spa, and tennis courts. A relaxed and beautifully landscaped home away from home with the Chattahoochee River Recreation Area only a short walk away.

THE HIGHLAND INN (C4), 644 N. Highland Ave., Atlanta 30306; (404) 874-5756. *I to M.* Located in the Poncey-Highland area near the Carter Presidential Center, this old European-style hotel was renovated for the Centennial Olympics and hosted the Japanese television contingent. Artists, punkers, and middle-class renovators share the eclectic neighborhood.

HILTON HOTELS. This premier international hotel company has impressive Atlanta credentials. Hilton hotels are stationed in downtown Atlanta, on the Perimeter I-285 next to Northlake Mall, off I-75 and Windy Hill Road, on Peachtree Industrial Boulevard in Norcross, and the newest near the airport, each a luxury accommodation in the respective areas. Room reservations worldwide (800) 445-8667.

ATLANTA AIRPORT HILTON & TOWERS (E3), 1031 Virginia Ave., Atlanta 30354; (404) 767-9000. *M-E.* Hilton's newest Atlanta location, this 17-story hotel offers the best of everything. Facilities and amenities include 503 beautifully appointed guest rooms with suites available, two restaurants, two lounges, indoor and outdoor swimming pools, a health club with Nautilus equipment, whirlpools and saunas, and lighted tennis courts. The 30,000-square-foot meeting and banquet space includes a complete business center designed for the business traveler.

Atlanta Hilton & Towers-Downtown (J10), 255 Courtland St., NE, Atlanta 30303; (404) 659-2000. E. The gleaming-white downtown Hilton Hotel is an imposing trylon with the Hilton logo a signal mark in the urban skyline. Inside, the atrium lobby is alive with flowers, sculpture, and inviting seating and meeting spaces, bordered by a promenade of gift shops. On this level is the Garden Terrace restaurant, downstairs is the world-known *Trader Vic's* restaurant, and atop the hotel is the famous Russian restaurant, *Nikolai's Roof*, plus a glittering disco lounge. This Hilton also offers resort-style facilities including two lighted tennis courts, a health club, and an outdoor jogging track and swimming pool. Foreign languages are spoken in this showcase luxury hotel of 1,224 rooms. The top three floors are designated the Towers—very special luxury lodging. The separate Towers lobby has a living-room atmosphere with help-yourself Continental breakfast, afternoon snacks, and a fully stocked bar available for guests' pleasure and convenience on the traditional honor system. A full-time concierge is on duty for personal attention and for immediate check-in and check-out. Suites available.

Hilton Atlanta Northeast 5993 Peachtree Industrial Blvd., Norcross 30092; (770) 447-4747. E. To visitors in the Norcross area, this beautiful hotel offers nearly 300 rooms. Other amenities include a restaurant, two lounges, an indoor-outdoor swimming pool, and complete health club facilities with sauna, Jacuzzi, and exercise equipment.

Hilton Atlanta Northwest (A2), 2055 South Park Place, Atlanta 30339; (770) 953-9300. M-E. At the intersection of I-75 and Windy Hill Road, another first-class Hilton is available for travelers in the northwest metro area. This Hilton offers an indoor-outdoor swimming pool and Jacuzzi, a lounge, and a restaurant, the *Gulf Street Grill*. Club level suites available.

HOLIDAY INNS. I-E. Whether you're looking for budget-minded accommodations or luxurious suites, this well-established chain will meet your expectations for excellent lodging. All properties have restaurants, pools, and entertainment. With numerous locations, Holiday Inn serves the entire metro Atlanta area. Call 1-(800) 327-0200 to ask for a Holiday Inn or Holiday Inn Express in the location you desire. A sampling is listed here.

Holiday Inn-Downtown (J9), 101 International Blvd., Atlanta 30303; (404) 524-5555.

Holiday Inn Select-Atlanta Airport South (E2), 4669 Airport Blvd., College Park 30337; (404) 763-8800.

Holiday Inn Select Perimeter/Dunwoody (B4), 4386 Chamblee-Dunwoody Rd., Chamblee 30341; (770) 457-6363.

Holiday Inn Select Atlanta/Decatur Conference Plaza (C4), 130 Clairmont Rd., Decatur 30030; 371-0204.

Holiday Inn Midtown North (C3), 1810 Howell Mill Rd. off I-75, Atlanta 30318; (404) 351-3831.

HOLIDAY INN EXPRESS HOTELS feature the same Holiday Inn quality with limited services for budget-minded travelers. Free Continental breakfast. *I-M.*

Holiday Inn Express-North Avenue (D5), 244 North Ave., NW, Atlanta 30313; (404) 881-0881.

Holiday Inn Express Stone Mountain (C6), 1790 E. Park Place Blvd., SW, Stone Mountain 30087; (770) 465-8847.

Holiday Inn Express Smyrna (B2), 1200 Winchester Pkwy., SE, Smyrna 30080; (770) 333-9910.

Holiday Inn Express Galleria Centre (B2), 2855 Springhill Pkwy., Smyrna 30080; (770) 435-4990.

HOWARD JOHNSON HOTELS. *I-E.* Howard Johnson's hotels are represented in Atlanta at several locations. Nationwide reservations are toll free (800) 446-4656.

Howard Johnson-Atlanta Airport (E10), 1377 Virginia Ave., Atlanta 30344, (404) 762-5111.

Howard Johnson Suites-Downtown (J10), 330 Peachtree St., NE, Atlanta 30308; (404) 577-1980.

HYATT REGENCY ATLANTA (J9), 265 Peachtree St., Atlanta 30303 (Downtown in Peachtree Center); (404) 577-1234 or toll free (800) 233-1234. *Very E.* This hotel with its soaring lobby started the international trend in open-atrium hotel design. The lobby is a thrilling place to meet for business, a social date, or sightseeing. Three restaurants, three cocktail lounges, and an outdoor pool with a Jacuzzi are among the pleasures here for hotel guests to choose.

HYATT REGENCY SUITES PERIMETER NW (A2), 2999 Windy Hill Rd., Marietta 30067; (770) 956-1234. *E.* Here you'll find 200 luxurious suites, an outdoor pool and a sauna, as well as a convenient restaurant and lounge.

LENOX INN (B4), 3387 Lenox Rd., NE, Atlanta 30326; (404) 261-5500. *M.* This attractive inn, across from Lenox Square, is a pleasant motel for out-of-town shoppers. Amenities include a restaurant, *The Black Bear*, pool, and tennis courts.

MARRIOTT HOTELS. In the 1960s, the Marriott Corporation established its first hotel in downtown Atlanta, signaling the beginning of Atlanta's blossoming hotel development. Building on its reputation for quality management and guest services, Marriott has continued to grow and expand in and around Atlanta and has become a leader in the city's booming hotel industry. Today, the Marriott's downtown location, the Atlanta Marriott Marquis, is the city's largest hotel and one of the largest in the country.

In addition to Marriott and Marriott Suite hotels, Atlanta is home to Courtyard Hotels, Fairfield Inns, and Residence Inns, all operated by Marriott. For Marriott reservations, call toll free (800) 228-9290. See separate listings for other property reservations.

Atlanta Marriott Northwest (A2), 200 Interstate North Pkwy., Atlanta 30339; (770) 952-7900 or toll-free (800) 228-9290. (Off I-75 at Windy Hill Rd. exit.) M-E. Marriott's Interstate North hotel, with its entry drive of rolling hills, features a restaurant and lounge, indoor-outdoor pool, tennis courts, and a health club.

J.W. Marriott at Lenox (B3), 3300 Lenox Rd., NE, Atlanta 30326; (404) 262-3444. This 371-room hotel is a hub of activity in the Lenox Square-Phipps Plaza shopping area. A restaurant, bar and lobby lounge cater to guests' comfort and a full health club, sky lit indoor pool, concierge services, and business center anticipate the needs of families and business travelers. Meeting space includes a grand ballroom that is a popular site for large functions.

Atlanta Marriott Gwinnett Place (A5), off I-85 North, 1775 Pleasant Hill Rd., Duluth 30096; (770) 923-1775. I-E. In the heart of Gwinnett County's rapidly expanding business and retail zone, the Marriott has 426 guest rooms, an indoor-outdoor pool, a variety of dining, a lounge with entertainment, lighted tennis courts, a health club, and other deluxe amenities.

Atlanta Airport Marriott (E2), 4711 Best Rd., College Park 30337; (404) 766-7900 or toll free (800) 228-9290. E. Located at I-285 and I-85, the Marriott is the giant of the airport hotels with 638 rooms and 24 suites, two restaurants, three lounges, and live entertainment. Recreational amenities include indoor-outdoor swimming pools, tennis courts, a weight room, and health club. Weekend package plans are available.

Atlanta Marriott Norcross (A5), 475 Technology Pkwy., Norcross 30092; (770) 263-8558. I-E. Five minutes north of I-285's exit 23 in rapidly growing Gwinnett County, the Marriott Peachtree Corners is part of Technology Park, a landscaped preserve with 75 high-tech research and development firms. The 224-room full-service hotel has a casual restaurant, lounge, meeting facilities, indoor heated pool, hydrotherapy pool, sauna, and health club.

Atlanta Marriott Marquis (J10), 265 Peachtree Center Ave., Atlanta 30303; (404) 521-0000. Very E. Designed by renowned Atlanta architect John Portman, the Marriott Marquis opened in 1985 and is Atlanta's largest hotel. In the spectacular sky lit atrium, 13 illuminated glass elevators deliver guests to the far corners of the 46-story complex.

This awe-inspiring yet hospitable hotel is located downtown. Many businesses and attractions are within walking distance. Hotel amenities include four restaurants, four lounges, an indoor-outdoor pool, a health club, a sauna, a whirlpool, valet parking, shopping, and concierge service. Business services are also available. Small pets allowed.

Marriott Perimeter Center (A4), 246 Perimeter Center Pkwy., Atlanta 30346; (770) 394-6500. E. (Off Ashford-Dunwoody Rd. exit from I-285.) Being situated next to Perimeter Center is a plus for this hotel. Sports facilities include lighted tennis courts, an indoor-outdoor swimming pool, a sauna, and a hydrotherapy pool.

MARRIOTT SUITES HOTELS. These all-suite properties provide guests with separate living rooms, marble baths, and in-room refrigerators. Other hotel amenities include indoor-outdoor pools, restaurants, and health clubs with saunas. Toll free (800) 228-9290.

Marriott Suites Atlanta Midtown (G11), 35 14th St., Atlanta 30309; (404) 876-8888.

OMNI HOTEL AT CNN CENTER (J8), 100 CNN Center, Atlanta 30335; (404) 659-0000 or toll free (800) 241-5500. E. The hotel is modern European elegance, with large abstract paintings, marble floors, and oriental vases. The design tone is complemented by a partly European, multilingual staff and the gourmet restaurant, *Prime Meridian*. The Omni Hotel is integrated into the Philips Arena, the World Congress Center, a convenient shopping mall, and office buildings that house the studios and offices of Cable News Network (CNN).

POST CORPORATE APARTMENTS. (770) 434-6494 or toll free (800) 643-POST. If you're planning to stay a month or more, Post Corporate Apartments offer a luxurious, spacious and homey alternative to hotel rooms. These apartment complexes, known for their high standards and spectacular landscaping, are available at 15 locations throughout the north Metro area. Linens and housewares are furnished and maid service is available. All apartments come equipped with color TV and every complex has an outdoor pool, tennis courts, and fitness center.

QUALITY INN-Downtown (J9), 89 Luckie St., Atlanta 30303; (404) 524-7991 or toll free (800) 228-5151. M. A small, personal downtown hotel, the Quality Inn was completely remodeled in 1997. Three blocks from Centennial Olympic Park, it sits directly across from the Rialto Center for The Performing Arts. It has a multilingual staff and serves a deluxe continental breakfast. The Quality Inn offers quiet, refined lodging especially attractive to international visitors who enjoy the personal touch. Some 30 restaurants are within easy walking distance.

RAMADA INNS. *I-M.* This moderate-price motel chain is known for cleanliness, good management, and strategic location. Toll-free (800) 282-2222. A few are listed here.
Ramada Inn Atlanta Airport South (F2), 1551 Phoenix Blvd. and I-285, College Park 30349; (770) 996-4321. *I-M.* Conveniently located in the airport area, Ramada Inn Airport South provides for corporate meetings with the *Phoenix* restaurant and the lounge *Sam's Place.* Added amenities are a swimming pool and free transportation to the airport.
Ramada Plaza Atlanta Airport (E2), 1419 Virginia Ave., Atlanta 30337; (404) 768-7800 or toll free (800) 476-1120. Free shuttle bus service to Atlanta Airport. Pool, restaurant, and lounge with entertainment.

RAMADA INN AND CONFERENCE CENTER, (C3), 418 Armour Circle, NE, Atlanta 30324; (404) 873-4661 or toll free (800) 282-2222. Convenient to Midtown, Downtown, Buckhead. Guests enjoy the pool, the restaurant, *Fountain Court Café,* and the *Reflections* lounge.
Ramada Inn Atlanta Six Flags (C1), 4225 Fulton Industrial Blvd., Atlanta 30336; (404) 691-4100. *I-M.* This modern 229-room chain motel, with pool, restaurant, and lounge, is convenient for those visiting Six Flags Over Georgia theme park, and conducting business in Fulton Industrial Park. Toll free (800) 272-6232.

RESIDENCE INNS BY MARRIOTT. These small hotels provide guests with a residential setting, perfect for extended stays. Amenities include fully equipped kitchens in every room, Continental breakfast in the lobby, and outdoor pools. Toll free (800) 331-3131. At last count there were 13 Metro Atlanta locations. Here are a few: (B1), Cumberland, 2771 Hargrove Rd., SE, Smyrna, (770) 433-8877; (A3), Perimeter West, 6096 Barfield Rd., NE, (404) 252-5066; (B5), Perimeter East, 1901 Savoy Dr., Chamblee, (770) 455-4446; (B3), Buckhead, 2960 Piedmont Rd., NE, (404) 239-0677; (H11), Midtown, 1041 W. Peachtree St., NE, (404) 872-8885; (E2), Airport, 3401 International Blvd., Hapeville (404) 761-0511; and Windward, 5645 Windward Pkwy. West, Alpharetta (770) 664-0664. M.

REGENCY SUITES HOTEL, (H11), 975 West Peachtree at Tenth St., Atlanta, GA 30309; (404) 876-5003. M. This all-suites hotel offers Midtown convenience adjacent to a MARTA rapid rail station.

RENAISSANCE HOTEL—Concourse, (E2), One Hartsfield Centre Parkway, Atlanta 30354; (404) 209-9999. M-E. This impressive hotel in the airport area has an elegant lobby, 404 rooms and suites, and an array of amenities including a health club, game room, indoor pool, sauna, and the Renaissance Club level with open bar and 24-hour concierge.

RENAISSANCE ATLANTA HOTEL—Downtown (I10), 590 W. Peachtree St., NW, Atlanta 30308; (404) 872-8046. *E.* Guests enjoy equal convenience to Downtown and Midtown and a perfect location for Georgia Tech football visits in this hotel with its 504 first-class guest rooms (including four suites with private balcony swimming pools). Large meeting and banquet facilities, two restaurants, a cocktail lounge, and a business center round out the impressive list of amenities.

THE RITZ-CARLTON (800) 241-3333. *E.* The Ritz-Carlton is now an Atlanta corporation. Introduced here in 1983, the Ritz-Carlton hotels are sited in two of Atlanta's prime locations, Downtown and across from Lenox Square.

Ritz-Carlton, Atlanta (J9), 181 Peachtree St., NE, Atlanta 30303; (404) 659-0400. *E.* The Ritz-Carlton brings old-fashioned opulence to the heart of the city, dressing its ultra modern comfort in mahogany, marble, and fine art. Rooms and suites are tailored to executive clientele as well as individual and international travelers seeking Old World elegance, impressive amenities, including two restaurants and a lounge, and attentive service.

Ritz-Carlton, Buckhead (B3), 3434 Peachtree Rd., NE, Atlanta 30326; (404) 237-2700. *E.* The Ritz-Carlton, a contemporary, upscale hotel, has three restaurants, two lounges, and proudly overlooks the South's honored Lenox Square-Phipp's Plaza shopping area. This dramatic luxury hotel with its handsome scalloped tower includes an executive health spa, sun deck, and multiple services and facilities for business conventions and social groups. The cuisine in the *Ritz Carlton Dining Room* is renowned. Make a reservation for the luxurious High Tea.

SHERATON HOTELS. *M-E.* The Sheraton Hotel company has a respected history of fine lodging here and abroad. Expect to find good restaurants and swimming pools in all locations along with personal attention. Toll free (800) 325-3535.

Sheraton Colony Square Hotel (G12), Fourteenth and Peachtree Sts., NE, Atlanta 30361; (404) 892-6000. *E.* The Colony Square Hotel is in the Midtown section of Atlanta, only a few miles from Downtown and from Buckhead. The hotel is situated on the southern end of a beautiful modern complex of office towers, condominiums, retail mall, and restaurants, and stands diagonally across from The Robert W. Woodruff Arts Center. The gracious restoration neighborhood of Ansley Park adjoins the northern flank, and the dramatic postmodern office buildings of Midtown lie to the north, south, and west. The fine Southern Conference Center is available with comprehensive business services.

Sheraton Gateway Atlanta Airport Hotel (E2), 1900 Sullivan Rd., College Park 30337; (770) 997-1100. *E.* The Sheraton Gateway's 400 guest rooms are complemented by a choice of restaurants, bar with entertainment, health club, pool, and direct connections to a major convention center.

Sheraton Suites Galleria (A2), 2844 Cobb Parkway SE, at I-75 Atlanta 30339; (770) 955-3900. *E.* In bustling Cobb County, 278 suites.

STONE MOUNTAIN INN (C6), P.O. Box 775, Stone Mountain Park Hwy. (78 East), Stone Mountain 30086; (770) 469-3311. *M.* Enjoy this lovely small motel in the Southern-plantation style, and the surrounding facilities and attractions of Stone Mountain Park. Swimming pool, tennis courts, golf course, and the lake and its beach await the sportsman, business person, and vacationer. The daily buffet at the Stone Mountain Inn restaurant is superb.

SWISSOTEL ATLANTA (B3), 3391 Peachtree Rd., NE, Atlanta 30326; (404) 365-0065. *Very E.* In the popular Buckhead area, this elegant, ultra modern hotel affords easy access to Lenox Square and Phipps Plaza. Pets are allowed. Enjoy fine dining at the *Palm Restaurant* or at numerous other restaurants in the area.

TERRACE GARDEN INN (B3), 3405 Lenox Rd., NE, Atlanta 30326; (404) 261-9250. *M-E.* The Terrace Garden Inn, across from Lenox Square shopping center and one block from Phipps Plaza, is a contemporary hotel combining informality and sophistication. The cafe allows superb Continental dining overlooking a waterfall and flower garden. The lounge is spacious and inviting, swimming and tennis is available, and courtesy transportation to Lenox, Phipps, and Buckhead is available for guests.

THE WESTIN PEACHTREE PLAZA HOTEL (J9), 210 Peachtree St., NW, at International Blvd., Atlanta 30303; (404) 659-1400. *E.* One of downtown Atlanta's most recognizable landmarks, the 73-story Peachtree Plaza soars over Peachtree Street like a colossal glass spacecraft. The hotel's public areas offer numerous secluded seating areas for conversation and drinks. The *Savannah Fish Company*, at street level, and *The Sundial*, a steak specialty restaurant that is the hotel's revolving 73rd floor, are very good. Guest rooms have panoramic views of downtown and the city's maze of freeways. Connected to the Atlanta Merchandise Mart and Macy's department store by enclosed walkways.

WYNDHAM GARDENS HOTEL (B2), 2857 Paces Ferry Rd., Atlanta 30309; (770) 432-5555. *E*. The glamorous Wyndham Garden, in suburban Vinings, is a convenient address for shopping, dining, and entertainment in the Cumberland Mall/Galleria area of Cobb County, and popular with those doing business at corporate headquarters that have proliferated hereabouts in recent years. The hotel has 150 deluxe guest rooms, a health club, tennis courts, restaurants, and lounges with live entertainment.

WYNDHAM GARDEN HOTEL BUCKHEAD (B3), 3340 Peachtree Rd., Atlanta 30326; (404) 231-1234. *E*. A medium-size hotel in the Buckhead area near the intersection of Piedmont and Peachtree roads. It is part of the Tower Place complex of office tower and mall, which is convenient to Lenox Square and Buckhead. The service is especially attentive; expect the nice touch of a complimentary newspaper and turned-down beds. *Savannah's* is an excellent hotel restaurant, and guests enjoy the conviviality of *Beauregard's Lounge*.

WYNDHAM GARDEN HOTEL PERIMETER NORTH (A3), 800 Hammond Dr., NE, Atlanta 30317; (404) 252-3344. *M-E*. This 143-room pink stucco hotel features a restaurant and lounge, an indoor-outdoor pool, an exercise room and spa, and 1,800 square feet of meeting space. Other hotel amenities include room service, valet service, guest laundry, and free parking. A pleasant and comfortable place to stay in North Atlanta.

WYNDHAM ATLANTA HOTEL (J9), 160 Spring St., NW, Atlanta 30303; (404) 688-8600. *E*. The location of this hotel is central to Downtown, across from the Greyhound terminal, and within a block of Peachtree Center and the Apparel and Merchandise Marts. Facilities include a restaurant, a lounge, and pool.

WYNDHAM GARDEN HOTEL MIDTOWN ATLANTA (J9), 125 10th St., Atlanta 30309; (404) 873-4800. *E*. In the midst of the Midtown area's theaters, restaurants, entertainment and corporate headquarters, the Wyndham Midtown is a contemporary gem, with 191 beautifully appointed guest rooms, an indoor pool and health club, and the comfortably chic *Juniper Street Cafe*.

UNIVERSITY INN AT EMORY (C4), 1767 N. Decatur Rd., NE, Atlanta 30307; (404) 634-7327. *M-E*. Despite its unassuming façade, this motel offers comfort and convenience, primarily to visitors to Emory University and Emory Hospital. It's also near the CDC, Fernbank Museum of Natural History, and Decatur. Includes a Continental breakfast. Ask about discounts, especially for hospital-related visits.

ALTERNATIVE LODGING

Bed-and-Breakfast Accommodations ———

Bed-and-Breakfast Atlanta (C3), 1608 Briarcliff Rd., Suite 5, Atlanta 30306; (404) 875-0525 or toll free (800) 967-3224. *I-E.* The British bed-and-breakfast tradition in lodging has come to Atlanta. More than 100 carefully chosen, meticulously inspected homes, guest houses and inns, many of them close to the downtown business area, others in lovely suburban communities, offer a private guest room with bath and Continental breakfast. The Bed-and-Breakfast organization brings the visitor who wishes to stay in a private home together with homeowners interested in housing guests overnight. Transportation accessibility, language needs, and attitudes about pets and smoking are all taken into consideration in matching host and guest. This is a person-to-person opportunity for Atlanta visitors.

Fallin Gate (L10), 381 Cherokee Ave., SE, Atlanta 30312; (404) 522-7371. *M.* This 1895 Victorian cottage in Historic Grant Park is ideally situated for a visit to see the pandas, Lun Lun and Yang Yang, at Zoo Atlanta. Also convenient to historic Oakland Cemetery, Turner Field, and the Cyclorama.

Gaslight Inn Bed & Breakfast (C4), 1001 Saint Charles Ave., NE, Atlanta 30306; (404) 875-1001. *M-E.* Three bedrooms and three suites in this lovely 1913 craftsman two-story home. Voice mail in all rooms. Short walk to popular Virginia-Highland area, Atlanta's SoHo, where you'll find great restaurants and unique shops. The inn is about halfway between downtown Atlanta and Decatur.

The Marlow House of Marietta/Atlanta (A1), 192 Church St., Marietta 30060; (770) 426-1887. *M.* Bed-and-breakfast lodgings are available in this lovely Victorian home near the restaurants and shops on Marietta's historic town square. The Marlow House is furnished with period antiques and oriental rugs. Prices include a Continental breakfast served in the dining room.

Shellmont Inn (J9), 821 Piedmont Ave., Atlanta 30308; (404) 872-9290. *M to E.* A splendid two-story Victorian home, built in 1891, has been given new life as a charming bed-and-breakfast inn. Near Midtown's eclectic array of restaurants, shops, and entertainment, the inn is a showcase of antiques, art works, stained and beveled glass, and gleaming hardwood floors. Look for the carved shell motif throughout. Three guest rooms are in the main house; a suite with a bedroom, separate living room, and kitchen is in the adjacent carriage house. Continental breakfast is included.

Sixty Polk Street (A1), 60 Polk St., Marietta 30064; (770) 419-1688 or toll free (800) 845-7266. M *to* E. This French-Regency Victorian home is a five-minute walk from Marietta Square. This charming home is on the National Register of Historic Places and is furnished with antiques and quality reproductions.

The Stanley House (A1), 236 Church St., Marietta 30030; (404) 426-1881. M. This four-story Victorian bed-and-breakfast lodge was originally built as the summer home for Woodrow Wilson's aunt. It is beautifully furnished with antiques and reproductions reminiscent of the turn-of-the-century period. The house has been operated as a bed-and-breakfast since 1985. The downstairs public rooms are available for parties. Rates include a full breakfast.

Woodruff Bed and Breakfast Inn (H11), 223 Ponce de Leon Ave., Atlanta 30308; (404) 875-9449 or toll free (800) 473-9449. M *to* E. This 1906 Victorian home, built by a prominent Atlanta family, is located conveniently in Midtown near fine restaurants and entertainment. Every room has a private bath. A full Southern breakfast is served to all guests.

Campgrounds

Atlantans have a number of campgrounds that provide rest and relaxation in a natural setting within an hour's drive from the city. Camping travelers can reverse this flow—come into the city at their leisure and then return to their campsite for lodging. We list three well-designed and -managed camping areas for your consideration. Rates are nominal.

Lake Lanier Islands Authority, 6950 Holiday Rd., Buford, GA 30518; (770) 932-7270 or toll free (877) 444-6777. *I.* Lake Lanier is managed by the U.S. Army Corps of Engineers and has 306 campsites for tents and trailers in the coves and on the points of this magnificent recreational lake. Every site has a picnic table and grill. Full hook-ups are available. Lake Lanier is northeast of the city; take I-85 north to GA 365, exit 2 onto Friendship Rd.

Red Top Mountain, 653 Red Top Mountain Rd., SE, Route 2, Cartersville, GA 30120; (770) 975-0055. *I.* This campground is 1 1/2 miles east of I-75; take the Red Top exit. Red Top has 92 campsites, four of them reserved for RVs. There are rental cottages in the park, plus a swimming beach, boating ramp and dock, and water sports. Full hook-ups available. Check in at the lodge or visitor's center.

Stone Mountain Park (C6), P.O. Box 778, Stone Mountain, GA 30086; (770) 498-5710 or toll free (800) 385-9807. *I.* This 500-site lakeside campground puts you within easy access of all the attractions and activities at Stone Mountain Park. Full hook-ups are available. See SIGHTS chapter.

Colleges and Youth Hostels

The **Atlanta International Youth Hostel** (H11), 223 Ponce de Leon Ave., Atlanta 30308; (404) 875-2882. *I*. Affiliated with Hostels America and Hostels Europe, this facility is three blocks from the Fox Theater and also near the Krispy Kreme Doughnut Co. The hostel's goal is to help promote world peace. It caters primarily to college students and other people visiting Atlanta to volunteer with non-profit groups such as Habitat for Humanity or as part of an educational program. Some 90 beds are available in small dormitory arrangements. Free coffee and, of course, doughnuts.

Georgia Institute of Technology (H9), 871 McMillan Street, Atlanta 30332; www.conference.gatech.edu or call (404) 894-2469. During the summer only, Georgia Tech rents rooms very inexpensively to groups of 25 persons or more with some kind of educational agenda. Linens are available but don't expect maid service. Available late May-early August. Restaurants and grocery on campus, or eat at one of the many restaurants in adjacent Midtown.

Paschal's Motor Hotel (D3), 830 Martin Luther King, Jr., Dr., SW, Atlanta 30314; (404) 577-3150. *I*. Paschal's has been serving the black community and visitors on the south side for many years. During the school year, it serves Clark-Atlanta University as a dormitory, but from June through August, its rooms are available to tourists at reasonable rates. Amenities include a restaurant and lounge, an outdoor swimming pool, and free parking.

Villa International, 1749 Clifton Rd., NE; (404) 633-6783. The Villa, supported by the Christian community, welcomes people from all religions, races, and political persuasions. Inexpensive rates for private room with bath; community kitchen. It's a 5-minute walk to the CDC and about 12 minutes on foot to the Emory campus. It's also on a MARTA bus line. Since 1972 the Villa has served more than 17,000 guests from 140 different countries.

RESORTS

Resorts around Atlanta encompass every kind of situation, from gardens to lakes to mountains, and are enjoyed by Atlantans as well as visitors. Check with the ONE-DAY EXCURSIONS chapter for more information on these resorts.

BIG CANOE, Big Canoe, GA 30143; (770) 804-4590 or toll free (877) 773-8732. M-E. Big Canoe is North Georgia at its best—7,000 acres of waterfalls, lakes, forests, and natural wildlife with the resort complex settled quietly in the center. Emerald golf greens overlook the blue lake; tennis, swimming, squash, platform tennis, fishing, sailing, and canoeing are offered in this idyllic setting. Accommodations in handsome one-, two-, and three-bedroom villas and condominiums are leased throughout the year on a daily and weekly basis. Big Canoe, a favorite second home community for Atlantans, 60 miles north of the city, will make you feel at home and at peace. Rates vary according to the seasons, so call in advance for reservations. On-season is March 15 through October. From Atlanta go north on GA 400, turn left at McFarland, Exit 8, and follow signs.

CALLAWAY GARDENS, Pine Mountain, GA 31822; (800) 225-5292. M-E. Callaway Gardens welcomes you into the west Georgia foothills of the Appalachian Mountains. This is a full-service resort with the Gardens an attraction at all seasons and four golf courses open all year.

Callaway Gardens offers three world-class golf courses, excellent tennis facilities, boating, fishing in stocked lakes, water-skiing, hiking, and a spectacular man-made beach.

Hundreds of acres of native Southern flowers, plants, and trees are beautifully cultivated in their natural setting. There are world-famous greenhouses, a jewel-like Gothic chapel nestled by a waterfall, and the breathtaking Butterfly Center, where visitors mingle with thousands of local and exotic butterflies in a natural enclosed setting.

The Inn's buffets are popular, and the lounge offers nightly entertainment. Rates vary with facility and season, and we recommend you call for current prices. Inn rooms, cottages, and villas are available. See ONE-DAY EXCURSIONS chapter for additional information.

CHATEAU ELAN WINERY AND RESORT, 100 Rue Charlemagne, Braselton, GA 30517; (770) 932-0900 or toll free (800) 233-WINE. E. Just 30 minutes north of Atlanta off I-85 at Exit 126 you'll find a fantasy resort built around a famed north Georgia winery. Guests choose from 274 deluxe guest rooms and suites. Attractions include six restaurants and lounges, championship golf course designed by Dennis Griffiths, Equestrian Show Center, and 25,000 square feet of meeting and conference space. There's also the charm of the winery itself and the beauty of the surrounding countryside in the mountain foothills.

LAKE LANIER ISLANDS, 7000 Holiday Rd, Lake Lanier Islands, (770) 932-7200, 45 minutes from Atlanta, is a popular recreational haven. *M-E*. Take I-85 north to GA 365, exit 2 on Friendship Rd., turn left and follow signs to Lake Lanier Islands and PineIsle, about four miles. Swimming at the lake beach, golfing at Emerald Pointe Golf Club, tennis, horseback riding, and boat rentals are available.

RENAISSANCE PINEISLE RESORT, Lake Lanier Islands, 9000 Holiday Rd., Lake Lanier Island, GA 30518; (770) 945-8921 or toll free (800) 327-7409. *M-E*. Stay at Stouffer's Resort Hotel for excellent cuisine at the *Grill Room Restaurant* and live entertainment in the *Championship Lounge*. Enjoy the active life with outdoor-indoor pools, tennis courts, golf course, health club, horseback riding, sail- and ski-boat rentals, trout grounds, water ski charters, and a super waterslide of 430 feet (131 meters). Rates vary according to seasons.

SKY VALLEY RESORT, Dillard, GA 30537; (800) 437-2416. *M-E*. Sky Valley is Georgia's prime snow-skiing lodge in winter and a beautiful North Georgia resort year-round. Two hours from Atlanta, it is in *Deliverance* country where the Burt Reynolds movie was filmed. And if you saw the movie and like white-water, try your skill rafting down the nearby Chattooga River. Guided tours available. The resort offers excellent golf, tennis, outdoor swimming, and horseback riding and boasts a popular restaurant and lounge. Nestled in the Georgia mountains, you can spend several hours nearby browsing and antiquing in the unusual areas and shops. See ONE-DAY EXCURSIONS chapter for additional information. Weekend package plans, and long-term rates are available. Rates vary with season so we recommend you call for current prices.

UNICOI LODGE AND CONFERENCE CENTER, Hwy. 356, Helen, GA 30545; call (706) 878-2201 or toll free (800) 573-9659 for reservations. *I-E*. This rustic modern lodge of diagonal wood and plate glass has rooms and two- and three-bedroom cottages snuggled into the northern woods. Dining is in the lodge restaurant. It is a mile from Helen and a stone's throw from Anna Ruby Falls. The lake provides swimming and boating, and nature trails abound. Color TV is in the lobby area. During the summer there are classes in pottery, macramé, as well as special dances. Unicoi is a quiet, spartan, and beautiful retreat center at very reasonable rates. Call for seasonal rates.

HOTEL SAFETY

As a public-safety service we include in this chapter the following guidance in case of a hotel fire. All information is taken from a publication of the National Safety Council.

Preliminary precautions start after you check into your hotel. Check the exits and fire alarms on your floor, count the doorways between your room and the exit, keep your key close to your bed, and take it with you if you leave your room in case you need to return. In case smoke blocks your exit, check the window latches and any adjoining buildings or decks for low-level escape.

In case of fire, take your key and crawl to the door. Don't stand; smoke and deadly gases rise.

If the doorknob is hot—*do not open*—stay in your room. Then open window, phone for help, hang a sheet from the window to signal for help, turn on the bathroom fan, fill the tub with water, wet towels and sheets to put around doors if smoke seeps in, and make a tent over your head with a blanket at a partially opened window to get fresh air.

If the doorknob is *not* hot, leave, close the door to your room, proceed to the exit, counting doorways in the dark, and walk down to ground level. If blocked at lower levels, turn around, walk up to the roof, and keep the roof door open to vent stairwell. Wait for help on the roof. **Do not use elevator. Remember to lie low to avoid smoke and gases.**

DINING

Atlanta is always in the midst of an exciting restaurant explosion, with hundreds of restaurants, a myriad of cuisines, and a range of ambience from environmental fantasies to storefront coziness. The restaurant world of Atlanta is flourishing, spinning, and lighting up the eager and hungry faces of Atlanta residents and visitors. We hope that selecting your restaurant in our guide will match the pleasure we have had in presenting these interesting eating establishments.

Atlanta had a small cadre of local restaurants for many years, but the development of the hotel industry dramatically expanded the quality and variety of international menus. Award-winning international chefs preside over top-rated restaurant kitchens within major hotels and have, in many cases, established their own unique restaurants in the city. Atlantans now enjoy a sophisticated dining scene appropriate to the city's international status.

Atlanta's Southern cooking institutions have increased in number, and new Atlantans immigrating from other cities in the United States and from other countries of the world have opened restaurants reflecting their own tastes and cultures. Cuisines proliferate, including Italian, both southern and northern; French; Spanish; Chinese, including Mandarin, Szechwan, and Hunan; Japanese; Indian; Cuban; Mexican; Greek; Russian; Korean; Thai; Vietnamese; Middle Eastern; Continental; and American.

With a simultaneous rediscovery of Atlanta's neighborhoods, the small and specialized restaurant business has found new places to thrive, new markets of young professionals who like to eat out consistently during the week. You will notice throughout this chapter the names of these neighborhood areas—Virginia-Highland, Inman Park, Decatur, Midtown, East Atlanta, and Buckhead. Notice also the names of Atlanta's outlying restaurant districts such as Marietta, Sandy Springs, and Roswell. South Atlanta is also enjoying a restaurant renaissance.

Regional and national chains have also moved to Atlanta. Two national chains, the Waffle House and Chick-Fil-A, deserve special note because they are Atlanta's own. Both originated in Atlanta and maintain headquarters here. Limitation of space does not allow us to include all the very fine chain restaurants; their regional and national reputations will serve as your guide in Atlanta. In an unusual case we reserve the right to make an inclusion. Most Atlanta hotels have quality restaurants that are convenient for the visitor. It is impossible to list them all; we have selected those we feel particularly worthy.

The dining guide includes restaurants, an Etcetera section of hard-to-categorize eateries, cafeterias, and brunch spots.

We include in the Marmac dining guide only those restaurants we can recommend, sketching for you the individual "personality" of each establishment, the raison d'etre for its inclusion among our selections. Keep in mind that new restaurants open every week, while old ones may close or change ownership and focus. However, one thing never changes: the endless possibilities. We include a quick reference for restaurants by area of the city. We have been careful to incorporate restaurants for a variety of occasions and pocketbooks. Our cost categories are listed below and coded directly following the address in the listings.

E   Expensive. Full dinner including appetizer, entree, and dessert (no beverage) over $35 per person

M   Moderate. Full dinner (no beverage), $20-$35 per person

I   Inexpensive. Full dinner (no beverage), under $20 per person

RESTAURANTS BY AREA

BUCKHEAD

Anthony's, Continental, E.
Atlanta Fish Market, Seafood, E.
Bacchanalia, American, M-E.
Bertolini's, Italian, M.
Bone's, American, E.
Boston Sea Party, Seafood, M-E.
Brasserie le Coze, French, E.
The Buckhead Diner, American, E.
Cafe Intermezzo, Continental, M.
Café Tu Tu Tango, Etcetera, I.
Carbo's Café, Continental, E.
Cassis, French, M to E.
Chops, American, E.
Ciao Bella, Italian, M to E.

Dante's Down the Hatch, American, M.
East Village Grille, American, I.
Eatzi's Market & Bakery, Etcetera, I-M
El Azteca, International (Mexican), I.
Hedgerose, Continental, E.
Houlihan's, American, I-M.
Houston's, American, I-M.
Jalisco, International (Mexican), I.
Kamogawa, Asian (Japanese), E.
McKinnon's Louisiane, Seafood, M-E.
Nava, International (Mexican), M.
103 West, Continental, E.

Pano's & Paul's, Continental, E.
Peachtree Café, American, I.
Peasant Uptown, Continental, M.
The Peasant, American, M-E.
Pricci, Italian, E.
Provino's, Italian, I to M.
Rio Bravo Cantina, International (Mexican), I-M.
Ruth's Chris Steak House, American, E.
Swan Coach House, American, M.
Toulouse, French, M.

DOWNTOWN

The Abbey, Continental, E.
Agatha's, A Taste of Mystery, American, E.
Avanzare, Italian, M.
Benihana of Tokyo, Asian (Japanese), M-E.
Chin Chin, Chinese, I.
City Grill, Continental, E.
Dailey's, Continental, M.
El Azteca, International (Mexican), I.
Hard Rock Café, American, I.
Hsu's, Asian (Chinese), M to E.
The Mansion, Continental, E.
Mary Mac's Tea room, Southern, I.
Nikolai's Roof, International (Russian), E.
Pacific Rim, Pan Asian, M.
Pittypat's Porch, Southern, M-E.
Pleasant Peasant, Continental, M.
Rio Bravo Cantina, International (Mexican), I-M.
The Sun Dial Restaurant, American, E.
The Varsity, Etcetera, I.

PEACHTREE, PIEDMONT, CHESHIRE BRIDGE (CORRIDORS BETWEEN MIDTOWN AND BUCKHEAD)

Benihana of Tokyo, Asian (Japanese), M-E.

Coco Loco, International (Cuban & Caribbean), I.
The Colonnade, American, I.
Dunk 'N Dine, American, I.
Happy Herman's, American, I.
Huey's, American, I.
Imperial Fez, International (Middle Eastern), E.
Jim White's Half Shell, Seafood, I-M.
LaGrotta Ristorante Italiano, Italian, I-E.
Lindy's, Italian, M-E.
Longhorn Steakhouse, American, M.
Marra's, Seafood, M.
Mick's, American, I to M.
The Melting Pot, American, M.
Nakato, Asian (Japanese), M.
Nino's, Italian, M-E.
Palisades, Continental, M.
Rocky's Brick Oven Pizzeria, American, I.

COBB COUNTY (MARIETTA, SMYRNA, VININGS)

Captain Billy's Fish House, Seafood, M.
Cherokee Cattle Company, American, M.
The Crab House, American, M-E.
Dave & Buster's, American, M.
1848 House, Southern, E.
Haveli, International (Indian), M.
Horseradish Grill, Southern, M-E.
House of Chan, Asian (Chinese), I-M.
Mt. Fuji, Asian (Japanese), M.
Picadilly, Cafeteria, I.
Ray's on the River, American, M.
The Vinings Inn, American, E.
Winfield's, Continental, M-E.

EAST ATLANTA, GRANT PARK, SOUTHEAST ATLANTA

Agave, Southern, *I*.
Burrito Art, Mexican, *I*.
Cabbagetown Grill, Southern, *I*.
Factory Barbecue, Southern, *I*.
Grant Central Pizza & Pasta, Italian, *I-M*.
Heaping Bowl & Brew, American, *I*.
Pastificio Cameli, Italian, *I-M*.

EMORY, DECATUR (AND ON TO STONE MOUNTAIN)

Basket Bakery and Café, German, *I*.
Benedetti's, Italian, *I*.
Café Alsace, French, *I-M*.
Café Lily, Mediterranean, *M-E*.
Crescent Moon, American, *M*.
DeKalb Farmer's Market, Etcetera, *I*.
Indian Delights, Vegetarian, *I*.
Mexico City Gourmet, International (Mexican), *I-M*.
Mick's, American, *I-M*.
Mosaic, Continental, *M*.
My Thai, Asian, *I*.
Our Way, Southern, *I*.
Pastries A-Go-Go, American, *I*.
Rainbow Grocery and Cafe, Vegetarian, *I*.
Sycamore Grill, Southern, *M to E*.
Watershed, American, *I to M*.
Ya-Ya's Cajun Café,, American, *I to M*.

MIDTOWN, VIRGINIA-HIGH-LANDS, INMAN PARK

Atkins Park Restaurant, American, *I*.
Babette's Café, Continental, *M-E*.
Baker's Café, Etcetera, *I*.
Bobby & June's Country Kitchen, Etcetera, *I*.

Brasserie, French, *I*.
Brother Juniper's, Etcetera, *I*.
Camille's, Italian, *M*.
Ciboulette, French, *E*.
The Country Place, Continental, *M*.
El Azteca, International (Mexican), *I*.
Floataway Café, Continental, *M-E*.
Flying Biscuit Café, American, *I*.
The Food Studio, American, *M*.
George's Restaurant, American, *I*.
Harvest, American, *M to E*.
Indigo, A Coastal Grill, Seafood, *M*.
The Majestic, American, *I*.
Mary Mac's Tea Room, Southern, *I*.
Mellow Mushroom, Etcetera, *I*.
Mirror of Korea, Asian (Korean), *I*.
Old Spaghetti Factory, American, *I*.
Partners, American, *M*.
The Patio, Italian, *M-E*.
Piccadilly, Cafeteria, *I*.
RJ's Uptown Kitchen & Wine Bar, American, *M*.
Ru San's, Asian (Japanese), *I*.
Silver Grill, Etcetera, *I*.
Soul Vegetarian, Vegetarian, *I*.
Surin, Thai, *M*.
Vickery's, American, *I*.

NORTHEAST ATLANTA

Asiana Garden, Asian (Japanese-Korean), *M*.
August Moon, Asian (Japanese), *I-M*.
Bambinelli's, Italian, *I-M*.
57th Fighter Group, American, *M*.
Five Sisters Café, Etcetera, *I*.
Harmony Vegetarian, Asian (Chinese), *I*.
Lawrence's Cafe, International (Middle Eastern), *I-M*.

Lettuce Souprise You, Cafeteria, *I*.
Little Szechuan, Chinese, *I*.
Mandarin Garden, Asian
   (Chinese), M.
Nicola's, International (Middle
   Eastern), *I*.
Oriental Pearl, Asian (Chinese), M.
Penang, Asian (Malaysian), M.
Pho Hoa, Asian (Vietnamese), *I*.
Phuket Thai Restaurant, Asian
   (Thai), *I*-M.
Petit Auberge, French, M-E.
Royal China, Asian (Chinese), *I*.
Song Long, Asian (Vietnamese), *I*.
South of France, French, M-E.
Thai Chili, Asian (Thai), *I*.
Thai Restaurant of Norcross,
   Asian (Thai), *I*.
Toyo ta ya Sushi Buffet, Asian
   (Japanese), *I*.
Violette, French, *I*.
Yen Jing, Asian (Chinese-Korean),
   I.

ROSWELL

Dick and Harry's, American, E.
Edelweiss, Continental, M.
Johnny Rockets, American, *I*.
Lickskillet Farm, Southern, M-E.
Public House, Continental, M-E.
Taxco, International (Mexican), *I*.

DUNWOODY

Chequers, American, M.
The Derby, American, *I*-M.
La Grotta Ravinia, Italian, E.
Mick's, American, *I*-M.

Old Hickory House, Southern, *I*.

SANDY SPRINGS

The Brandy House, American, *I*-
   M.
Café Prego, Italian, *I*-M.
Café Sunflower, Vegetarian, *I*.
Café 290, American, M-E.
Chopstix, Asian (Chinese), *I*-M.
Edelweiss, Continental, M.
El Toro, International (Mexican),
   I.
The Embers Seafood Grille,
   Seafood, M.
Kobe Steaks, Asian (Japanese), M-
   E.
Ming Garden, Asian (Chinese), *I*.
Ruth's Chris Steak House,
   American, E.
Tanner's, American, *I*.

SOUTH ATLANTA

Café at the Corner, French, *I*.
Folks Southern Kitchen, Southern,
   I.
Harold's, Southern, *I*.
Paschal's, Southern, M-E.
Pilgreen's, American, M.
Soul Vegetarian, Vegetarian, *I*.
Thomas Marketplace, Southern, *I*.
Zab-E-Lee, Asian (Thai), M.

BEYOND ATLANTA

Blue Willow Inn, Southern, *I*-M.
Sprayberry's Barbecue, Southern,
   I.
Yesterday Café, American, *I*-M.

RESTAURANTS

American ——————————————

Agatha's: A Taste of Mystery (C3), 693 Peachtree St.; (404)
875-1610. E. At this unusual dinner theater, diners participate in

mystery-solving with costumed actors and actresses. Each guest is given new identity papers at the door and spends the rest of dinner trying to figure out "who dunnit." Nightly. Call for reservations.

Atkins Park Restaurant (C4), 794 N. Highland Ave., NE; (404) 876-7249. *I to* M. Atkins Park is a restored jewel from Atlanta's 1920s past. First a deli, then a neighborhood beer and wine tavern, and later a dining room as well, Atkins Park has the oldest (1927) beer and wine license in Atlanta. Atkins Park serves American and continental fare in its cozy, fun, and eclectic environment. Lunch and dinner daily.

Bacchanalia (B3), 3125 Piedmont Rd., NE; (404) 365-0410. M *to* E. The contemporary American menu selections at this Wine Country cottage are not only delicious, they're organic whenever possible. Small portions, large flavors, a selection of off-beat West Coast wines. Don't miss the venison with sweet potato puree and dried fruit, or the fois gras with caramelized turnips and ginger-rosemary sauce. Dinner.

Bone's (B3), 3130 Piedmont Rd., NE; (404) 237-2663. E. Bone's is synonymous with steak, some of the juiciest and thickest in town, and live lobster flown in daily. Highlighting the Victorian decor is the wonderful gallery of autographed photos of famous patrons. This is a place to enjoy both a congenial business meal and a family gathering. Lunch Mon-Fri, dinner daily.

Brandy House (B3), 4365 Roswell Rd., NE; (404) 252-7784. *I to* M. Another W. D. Crowley restaurant, the Brandy House is popular with young singles looking for dapper environs, a cross section of foods from burgers to crabs, and each other. Lunch Mon-Fri, dinner Mon-Sat.

The Buckhead Diner (B3), 3073 Piedmont Rd.; (404) 262-3336. M *to* E. All decked out in shiny stainless steel, neon, and comfy leather booths, the Buckhead Diner is a gleaming monument to American culinary chic from Atlanta restaurateurs Paul Albrecht and Pano Karatossas (103 West, Pano's and Paul's, etc.). One of the city's top locations for celebrity spotters, the Buckhead Diner pleases faddish palates with such treats as baked grouper with ground hazelnuts, linguini with butter clams, and risotto with wild mushrooms, asparagus, basil, and parmesan. Lunch and dinner Mon-Sat.

Cafe 290 (A3), 290 Hildebrand Ave., Sandy Springs; (404) 256-3942. M *to* E. Casually elegant suburban restaurant serves steaks, seafood, chicken and pasta dishes, salads, and appetizers. After dinner, enjoy live jazz in the lounge. Dinner Mon-Sat.

Chequers (A4), 236 Perimeter Center Pkwy.; (770) 391-9383. M. The menu at this popular dining choice offers an extensive selection of fish and seafood, along with certified angus beef and regional specialties. The food is prepared simply and carefully with all fresh ingredients, in the tradition of a classic American grill. Lunch and dinner daily, Sunday brunch.

Cherokee Cattle Co., 2710 Canton Rd. (Hwy. 5), Marietta; (770) 427-0490. M. Texas-style mesquite-grilled steaks, chicken, mixed drinks, and a friendly Western atmosphere. Lunch Mon-Fri, dinner daily.

Chops (B3), 70 West Paces Ferry Rd., NW; (404) 262-2675. E. Great steaks, big drinks, clubby atmosphere. Perfect for wining and dining on the company expense account.

The Colonnade, (C4), 1879 Cheshire Bridge Rd.; (404) 874-5642. I. One of Atlanta's favorite restaurants for more than 25 years. Excellent seafood, steaks, chops, Southern-fried chicken and vegetables, in a friendly family-type atmosphere. Breakfast, lunch, dinner daily. No credit cards.

The Crab House Seafood Restaurant (A1), 2175 Cobb Pkwy. (U.S. 41), Smyrna; (770) 955-CRAB. M to E. Choose your favorite seafood dish from a menu that includes Florida grouper, red snapper, salmon, amberjack, trout, pompano, Maryland-style garlic crabs, and live Maine lobster. Lunch and dinner daily.

Crescent Moon (C5), 174 W. Ponce de Leon Ave., Decatur; (404) 377-5623. I. Downtown Decatur's favorite little eatery, this bustling diner serves up delicious breakfasts, gourmet salads, sandwiches, huge burgers, pastas, and seafood dishes with a very upbeat flair. Breakfast, lunch, and dinner Tue-Sat.

Dante's Down the Hatch in Buckhead (B3), 3380 Peachtree Rd., NE; (404) 266-1600. M. An Atlanta institution, Dante's is both nightclub and specialty restaurant in an incredible nautical setting. Dante's specializes in fondue—cheese and beef and chocolate—all designed for the comradeship of eating from the same pot. Take a cheese tour and a wine tour of the world with Dante's broad selection of cheeses and wines. The restaurant is open for cocktails and dinner Mon-Sat. See the Music section of the NIGHTLIFE chapter.

Dave & Buster's (A1), 2215 D&B Drive, SE, Marietta; (770) 951-5554. I. 50,000 square feet of great food and fun. Includes conventional dining, as well as a mystery dinner theater. Don't miss the fajitas, the pasta, the pizza, or the baby back ribs. And don't miss the incredible game room either.

The Derby, 7716 Spalding Dr.; (770) 448-2833. I to M. In the Spalding Corners Shopping Center of Dunwoody, the Derby is a popular luncheon and dinner spot for business people and area residents. The mood is friendly and jovial; the fare is All-American. Lunch and dinner daily, brunch Sun.

Dick and Harry's (A3), 1570 Holcomb Bridge Rd., No. 810; (770) 641-8757. M to E. Contemporary American cuisine at Dick and Harry's includes chops, pastas, steaks, and lots of seafood. Sushi bar. Tasty veggies. Award-winning desserts include homemade ice creams. Serves lunch and dinner Mon-Sat.

Dunk 'n' Dine (C4), 2277 Cheshire Bridge Rd., NE; (404) 636-0197. Dunk 'n' Dine is a *real* diner, the kind of diner we had before diners were cool. The place is open around the clock. They've got great coffee and what may be the best-value breakfast around.

East Village Grille (B3), 248 Buckhead Ave.; (404) 233-3345. *I*. Down-home, moderately priced chow such as barbecue, fried chicken, meatloaf, and vegetables, plus a usually jam-packed bar, make this cunningly converted old firehouse one of Buckhead's hottest destinations. Lunch and dinner daily.

57th Fighter Group (B4), 3829 Clairmont Rd.; (770) 457-7757. *M*. Airplanes and nostalgia come together in a unique ambience for this All-American restaurant next to DeKalb Peachtree Airport. Enjoy thick steaks, fresh seafood, and succulent poultry as you watch the planes take off and land. A spacious outdoor patio bar and a large dance floor add to the mystique.

The Flying Biscuit Cafe (C4), 1655 McLendon Ave.; (404) 687-8888. *I*. Mostly breakfast-type items, for lunch and dinner, too. Healthy and delicious menu features organic oatmeal pancakes, Mexican-style eggs on black bean-cornmeal cakes, chocolate bread pudding, and of course lots of biscuits. Tight tables, neighborhood ambience. Breakfast, lunch, dinner.

George's Restaurant (C4), 1041 N. Highland Ave.; (404) 892-3648. *I*. This is one of Atlanta's best-known neighborhood bar-and-restaurant settings. The haunt of politicians, writers, and neighborhood activists, George's was immortalized in the "Hardman" detective novels of the early 1970s, created by the late Ralph Dennis, a regular.

Hard Rock Café (C3), 215 Peachtree St.; (404) 688-7625. *I*. In the center of town. Depend on it for juicy burgers and star-studded décor of the rock-music culture. Get your T-shirt here. Open daily until 2 a.m.

Happy Herman's (C4), 2299 Cheshire Bridge Rd.; (404) 321-3012. *I*. Established in 1948, this popular kosher-style deli has a serve-yourself dining area. Delicious prepared dinners, salads, pastas, and sandwiches. Mouth-watering desserts, too. Take home a gourmet gift basket, a selection of chocolates, or other goodies from the gifts section. Two other locations. Call for directions.

Harvest (C4), 853 N. Highland Ave.; (404) 876-8244. *M to E*. Arts and Crafts furniture and fireplaces give this lovely restaurant in a two-story house added appeal. Varied menu includes pecan roasted rainbow trout and grilled Argentine beef tenderloin. Try the buttermilk mashed potatoes. Serves lunch Mon-Fri; dinner daily; Sunday brunch.

The Heaping Bowl & Brew (D4), 469-A Flat Shoals Ave.; (404) 523-8030. *I*. Their slogan is "Everything's good in a bowl," and so it is at this comfortable neighborhood café in East Atlanta Village. Mashed potato bowl, Asian pots, as well as a spicy turkey burger, hearty soups and sweet potato fries. Try "Izzy's Banana Pudding." As for the brew, it's two bucks a pint on Tuesdays and Thursdays, and Margaritas are $3 on Mon and Wed.

Houlihan's (B3), Colony Square, 1197 Peachtree St.; (404) 873-1119. Park Place, 4505 Ashford-Dunwoody Rd.; (770) 394-8921. *I to M.* Dark walls, Tiffany lamps, Victorian memorabilia, and fluffy green plants provide a warm clublike restaurant and bar, where the twenties to forties set mingles over drinks and a menu from quiches to steaks, burgers to seafood. Lunch, dinner, and late night daily, brunch Sun.

Houston's (B3), 3525 Piedmont Rd.; (404) 231-3564. 4701 Ashford-Dunwoody Rd.; (770) 512-7066. *I to M.* Houston's is where you'll find some of Atlanta's finest preppies and young career types. The restaurant has the sophisticated dark-green and beige treatment popular in the last few years, and the fare includes light meals such as quiches, salads, burgers, and soups. Lunch and dinner daily.

Huey's (C3), 1816 Peachtree Rd.; (404) 873-2037. *I.* Casual New Orleans fare includes flaky *beignets,* red beans and rice, po' boy and muffaletta sandwiches. Small, casual place also serves breakfast and has outside tables during warm weather. Breakfast Tue-Fri, brunch Sat-Sun, dinner Tue-Sun. No credit cards.

Johnny Rockets (A3), 6065 Roswell Rd.; (404) 257-0677. Other metro area locations. *I.* Born on L.A.'s trendy Melrose Avenue, Johnny Rockets is a whimsical, and delicious, time trip back to the 1940s malt shops, where you may enjoy a chocolate shake, a root beer float, or a cheeseburger with fries to the music of the Andrews Sisters. Lunch and dinner daily.

Longhorn Steakhouse (C3), 2151 Peachtree Rd., NE; (404) 351-6086. (A3), 4721 Lower Roswell Rd., Marietta; (770) 977-3045. Eleven other locations in metro Atlanta. *M.* Choice steaks at choice prices in the atmosphere of a Texas saloon and steakhouse—that's Longhorn Steaks. Rustic wood stalls, beer signs, and cheerful waitresses accompany the savoring of good beef steaks. Lunch Mon-Fri, dinner daily.

The Majestic (C3), 1031 Ponce de Leon Ave.; (404) 875-0276. *I.* This landmark diner, a.k.a. Majestic Food Shops, has been around since the 1920s. Although renovated and redecorated, it keeps its enduring ambience. Especially colorful after midnight, when children of the night drop by for eggs, waffles, apple pie, and steaming hot coffee. Open all the time.

The Melting Pot (B3), 857 Collier Rd.; (404) 351-1811. *M.* Beef, chicken, seafood, cheese and chocolate fondues prepared at tableside, with a large choice of wines by the glass. Dinner nightly.

Mick's (I10), 557 Peachtree St.; (404) 875-6425. (B4), Lenox Square Mall; (404) 262-6425. (A4), Park Place Shopping Center,

Ashford-Dunwoody Rd.; (770) 394-6425. (C3), Peachtree at Bennett Street; (404) 351-6425. (C5), Decatur; (404) 373-7797. Other locations. *I to M*. Casual, trendy, California-style dinners delight SRO crowds with oversized burgers, grilled chicken, pizza, pasta, salads, and sundaes. Continuous service daily.

NAVA (B3), 3060 Peachtree Rd; (404) 240-1984. M. Latin and Native American touches enhance the seafood, meat, and game dishes at this new Buckhead hot spot. Lunch Mon-Sat. Dinner daily.

The Old Spaghetti Factory (C3), 249 Ponce de Leon Ave.; (404) 872-2841. *I*. Old World antiques, good food, and good fun mark this intown dining spot.

Partners Morningside Cafe (C4), 1399 N. Highland Ave.; (404) 875-0202. M. One of the city's favorite neighborhood restaurants, trendy, upbeat Partners treats nightly SRO crowds to house-made pastas, seafood, lamb, beef, and stir-fried dishes. Dinner Tue-Sat.

Pastries A-Go-Go (C4), 250 W. Ponce de Leon Ave.; Decatur (404) 373-3423. *I*. Fine things really do come in small packages, as evidenced by this superb bakery and café owned by pastry chef Bob Light. He serves a heavenly breakfast, lunch, and weekend brunch. Homemade sausage, croissants made with sweet cream, southwestern omelets, malted Belgian waffles, delectable sandwiches and soups. Dieters can get hearty salads, but beware of that pastry counter. Most people leave with a take-out bag of goodies.

Peachtree Cafe (B3), 268 E. Paces Ferry Rd., NE; (404) 233-4402. *I*. This extremely popular eatery, one block off Peachtree in Buckhead, combines light fare of burgers, pocket sandwiches, baked potatoes, soups, salads, and desserts with 24 imported beers and a good selection of wines. Lunch and dinner Mon-Sat.

The Peasant (B3), 3402 Piedmont Rd.; (404) 231-8740. M to E. Founded by Atlanta's Peasant Corporation, this trendy spot caters lavishly to Buckhead's fashion-conscious winers and diners with such fare as pork satay with mango sauce, duck and sesame tacos, and whole steamed snapper with black sesame seeds. Lunch and dinner daily.

Pilgreen's (D3), 1081 Lee St., SW; (404) 758-4669. 6335 Jonesboro Rd.; (770) 961-1666. M. The house specialty in this longtime favorite of south Atlantans is the T-bone steak, but all steaks are recommended and big steak lovers can special-order a three-pounder. Lounge accompanies restaurant. Lunch and dinner Tue-Sat.

Ray's On The River (A2), 6700 Powers Ferry Rd., SE, Marietta; (770) 955-1187. M. Fresh seafood and steaks in "Atlanta's most spectacular setting!" Nestled on the banks of the Chattahoochee. Lunch Mon-Sat, dinner daily, Sunday brunch.

RJ's Uptown Kitchen and Wine Bar (C3), 870 N. Highland Ave.; (404) 875-7775. *I to M*. A 1940s service station has been cleverly reborn as a trendy cafe and wine shop. Dine on seafood, pasta, chicken, and other entrees, with a choice of 40 wines by the glass, in the former service bay or outdoor patio where the gas pumps once stood. Bottle wines from around the world are sold in the station's former office. Lunch and dinner Tue-Sun, brunch Sun.

Rocky's Brick Oven Pizzeria (C3), 1770 Peachtree St. at 26th St.; (404) 870-7625. *I.* Some of Atlanta's most delicious pizza comes out of the European-style wood-burning brick ovens at this very popular, very casual pizzeria between Downtown and Buckhead. Lunch and dinner daily.

Ruth's Chris Steak House (B4), 950 E. Paces Ferry Rd., across from Lenox Square; (404) 365-0660. (A3), 5788 Roswell Rd., NW, Sandy Springs; (404) 255-0035. *E.* Extra-select U.S. prime beef is the hallmark of this gorgeous contemporary dining room. The menu includes fresh seafood and a large selection of domestic and imported wines. Lunch Mon-Fri, dinner daily.

The Sun Dial Restaurant and Lounge (J9), Westin Peachtree Plaza Hotel, Peachtree St. at International Blvd.; (404) 589-7505. *E.* Savor prime steaks and hickory-smoked prime ribs as you revolve atop the 73-story Peachtree Plaza. Lunch Mon-Sat, dinner daily.

Swan Coach House (B3), Atlanta History Center, 3130 Slaton Dr., NW; (404) 261-0636. *M.* This charming coach house for the elegant 1920s Swan House on the Atlanta Historical Society grounds is a perfect luncheon spot in Buckhead. The food is delectable; the atmosphere genteel. Lunch Mon-Sat.

Tanner's (A3), 350 Northridge Rd., between GA 400 and Roswell Rd.; (770) 642-7777. Several other metro locations. *I.* Casual, friendly neighborhood restaurant features delicious rotisserie chicken, fresh vegetables, daily lunch specials, and draft beer. Lunch and dinner daily.

Vickery's (G11), 1106 Crescent Ave., NE; (404) 881-1106. *I.* Mrs. Vickery's turn-of-the-century house and antique store has been given a soft art deco interior treatment and, presto, one of the friendliest bars and eateries in Midtown. In fair weather, have your meal on the brick patio under the spreading oak. Lunch, dinner, and late night Tue-Sun.

The Vinings Inn (B2), 3011 Paces Mill Rd.; (770) 438-2282. *E.* Contemporary Southern cuisine in a charming 130-year-old house in the historic village of Vinings. Consider the peach barbecue prawns on cheese grits. Renowned lump crab cakes. Live entertainment nightly in the attic bar. Lunch and dinner Mon-Sat.

Watershed (C4), 406 W. Ponce de Leon Ave., Decatur; (404) 378-4900. *I to M.* Inventive, American cuisine is served for the sophisticated palate in this wine shop/restaurant/gift boutique. Sip your wine or browse the boutique while waiting for incredible sandwiches and entrees, sinful desserts, including a chocolate cake that will set your heart racing. Mon-Sat 11 am-10 pm.

Ya Ya's Cajun Cuisine (C4), 426 W. Ponce de Leon Ave., Decatur, (404) 373-9292. *I to* M. Authentic, traditional Cajun cuisine is served in this lively restaurant with a carnival ambiance. Seafood reigns, of course, but some tasty chicken and veggie dishes are available, too. Serves lunch and dinner daily. Live blues music on weekends.

Asian

Asiana Garden (B5), 5150 Buford Highway, Doraville; (770) 452-1677. M. Korea meets Japan in this highly rated restaurant. Diners enjoy an assortment of Korean delicacies served with each meal (don't miss the pickled lotus root), as well as a broad selection of Japanese and Korean entrees. The house specialty is beef or fish prepared at your table—the table top is a grill. Lunch Mon-Fri. Dinner nightly.

August Moon (A5), 5715 Buford Highway, Doraville; (770) 455-3464. *I to* M. This Japanese restaurant is a really top-notch sushi bar that also excels in hibachi cooking and other traditional Japanese fare. Come early to avoid a wait on weekends. Dinner Mon-Sat.

Benihana of Tokyo (J9), Peachtree Center, (404) 522-9629. (C3), 2143 Peachtree Rd., NE; (404) 355-8565. M *to* E. For Downtowners with a lust for raw seafood and for those who want the opportunity to try this exotic fare, the sushi bar at Benihana's at Peachtree Center is a special treat from Japan. The first Benihana in Atlanta, at 2143 Peachtree Road, is a recreated, 17th-century Japanese palace, hand-built by Japanese craftsmen with materials made in Japan. This restaurant and the newest location at Peachtree Center feature tabletop teppan-yaki cooking at your table with an expert flourish of the knives. Lunch Mon-Sat, dinner daily.

Chin Chin (C3), 699 Ponce de Leon Ave., just east of City Hall East; (404) 816-1511. *I.* Four other locations. Chef John Kuan, formerly of New York's five-star Sun Lee, serves up tasty low-cal seafood and vegetable dishes. Open-kitchen setting. Lunch and dinner daily. Call for hours.

Chopstix (A3), 4279 Roswell Rd.; (404) 255-4868. *I to* M. Delicious Cantonese and Szechwan cooking, in a refined Continental setting, attracts appreciative crowds of Occidentals and Orientals. Lunch Mon-Fri, dinner daily.

House of Chan (B2), 2469 Cobb Pkwy. (U.S. 41), Smyrna; (770) 955-9444. *I to* M. One of the metro area's very best Chinese restaurants, specializing in Mandarin, Szechwan, and Hunan cuisine. Lunch and dinner Mon-Sat.

Hsu's at Peachtree Center (J9), 192 Peachtree Center Ave., NE; (404) 659-2788. M *to* E. Peking duck, shrimp cooked in ginger and garlic, and stir-fried cashew chicken are a few of the enticing specialties at this up-scale Cantonese restaurant in the heart of Downtown. Lunch Mon-Fri, dinner daily.

Kamogawa (B3), 3300 Peachtree Rd., NE, in Grand Hyatt Atlanta Hotel; (404) 841-0314. *E.* Traditional Japanese dining in an elegant setting. Order from the menu or, for a truly memorable evening, schedule a Kaiseki dinner for four or more in your own private tatami room. The Kaiseki dinner is highly traditional and its many courses represent a near-complete sample of the various types of dishes in Japanese cuisine. This leisurely dining experience is a favorite method among Japanese executives for entertaining clients. Lunch is served Mon-Fri. Dinner is served daily. Reservations are recommended.

Kobe Steaks (A3), the Prado Shopping Center, 5600 Roswell Rd., NE; (404) 256-0810. *M to E.* Kobe Steaks is in the tower plaza of the Prado Center, a few blocks from the perimeter I-285, and therefore convenient to the north side of town. The milieu is authentic Japanese designed by one of Japan's leading architects. Enjoy a gracious display of teppan-yaki table cooking, Oriental decor, and polished service from the kimono-clad waitresses. Kobe steak is the specialty, the ultimate in the choicest beef, as the name says, but seafood and chicken dishes are also offered. Dinner daily.

Little Szechuan (A5), 5091-C Buford Hwy., Doraville; (770) 451-0192. *I.* Don't let the storefront ambience fool you. This is top-ranked Chinese cuisine. Portions are large. Don't miss the spicy won tons or dry-fried Szechwan green beans with minced pork. Lunch and dinner daily except Tuesdays.

Mandarin Garden (A5), 6180 McDonough Blvd., Norcross; (770) 246-0406. *M.* At Mandarin Garden you'll find traditional Chinese dishes made using the highest quality natural ingredients and the most healthful preparation methods. Lunch and dinner are served daily. Reservations are recommended.

Ming Garden (A3), 5006 Roswell Rd., (404) 255-4515. *I.* Chef's specialties cover all geographical regions of China. Try family dinners, the Emperor's Feast, and Banquet Royale for parties. Lunch Mon-Fri, dinner daily.

Mirror of Korea (C3), Plaza Shopping Center, 1047 Ponce de Leon Ave.; (404) 874-6243. *I.* Korean and Chinese dishes and a sushi bar are in a room designed to look like a Korean village. Choose the dining room or a private booth. Lunch and dinner Tue-Sun.

Mt. Fuji (A1), 180 Cobb Pkwy. South, Marietta; (770) 428-0955. *M.* Dinner is prepared at your table in this steakhouse-sushi bar that is one of Cobb County's finest Asian restaurants. Dinner daily. Reservations recommended.

My Thai (C4), 1248 Clairmont Rd.; (404) 636-4280. *I.* Always fresh ingredients go into the dishes at this popular Thai restaurant. Three levels of "hot" satisfy the timid to the bold palate. Lunch served Mon-Fri.; dinner daily. Come early on Saturdays to avoid the crowd.

Nakato (C3), 1776 Cheshire Bridge Rd., NE; (404) 873-6582. M. Nakato has three dining rooms for three different Japanese cuisines. Teppan-yaki cooking features steel tables where the food is prepared, cooked, and individually served by the chef. Sukiyaki dinners include thin strips of beef simmered in special Nakato sauces with vegetables, shirataki noodles, and mushrooms cooked at your table. Tempura features shrimp, seafood, and vegetables deep fried with a crispy thin golden batter at the tempura bar. Choose one of Nakato's dining experiences and come back for another. Dinner daily.

Oriental Pearl (B5), 5399 New Peachtree Rd., Chamblee; (770) 986-9866. M. This elegant Chinese restaurant, with its white tablecloths and art deco design, is an institution in Atlanta's Chinese community and a popular spot with non-Asian residents as well. Lunch Mon-Fri. Dinner nightly.

Penang Malaysian Cuisine (A5), 4897 Buford Hwy.; (770) 220-0308. *I* to M. Spicy delights. Seafood is the specialty here from various seafood soups to squid in lemon grass sauce or deep fried fish in Thai sauce. Satays, too. But noodles, beef, chicken, and vegetables also whet the appetite. Located in the Orient Center in Chamblee. Open daily from 11 am. Sunday brunch.

Pho Hoa (B5), 5150 Buford Highway, Doraville; (770) 455-8729. *I.* This authentic Vietnamese noodle shop, with its lively neon-and-glass-block decor, is part of a national chain of similar restaurants. You'll find great Asian noodle soup (the house specialty), along with other selections. The budget prices make this a popular eatery with Atlanta's young Asians. Lunch and dinner daily.

Phuket Thai Restaurant (C4), Clocktower Peachtree Creek Shopping Center, 2839 Buford Hwy.; (404) 325-4199. *I* to M. An exotic 60-item menu, prepared by owners from the Thai resort city of Phuket (pronounced Poo-get), ranges the spicy scale from medium warm to three-alarm. The owners will happily guide you through a memorable adventure. Lunch and dinner daily.

Royal China (B4), 3295 Chamblee-Dunwoody Rd., Chamblee; (770) 261-9933. *I.* The kind of place you'd expect to find in Hong Kong or San Francisco's Chinatown, this spartan suburban restaurant specializes in fresh seafood and many unusual dishes. Definitely not the same-old sweet-and-sour. Lunch and dinner daily.

Ru San's (H11), 1529 Piedmont Rd.; (404) 875-7042. *I.* The excellent sushi bar and succulent noodle dishes and yakitori meats make this a restaurant of choice among Midtown's Generation X-ers. The walls are enlivened with great Japanese caricatures. Lunch and dinner daily.

Song Long (A5), 4166 Buford Hwy.; (404) 320-9772. *I*. New and already popular eatery in the Oriental Mall, Song Long combines tasty food with music videos. Try the cha gio (Vietnamese fried spring rolls) or any of the rice-noodle soups.

Surin (C3), 810 N. Highland Ave.; (404) 892-7789. *I to M*. This elegantly simple Thai restaurant has a long record of satisfying its customers. Beautiful Thai wall hangings and original pressed tin ceiling add to a lovely dining experience. Known for their fresh basil rolls with plum sauce. We recommend the coconut soup, too. Lunch and dinner daily. Come early to avoid a long wait for dinner.

Thai Chili (C4), 2169 Briarcliff Rd., NE; (404) 315-6750. *I*. A family-run restaurant by a veteran of Atlanta's reigning Thai restaurants. Delicate flavors, upscale curries, and spicy accents make meals here particularly memorable. Lunch and dinner.

Thai Restaurant of Norcross (A5), 6065 Norcross-Tucker Rd., Norcross; (770) 938-3883. *I*. Delectable Thai cuisine and Chinese dishes in a friendly suburban location. Lunch and dinner daily.

Toyo ta ya Sushi Buffet (A5), 5082 Buford Highway, Doraville; (770) 986-0828. *I*. Famed for its sushi buffet, this attractive restaurant also offers miso soup, yakitori, tempura, and other Japanese items in an all-you-can-eat cafeteria setting for a most reasonable fixed price. Live piano entertainment adds a continental touch to the setting. Lunch and dinner daily.

Yen Jing (A5), 5302 Buford Highway, Doraville; (770) 454-6688. *I*. Yen Jing is located in Atlanta's Koreatown Mall and serves Chinese food with a Korean flair. The portions may be the most generous we've found anywhere in the city, and the pot stickers are out of this world. Lunch Mon-Fri. Dinner nightly.

Zab-E-Lee (E2), 4835 Old National Highway, College Park; (404) 768-2705. *I*. Enthusiastic adherents claim this small neighborhood establishment serves the best Thai cuisine in the Southeast. Dishes are authentic, rather than trendy. Try the green papaya salad or the duck curry with steamed rice. Lunch and dinner daily except Sundays.

Continental

The Abbey (I11), 163 Ponce de Leon Ave.; (404) 876-8532. *E*. Housed in a landmark downtown church with vaulted ceilings and stained-glass windows, the Abbey restaurant brings you continental cuisine and a wine list considered one of the best in the city. The staff serves in monks' habits and your candlelit dinner is accompanied by the delicate sounds of the Abbey harpist. The lounge is open every evening. Dinner daily.

Anthony's (B3), 3109 Piedmont Rd., NE; (404) 262-7379. *E*. Dine at one of the nation's foremost Continental restaurants in the gracious setting of an antebellum plantation home. The house was carefully removed brick by brick and plank by plank from nearby Washington, Georgia, in the 1970s and relocated at the present four-acre site on Piedmont Road. It is handsomely decorated with period antiques and reproductions in both art and furnishings. Dinner Mon-Sat.

Babette's Cafe (C4), 471 N. Highland Ave.; (404) 523-9121. M *to* E. Inspired by the book and movie, *Babette's Feast*, this restaurant lives up to the name. Intimate setting, elegant food make it a winner. Homemade pastas vie with cassoulet for popularity at dinner, and Babette's Benedict and a *crème fraiche* omelet make the Sunday brunch divine.

Basket Bakery and Café (C6), 6655 James B. Rivers Dr. at The Village Corner, (770) 498-0329. *I*. Tasty German food in a charming setting at the edge of Stone Mountain Village. No skimping here on portions. After an excellent meal, get some homemade bread to take home. Then walk off any excess indulgence in the historic cemetery across the street.

Cafe Intermezzo (C3), 1845 Peachtree Rd.; (404) 355-0411. (A4), Park Place, 4505 Ashford-Dunwoody Rd.; (770) 396-1344. M. Chic European-fashion cafe/bars are a favorite haunt of Atlanta's glamorous children of the night. Theater and ballet-goers, and others out on the town, drop by to peruse more than 30 luscious desserts, enjoyed with wines, cocktails, and a host of teas and coffees. Other offerings include salads, quiche, and jaffle—European stuffed sandwiches grilled to a flaky puff. Open nightly until 3-4 am.

Cafe Lily (C4), 308 W. Ponce de Leon Ave., Decatur, (404) 371-9119. M *to* E. Original classic and family recipes from Italy, Morocco, Greece, France and Spain. Enjoy the intimate bistro setting indoors or alfresco. We recommend the tuna steak. Piquant lemon-garlic potatoes come with several entrees. Desserts are delicious, too. Lunch Mon-Fri.; dinner daily; Sunday brunch.

Carbo's Cafe (B3), 3717 Roswell Rd.; (404) 231-4433. *E*. This 80-seat restaurant is a jewel—intimate and elegant with the distinctive personal touch of the owner's art collection, a fresh rose on each table, and sparkling cut crystal and silver. Continental fare includes fresh seafood, veal, fowl, and steaks. Complete a superb meal at the cappuccino and espresso bar. A visit to the piano bar is an after-dinner favorite with regular patrons. Piano bar and dinner daily.

City Grill (J9), 50 Hurt Plaza; (404) 524-2489. *E*. Located in the beautifully renovated Hurt Building, downtown Atlanta, the City Grill offers sophisticated and elegant dining. A selection of deliciously prepared prime beef, chops, and fresh fish. Diners dress for the occasion here! Reservations encouraged. Lunch and dinner daily.

The Country Place (G12), Colony Square, 14th St. and Peachtree St., NE; (404) 881-0144. M. Portuguese tiles, large terra-cotta pots of greenery, and European country furniture transform this space in the Colony Square mall into clear Mediterranean ambience. Enjoy piano music in the lounge, a popular after-work spot for Colony Square tenants and residents. Lunch Mon-Fri, dinner daily, brunch Sun.

Dailey's (J9), 17 International Blvd.; (404) 681-3303. M. The Downtown link in the Peasant restaurant chain is next to Peachtree Center in a warehouse restored to turn-of-the-century character with brick walls, skylights, wide floorboards, antique carousel horses, and baskets of plants. The fare is creative Continental in the upstairs restaurant. Street level is Dailey's bar and grill with piano entertainment and grill food service until 1 am. Sunday brunch is a special feature. Upstairs or downstairs Dailey's is a great place to be. Lunch Mon-Sat, dinner daily, brunch Sun.

Edelweiss, 6075 Roswell Rd., Sandy Springs; (404) 303-8700. M. German and American fare are the order of the day in this award-winning restaurant. Check out the wiener schnitzel, sauerbraten, bratwurst, and venison.

Floataway Café (C4), 1123 Zonolite Rd., Suite 15; (404) 892-1414. M to E. Inventive dishes from two of Atlanta's top chefs always give this trendy retro-industrial café rave reviews. Fresh, often organic ingredients are half the secret, presented with panache. Piccolo Fritto is their famous fresh-from-the-sea squid appetizer. Be sure to try the Bourride and the rosemary rolls. Serves lunch and dinner Tues-Fri.; dinner only Sat.

Hedgerose (B3), 490 E. Paces Ferry Rd., NE; (404) 233-7673. E. The Hedgerose is an inviting, polished place for gourmet dining in the European tradition. This small, intimate restaurant will charm you with its peach and white decor, courteous service, and brilliant Continental menu. Pheasant with a velvety morel sauce and medallions of venison from northeastern Italy exemplify the range of delights in selecting an entree. Hors d'oeuvres include piroshki topped with sauce béarnaise. For a return to elegant, expert, and beautiful wining and dining, reserve your table at the Hedgerose. Dinner Mon-Sat.

The Mansion (I11), 179 Ponce de Leon Ave., NE; (404) 876-0727. E. The Mansion is the former estate house of one of Atlanta's oldest families. This Queen Anne-style residence of Edward C. Peters was built in 1885 and is listed in the National Register of Historic Places. Now visitors and Atlantans "come to dinner" at the Mansion, a Victorian delight of red brick, stone, and half-timbered gables with the interior restored to the style of Atlanta's gilded age. Continental fare is served in the first-floor rooms with their ornate crown moldings, Tiffany lamps, and crystal chandeliers, and also on the greenhouse veranda. Lunch Mon-Fri, dinner Mon-Sat, brunch Sat-Sun.

Mosaic (C4), 308 W. Ponce de Leon Ave., Decatur, (404) 373-9468. M. Serving southern European cuisine in a colorful atmosphere, Mosaic offers great variety. Latin nights on Thursdays feature paella and live music. Try Zac's renowned banana pudding, or ask about daily desserts. Lunch Tues-Fri., dinner Tues-Sat., and brunch on Sat and Sun.

Pacific Rim (C3), 6303 Peachtree Center Ave.; (404) 893-0018. M. A mix of southeast Asian flavors creates the "fusion" menu. Enjoy a sushi bar, satay bar, and alfresco dining. Lunch Mon-Fri; dinner nightly.

103 West (B3), 103 W. Paces Ferry Rd., NW; (404) 233-5993. E. This fine restaurant is owned and run by two of Atlanta's renowned restaurateurs. It joins Pano's and Paul's and the Fish Market with the same creative Continental cuisine and excellent service. Marble and mirrors, floral prints, and the gray and mauve decor add sensuous flair to the interior. The wines are superior. The menu is exciting, from venison to hot amaretto soufflé. Servings are beautifully presented for each course. Dinner Mon-Sat.

Palisades (C3), 1829 Peachtree Rd., NE; (404) 350-6755. M. Understated elegance in a *tres chic* Atlanta neighborhood includes reservations and valet parking. The straightforward Continental menu features such instant classics as seared-and-baked sea bass and mashed potatoes or angel hair pasta with tomatoes and basil. Dinner.

Pano's and Paul's (B3), 1232 W. Paces Ferry Rd., NW; (404) 261-3662. E. Pano's and Paul's is a restaurant in vogue with the residents of northside Atlanta and for good reason. The Victorian elegance of print-draped booths and brass and glass Edwardian appointments is a plush setting for the wide selection of Continental and American cuisine. Dinner Mon-Sat.

The Peasant Uptown (B3), Phipps Plaza, 3500 Peachtree Rd., NE; (404) 261-6341. M. Part of the Peasant chain, the Peasant Uptown is on the upper level of Phipps Plaza. With a 100-foot greenhouse atrium that resembles a New Orleans courtyard, the ambience is casual and spatial elegance. The Continental cuisine is creative and cool, and hot piano is featured in the lounge. While at Phipps don't miss dining at this excellent restaurant. Lunch and dinner daily.

The Pleasant Peasant (H11), 555 Peachtree St.; (404) 874-3223. M. This small, wonderful restaurant in an old drugstore storefront on Peachtree was a trend-setter and tastemaker for Atlantans in the last decade. The Pleasant Peasant, a favorite for the local residents, was the first of the Peasant group chain. The interiors are charming and cheerful, the management is meritorious, and the Continental fare is deliciously inviting and consistent. Dinner daily.

The Public House, on Roswell Town Square; (770) 992-4646. M. The Peasant restaurant group restored an antebellum brick structure on

Roswell Square, just north of Atlanta, and called it the Public House. Nearby residents and visitors come in droves for the quality Continental fare, to see each other, and to listen to the pianist in the loft. No reservations. Lunch Tue-Sat, dinner Mon-Sat.

Winfield's (B2), One Galleria Pkwy.; (770) 955-5300. M to E. Winfield's anchors the west end of the Galleria shopping center with its bright red-orange awnings and handsome deep green interior. The bar and lounge to the left feature some of Atlanta's finest talent. The restaurant is one of the Atlanta-based Peasant chain, a sterling addition to Cobb County dining. Lunch Mon-Sat, dinner daily, brunch Sun.

French

Brasserie Le Coze (B3), 3393 Peachtree Rd., NE; (404) 266-1440. M. Just the kind of French restaurant that ought to be right around the corner from Neiman Marcus at Lenox Square, which is where it is. This is French fare with a New York flair, a patio and valet parking. The creamed soups are a special treat.

Cafe Alsace (C4), 121 E. Ponce de Leon Ave., Decatur, (404) 373-5622. M. Co-owners Benedicte and Marceau of Strasbourg bring a touch of Europe to Decatur at this delightful bistro on the square. The unpretentious décor gives a definite flavor of French café, and the delicious food lives up to the look. Start with an Alsatian onion pie, move on to butterfly trout or lamb chops or Marceau's always tasty crepe du jour, and finish with an exquisite fruit tart. Lunch Tues-Fri, dinner Tues-Sat, Sunday brunch.

Cafe at the Corner (E2), 636 S. Central Ave., Hapeville, (404) 766-1155. I. This charming bistro has served southside Atlanta for nearly a decade. The French owner serves her family recipes. Crepes, soups, and handmade pastries are especially popular. Lunch Mon-Fri.

Cassis (B3), 3300 Peachtree St., in the Grand Hyatt Atlanta; (404) 365-8100. M to E. Delicious selections from the South of France. A lovely choice for an elegant dining experience in the heart of Buckhead's financial district. Lunch and dinner daily.

Ciboulette (C3), 1529 Piedmont Ave., NE; (404) 874-7600. E. Trend-setting dishes are served up by a talented staff in a toney setting. Prices are high, but portions are large. A four-course meal can feed two. So put on your dress-up clothes and come on down. Dinner daily except Sundays.

Petite Auberge (C4), 2935 N. Druid Hills Rd. in Toco Hills Shopping Center; (404) 634-6268. M to E. This "little inn" restaurant sits incongruously in a suburban shopping mall attracting a loyal clientele and offering the visitor a superior dining experience in French cuisine with

German specials on Friday nights. The dining rooms are handsome and elegantly appointed, the service is winning, and the food is infallibly good. Entrees range from pink salmon with sauce sorrel to such delicacies as braised sweetbreads in cognac sauce and rack of lamb. Lunch Mon-Fri, dinner Mon-Sat.

South of France (C4), 2345 Cheshire Bridge Rd., NE, in the square; (404) 325-6963. M *to* E. The decor is unmistakably Country French: stucco walls, half-timbers, and a marvelous stone double fireplace. The three French owners are brothers who bring to Atlanta a southern French cuisine of excellence and extend a warm welcome as you enter. For a casual evening of relaxed and friendly dining, go to the South of France. Dinner by the fire in the winter months is a lovely seasonal garnishment. Lunch Mon-Fri, dinner daily.

Toulouse (C3), 2293-B Peachtree Rd., NW; (404) 351-9533. M. French-American food is served in a sociable atmosphere where the kitchen is part of the show. Don't miss the beef filet with mushrooms, Montrachet, and cognac. Dinner daily.

Violette (B4), 3098 Briarcliff Rd., NE, at Clairmont Rd.; (404) 633-3323. I. The hearty bistro fare makes this Left Bank look-alike a favorite with locals who appreciate good French food in a casual setting.

International

Burrito Art (D4), 1259 Glenwood Ave.; (404) 627-4433. I. More than your ordinary burrito, these feature barbecued chicken, roast pork, chili relieno and the like. Paintings by local artists add visual interest to a cozy if somewhat cramped space. The restaurant's success in quixotic East Atlanta Village has spawned two other locations: (B3) 3365 Piedmont Rd. (404) 237-0095; and (C4) 1451 Oxford Rd. (404) 377-7796.

Coco Loco Cuban and Caribbean Cafe (C3), 2625 Piedmont Rd., NE; (404) 364-0212. M. This friendly restaurant offers a broad menu that includes items from Mexico, Jamaica, and various Latin American countries. A terrific place to experiment with foods from different countries in a setting that feels like Little Havana.

El Azteca, Several metro Atlanta locations, including (B3), 3424 Piedmont Rd., NE, (404) 266-3787; and (H11), 939 Ponce de Leon Ave., NE, (404) 881-6040. I. These fun Mexican restaurants are simple, fast, and good. Outdoor tables make a good place to sit, sip, and watch the traffic go by.

El Toro, I. In 1974, El Toro was one of Atlanta's first Mexican restaurants. Today, success has bred success—10 El Toros throughout the metro area, including one at (A3) 5899 Roswell Rd. in Sandy Springs, (404) 257-9951.

Haveli (B1), 2706 Cobb Pkwy. (U.S. 41), Smyrna; (770) 955-4525. M. Outstanding Indian restaurant serves a broad range of tandoori, curry, seafood, lamb, vegetarian dishes, and breads. Luncheon buffet is an excellent way to sample the menu. Lunch Mon-Sat, dinner Tue-Sat.

The Imperial Fez, (C3), 2285 Peachtree Rd., NE; (404) 351-0870. M to E. Spend a fantasy evening in a sultan's tent. Sit around low tables on plush Oriental carpets and enjoy the finest Middle Eastern food and service. The succulent selection of courses offers choices for meat lovers and vegetarians alike. And the belly dancer puts on a delightful show. Dinner nightly. Reservations suggested.

Jalisco (C3), 2337 Peachtree Rd., NE; (404) 233-9244. I. Tucked near the elbow of the Peachtree Battle Shopping Center, Jalisco is a cheerful Mexican restaurant with a very reasonable price range and tasty South-of-the-Border specialties. Dinner 5-10:30 pm daily.

Lawrence's Cafe (B4), 2888 Buford Hwy.; (404) 320-7756. I to M. A small Middle Eastern restaurant named for Lawrence of Arabia. A succulent selection of Middle Eastern delicacies highlighted with belly dancing on Friday and Saturday evenings. Lunch Mon-Fri, dinner Mon-Sat.

Nicola's (C4), 1602 LaVista Rd., NE; (404) 325-2524. I. Hummus, tabouli, great stuffed grape leaves, and other tasty Middle Eastern dishes are served in an informal family setting. This long-standing restaurant is a dependable favorite with a substantial local following.

Nikolai's Roof (J10), Atlanta Hilton Hotel, Courtland and Harris Sts.; (404) 221-6362. E. At Nikolai's Roof you will usually need reservations in advance, and men must wear jackets and ties. Atop the Atlanta Hilton Hotel, Nikolai's Roof brings you a five-course dinner fit for a czar, with a verbal menu, which rotates every month, recited by your waiter in an opulent environment reminiscent of czarist Russia. Flavored Russian vodka, rare wines, and a splendid series of culinary offerings—have it all at Nikolai's Roof. Prix fixe.

Rio Bravo Cantina (B3), 3172 Roswell Rd.; (404) 262-7431. (J10), 240 Peachtree St., NW; (404) 524-9224. Other Atlanta locations. I to M. Campy Mexican surroundings and simply wonderful fajitas, quesadillas, burritos, and chiles rellenos await all who enter here. Lunch and dinner Mon-Sat.

Taxco (A3), 4500 Roswell Rd., NE (2 miles inside I-285); (404) 255-9933. I to M. Superb Mexican fare prepared with the freshest of ingredients is the hallmark of these restaurants, which also claim the best margaritas in Atlanta. Lunch Mon-Sat. Dinner daily.

Touch of India Tandoori (H11), 1037 Peachtree St., at 10th St.; (404) 876-7777. I. One of Atlanta's most outstanding ethnic cafes, this busy little place serves spicy curries, tandooris, vegetarian dishes, and breads to appreciative midtown patrons. Lunch and dinner daily.

Italian

Avanzare (J10), 265 Peachtree St. in the Hyatt Regency; (404) 577-1234. M. Contemporary Italian restaurant with a large saltwater aquarium. Veal, seafood, and pasta are specialties. Lunch Mon-Fri, dinner nightly.

Bambinelli's (B5), 3202 Northlake Pkwy., NE; (770) 493-1311. *I to M*. This family-owned restaurant serves up pizza, pasta, and seafood in a location convenient to suburban Northlake Mall. Lunch and dinner daily.

Benedetti's (C4), 2064 N. Decatur Rd.; (404) 633-0408. *I.* Italian bistro fare in an art deco setting makes this popular eatery especially memorable. Sample the luncheon specials or enjoy dinner daily.

Bertolini's of Phipps Plaza (B3), 3500 Peachtree Rd.; (404) 233-2333. M. Located in Atlanta's ritziest shopping mall, Bertolini's provides foot-weary shoppers with authentic Northern Italian cuisine that includes fresh pasta and signature desserts. Lunch and dinner daily.

Cafe Prego (A3), 4279 Roswell Rd. (Chastain Square); (404) 252-0032. *I to* M. A festive awning sets the tone for this comfortable neighborhood restaurant which is highly popular with nearby north Atlantans. Lunch Tue-Fri, dinner Mon-Sat.

Camille's (C4), 1186 N. Highland Ave., (404) 872-7203. M. Very New York-y Italian cafe in the trendy Virginia-Highland neighborhood serves excellently sauced lasagna, linguini, seafood, chicken dishes, and pasta to nightly SRO crowds. All-weather outdoor patio. Lunch and dinner daily.

Ciao Bella (B3), 309 Pharr Rd., (404) 261-6013. (A6), 10350 Medlock Bridge Rd. in Duluth, (770) 418-0448. M *to* E. Classy trattorias with slightly different menus at each of its two locations. Lunch and dinner. Reservations suggested.

Everybody's Pizza (C4), 1593 N. Decatur Rd.; (404) 377-7766. (C4) 1040 N. Highland; (404) 873-4545. *I.* Some of the best pizza in Atlanta. When the original building burned to the ground, the owners built a bigger, brighter restaurant with patio that draws huge crowds, so it's wise to go early or late. Great salads, too. Open daily. They also deliver.

Grant Central Pizza & Pasta (D3), 451 Cherokee Ave.; (404) 523-8900. *I to* M. Gourmet pizzas vie with salmon specials and hefty sandwiches to seduce the diner's tastebuds. If not sufficiently tempted, try the lasagna of the day. There's also a comfortable bar area. Located in the Historic Grant Park neighborhood.

La Grotta Ravinia Ristorante Italiano, (A4), 4355 Ashford-Dunwoody Rd., NE, at Crown Pointe Ravinia; (770) 395-9925. E. Among Atlanta's finest restaurants, regardless of cuisine. The veal, seafood, pasta, and desserts are uniformly excellent. Dinner Tue-Sat.

La Grotta Ristorante Italiano (C3), 2637 Peachtree St.; (404) 231-1368. M *to* E. Atlantans have named this their favorite Italian restaurant for the past 14 years. Northern Italian cuisine with homemade pasta. Delicious veal and seafood. Excellent wine list. Dinner Mon-Sat. Reservations recommended.

Lindy's (C3), 10 Kings Cir.; (404) 231-4112. M *to* E. Sumptuous Italian cooking, topped by marvelously rich desserts, in a trendy chintz living room ambience. In favorable weather, ask for a table on the upstairs outdoor terrace. Lunch Mon-Fri, dinner daily.

Nino's (C4), 1931 Cheshire Bridge Rd., NE; (404) 874-6505. M *to* E. Looking for that little Italian restaurant for an intimate evening of conversation, unsurpassed Italian cuisine, and friendly service? Nino's is your place with veal saltimbocca the chef's specialty. Dinner daily.

Pastificio Cameli (D4), 1263 Glenwood Ave., SE; (404) 622-9926. I *to* M. Handmade pastas, grilled steaks and seafood top the list at this excellent trattoria in funky East Atlanta Village. Dine alfresco on the private deck. Choose from an extensive wine list. Dinner Tues-Sat.

The Patio (D4), 1029 Edgewood Ave.; (404) 584-8945. I *to* E. People wax rhapsodic over the atmosphere of this restaurant just across from the Inman Park MARTA station. Yes, there's a patio, a magical spot for dining. The Italian cuisine adds to the love affair. Wide assortment of delectable pasta dishes, as well as pizza and sophisticated entrees. Good wine list to match.

Pricci (B3), 500 Pharr Rd.; (404) 237-2941. E. The *in* Italian restaurant in trendy Buckhead is known for its food, for its whimsical ambience, and for its delicious breads and pastries baked on the premises. Lunch Mon-Fri. Dinner nightly.

Provino's (B3), 4387 Roswell Rd. at Weiuca Rd.; (404) 256-4300. Plus five more metro Atlanta locations for this highly successful restaurant. I *to* M. Provino's has southern Italian fare for the budget-minded traveler, for families, and for those who have a penchant for pasta and rich sauces. Dinner Mon-Sat.

Seafood

Atlanta Fish Market (B3), 265 Pharr Rd., NE; (404) 262-3165. E. Gourmet seafood in high style. The Atlanta Fish Market offers guests an extensive menu and an equally extensive wine list. Lunch Mon-Sat. Dinner nightly. Reservations recommended.

Boston Sea Party (B3), 3820 Roswell Rd.; (404) 233-8766. M-E. This nautically-minded restaurant serves up a spectacular seafood buffet on white linen tablecloths in candlelit elegance. Dinner nightly. Reservations recommended.

Captain Billy's Fish House (A1), 10 Whitlock Ave., SW, Marietta; (770) 423-7171. M. Seafood on Marietta's historic square. Dinner Thu-Sun.

The Crab House (B1), 2175 Cobb Pkwy., SE, Smyrna; (770) 955-2722. *I*. The Crab House caught on quickly in Atlanta because of its extensive menu and relaxed, friendly atmosphere. Lunch Mon-Fri. Dinner nightly.

Embers Seafood Grille (A3), 234 Hildebrand Dr.; (404) 256-0977. M. Residents of Sandy Springs nightly patronize this small, select seafood restaurant. Grilled fish, mussels, conch chowder, and the taramasalata dip add up to a fine treat. Dinner daily.

Indigo, A Coastal Grill (C4), 1397 N. Highland Ave.; (404) 876-0676. M. A campy blend of the Caribbean and Key West, and an intriguing menu of fresh seafood, has made this one of the city's most popular neighborhood dining places. Start with Bahamian conch fritters or tangy lime soup and go from there to steamed or broiled fish. Dinner Tue-Sat.

Jim White's Half Shell (C3), Peachtree Battle Shopping Center, 2349 Peachtree Rd., NE; (404) 237-9924. *I-M*. The Half Shell is an informal neighborhood restaurant, a pioneer in seafood establishments in Atlanta. Its location in the Peachtree Battle Shopping Center is convenient to Downtown and the suburbs. For an evening of solid seafood satisfaction and atmosphere, have dinner at the Half Shell. Dinner Mon-Sat.

Marra's (C3), 1782 Cheshire Bridge Rd., NE; (404) 874-7347. M. Seafood at Marra's is charcoal-grilled with an Italian accent. Pasta accompanies fish. Mako shark, mussels, antipasto, and cioppino complement the regular menu of seafood. Seating is on two levels in this attractive, small house-restaurant. Dinner Mon-Sat.

McKinnon's Louisiane (B3), 3209 Maple Dr.; (404) 237-1313. M-E. McKinnon's was treating Atlantans to spicy Creole and Cajun cuisine long before it became a nationwide sensation. After your jambalaya, crawfish pie, and filé gumbo, join the crowds around the sing-along piano in the lounge. Dinner Mon-Sat.

Southern

Agave (D3), 242 Boulevard, SE; (404) 588-0006. *I*. A funky downhome diner that's popular with neighborhood residents and uptown sophisticates alike. An eclectic menu ranges from burgers to Appalachian pan seared trout, with special features advertised on a hand-lettered board in front. Cocktails, too. Breakfast served anytime.

It's worth a visit just to meet the servers, a motley but cheerful crew. Located across from historic Oakland Memorial Cemetery and near Grant Park and Zoo Atlanta.

Cabbagetown Grill (D3), 727 Wylie St.; (404) 525-8818. *I.* A true neighborhood eatery with an ambience that defies description. Someone did some excellent wood carving for the door and the bar. Food ranges from a black bean burger to herb-baked chicken and pork loins. Try the jalapeno cornbread. Open 11 to 11 Mon-Sun.

1848 House (A1), 780 S. Cobb Dr., SE, Marietta; (770) 428-1848. *E.* Hailed by *Travel and Leisure* as "one of the hottest new restaurants in the nation," 1848 House Restaurant and Conference Center occupies a historic home and the last remaining 13 acres of what was an upland plantation. The Greek Revival home is on the National Register of Historic Places, and the grounds were the site of a Civil War battle. Civil War artifacts are on display—but come for the food, which is certified "nouvelle Southern." Examples include pork tenderloin marinated in bourbon, a Vidalia onion tart, and pan-fried crab cakes with oven-dried tomato mayonnaise and sweet and sour chow-chow. Open for dinner and Sunday brunch. Closed Mondays. Make reservations in advance.

Evan's Fine Foods (C4), 2125 N. Decatur Rd.; (404) 634-6294. *I.* Popular with young families and the older set, this long-time restaurant serves good, basic Southern fare with surprising variety on the menu. Friendly staff may call you "Hon." A complete meal costs $7 or less. Easy parking, too.

Factory's BBQ (D3), 428 Boulevard, SE; (404) 627-8448. *I.* It looks like a tornado just dropped it at random, but a breeze scented with hickory smoke gives it away. Menu ranges from chopped pork or beef sandwiches to a half slab of ribs. Reasonable prices and yummy aromas make it hard to choose just one selection. Four side dishes include potato wedges. They claim the tangy sauce is a secret family recipe from the 1950's. Limited seating, but it's close to Grant Park, so order a takeout and go find the picnic area. Open Tue-Sat.

Folks Southern Kitchen (E2), 6564 Tara Blvd., Jonesboro; (770) 968-8965. *I.* Check the telephone Yellow Pages for other metro Atlanta locations. OK, so this is a chain. But some local wags insist they've got some of the best fried chicken hereabouts. The iced tea, served in Mason jars, gets a thumbs up, too. Lunch and dinner daily.

Food Studio (C3), 887 W. Marietta St.; (404) 815-6677. *I-M.* Located in the King Plow Arts Center, this café includes old plow machinery in its creative décor. The New Southern cuisine is equally inventive, mixing Mediterranean and Southwestern tastes with more traditional fare for delightful combinations. Cosmopolitan wine bar. Dinner nightly.

Harold's (D2), 171 McDonough Blvd. SE; (404) 627-9268. *I.* This Southern barbecue restaurant, established nearly 50 years ago in south Atlanta, brings in the faithful from Atlanta and surrounding counties. Lunch and dinner Mon-Sat.

Horseradish Grill (B3), 4320 Powers Ferry Rd., NW; (404) 255-7277. M *to* E. This "Southern Revival" restaurant is proving itself a worthy successor to the classic Red Barn Inn, whose picturesque building it now occupies. Low Country shrimp paste on grits with toast points, Vidalia onion soup, and group fritters have spawned a coterie of regulars. Dinner. Also Sunday "Southern Brunch." As they say, "It's not just grits!"

Lickskillet Farm, 1380 Old Roswell Rd., Roswell; (770) 475-6484. M *to* E. This pre-Civil War farmhouse is rural eloquence. Enjoy cocktails in the gazebo overlooking Foekiller Creek before stepping back to the restaurant for a select country menu of chicken, steaks, and seafood. A roaring fire in winter and piano entertainment in the evening make Lickskillet Farm a special place. Dinner Tue-Sat, champagne brunch Sun.

Mary Mac's Tea Room (I11), 224 Ponce de Leon Ave., NE; (404) 876-1800. *I.* If you've never been to the South, Mary Mac's will thrill you, and if you're from the South, especially any small town that has its local restaurant, you'll be right at home at Mary Mac's. The food is country Southern. Lunch and dinner until 8 pm Mon-Fri.

Old Hickory House (C3), 5490 Chamblee-Dunwoody Rd., Dunwoody; (770) 671-8185. *I.* Call for other locations throughout metro Atlanta. Old Hickory House is an Atlanta barbecue institution, family-owned and operated, with some of the best secret barbecue recipes in the South. Try pork, beef, or chicken with or without jalapeno peppers, special slaw, and the famous Old Hickory House Brunswick stew. Breakfast, lunch, and dinner daily.

Paschal's (D3), 830 Martin Luther King, Jr. Dr., NW; (404) 577-3150. M-E. Paschal's is a landmark in Atlanta's black heritage, a thriving restaurant in the Atlanta University section of the city. Frequented by politicians, businessmen and businesswomen, and visiting entertainers, Paschal's introduces you to the pleasures of Southern fare and to the traditional meeting place and forum for the black community. The restaurant, which is part of Paschal's Motor Inn, is open for breakfast, lunch, and dinner daily.

Pittypat's Porch (J9), 25 International Blvd.; (404) 525-8228. M-E. The tone is antebellum "Old South" at Pittypat's Porch with original Southern antiques, period memorabilia, rocking chairs, and the staff in full costume. Traditional Southern cooking is the main attraction, although American and continental dishes are also on the menu. Dinner daily.

Sycamore Grill (C6), 5329 Mimosa Dr., Stone Mountain; (770) 465-6789. M-E. Located in historic Stone Mountain Village, Sycamore Grill is a white clapboard hotel built about 1836 in a Charleston townhouse style. Once used as a Confederate hospital, its name derives from a 150-year-old tree next to the veranda. Try the crab cakes with a glass of sweet tea. Serves lunch and dinner Tue-Sat.

Thomas Marketplace (F3), 16 Forest Parkway; (404) 361-1367. I. This is the real thing. A family-owned homestyle restaurant that's been pulling people in for more than 30 years with good food, friendly service, and a casual setting at the state farmer's market. Breakfast, lunch, and dinner served daily.

Vegetarian

Café Sunflower (A3), 5975 Roswell Rd.; (404) 256-1675. I. This upscale restaurant caters to its Sandy Springs clientele with a combination of culinary influences from Asia, the Mediterranean, and Mexico. Be sure to try the Sandy Springs rolls, red pepper hummus, and eggplant and wood-ear mushrooms in garlic and ginger sauce with short-grain brown rice. Lunch and dinner.

Harmony Vegetarian (A5), 4897 Buford Hwy.; (770) 457-7288. I. For the purist, Harmony serves no meat at all in its traditional Chinese dishes. Imitation chicken, beef, pork, and seafood do the honors instead. Vegetables in curry sauce are especially good. Friendly family atmosphere. Open daily except Tuesday for lunch and dinner.

Indian Delights (C4), 1707 Church St., Decatur; (404) 296-2965. I. Indian food with a bit of a different slant. The Decatur location has only a small dining area, but does a bustling business in take-out. Lunch and dinner daily.

The Rainbow Grocery and Café (C4), 2118 N. Decatur Rd., NE; (404) 633-3538. I. Natural foods, fresh produce, cosmetics, and vitamins are sold in the grocery. The café at the back has wonderful hot entrees, soups, salads, sandwiches, and desserts, naturally. No smoking. Lunch and early dinner Mon-Sat.

Soul Vegetarian Restaurant, (D3), 879 Ralph D. Abernathy Blvd., SW; (404) 752-5194. (C4), 652 N. Highland Ave., NE; (404) 875-4641. I. Proof positive that veggies can be delicious and satisfying food for the soul.

ETCETERA

Here is a grab bag of interesting but difficult-to-define items in the

Atlanta restaurant scene: some gourmet fast foods, natural-food eateries, unique menus, and hamburger joints. Take your pick.

The Baker's Café (D3), 1134 Euclid Ave., NE; (404) 223-5039. *I*. It's a deli with delicious desserts, great sandwiches, and dinner pasta, chicken, and beef specialties. This is a regular haunt for the neighborhoods of Inman and Candler Park in the Little Five Points intersection. Bring your own beer or wine. Lunch and dinner Mon-Sat. Brunch Sun.

Brother Juniper's (G12), 1037 Peachtree St., NE; (404) 881-6225. *I*. This bright breakfast and lunch spot in Midtown is run by a Catholic brother offering good cheer, deli sandwiches with homemade bread in two sizes, whole and half, desserts such as poppy-seed cake, and beverages that include fresh lemonade, hot spiced cider, and red zinger tea. Eggs, waffles, and omelets are for breakfast. Breakfast and lunch Mon-Fri.

Café Tu Tu Tango (B3), 220 Pharr Rd.; (404) 841-6222. *I*. Local artists paint and sell their work at this lively café in the heart of Buckhead. Mexican, pizza, and American fare are served in appetizer portions. Order several and share. Award-winning Sangria. Open until 2 am on Fri and Sat.

EatZi's Market & Bakery, 3221 Peachtree Rd.; (404) 237-2266. *I-M*. It's a bit like walking into the middle of an operetta. Colorful food, gourmet takeouts, or all the fixin's if you prefer to make your own. Classical music plays. Chefs call out their specialties like carnival barkers. Daily 7 am-10 pm.

Five Sisters Café (C5), 2743 LaVista Rd.; (404) 636-6060. *I*. This offbeat neighborhood bistro is located in the Oak Grove Shopping Center. Good salads, unique sandwiches, and dinner entrees that change weekly. Yes, there are five real sisters, at least one of whom will be present to greet and chat with diners. Mon-Sat.

Mellow Mushroom (C3), 931 Monroe Dr., NE; (404) 874-2291. *I*. A little bit of local color that's a holdover from Atlanta's Hippie era. It's good pizza, and they shape the crust the old-fashioned way—tossing it in the air in full view of the customers. Call for six other locations. Lunch and dinner daily.

Try the following for breakfast or lunch. The Silver Grill and Our Way are also open for dinner, or as they might say, supper.

Bobby & June's Country Kitchen (C3), 375 Fourteenth St., NW; (404) 876-3872. **Our Way** (C4), 303 E. College Ave., Decatur; (404) 373-6665. **Silver Grill** (C3), 900 Monroe Dr., NE; (404) 876-8145.

The Varsity (I10), 61 North Ave., NW; (404) 881-1706. *I*. The Varsity is an Atlanta landmark next to Georgia Tech. The shiny red enamel art deco exterior, the jazzy curb service, and the TV rooms are part of Atlanta's fast-food history. Chili dogs are a must before Georgia Tech football games. Service is 24 hours. Also visit the **Jr. Varsity** (C3),

1085 Lindbergh Dr., NE; (404) 261-8843. The newest Varsity is the **Varsity Gwinnett** (A6), 6045 Dawson Blvd., Norcross, (770) 840-8519.

CAFETERIAS

Cafeterias have many selections of meats, seafood, vegetables, and desserts at inexpensive prices. Children are welcome, and many older Atlantans still have the habit of eating regularly at their favorite cafeteria. Below are our choices.

DeKalb Farmers Market (C5), 3000 E. Ponce de Leon Ave.; (404) 377-6400. *I.* For a truly international atmosphere, nothing beats the DeKalb Farmers Market, and the cafeteria is a real bargain. Dine first, then stock up on your weekly groceries. Don't expect designer décor, but the food is both good and nutritious. Two lines include a salad bar, freshly made soups, meat, vegetables, sandwiches, wraps, fresh breads, and just-squeezed juices. With the market just across the aisle, everything is fresh, and there's a lot of variety, from fried sweet potatoes to roasted duck to vegetarian sausage. Very reasonable rates. Open daily 11 am-8 pm.

Lettuce Souprise You (C4), 2470 Briarcliff Rd.; NE; (404) 636-8549. *I.* Great salad fixings, selection of hearty soups, pastas, muffins, fresh fruit, all served up cafeteria style in a health-conscious, smoke-free environment. Lunch and dinner daily.

Piccadilly Cafeteria (C3), Ansley Mall, 1544 Piedmont Ave., NE; (404) 872-8091. Many other locations. *I.* Convenient to neighborhoods in and around the city, Piccadilly is both comfortable and famous for its variety. Open 11 am-8:30 pm. Check telephone white pages for a Picadilly near you.

Whole Foods Market (C4), 2111 Briarcliff Rd.; (404) 634-7800. *I-M.* Part of a healthy-foods supermarket, this cafeteria serves food so good you won't realize it's good for you as well. Choose your feast and take it home, or eat at the market in booths located by the front windows. Entrees include citrus glazed salmon, free-range chicken stuffed with roasted red pepper, and herb crusted tofu. Tasty appetizers and side orders and, yes, even healthful desserts. Open daily.

BRUNCH

Sunday brunch—that wonderful contraction of breakfast and lunch in a midday meal—has become a fashionable leisure activity for apres-church or following a morning of rest. For the traveler, brunch can be a welcome shift in dining, leaving the morning and evening free. Remember that liquor cannot be served in Atlanta until after 12:30 on Sunday. We list below some selected brunch spots in the city. Many others abound. Call to check specific times and refer to restaurant listings for further information.

Café Marmalade (A4), Doubletree Hotel, 7 Concourse Pkwy.; (770) 395-3900. *I*. One of Northside Atlanta's most popular brunches. Hot entrees, omelets cooked to order, salads, fruits, carved meats. All this and live piano music.

Park 75 (H11), 75 Fourteenth St.; (404) 253-3840. *E*. As you might expect, champagne Sunday brunch at the sumptuous Four Seasons Hotel features all the flavors of Europe in an eye-popping spread.

Cassis (B3), Peachtree at Piedmont; (404) 365-8100. *M*. A glass of champagne accompanies a delectable variety of chef's creations in an atmosphere of casual elegance.

The Country Place (G12), Colony Square, Fourteenth St. and Peachtree St., NE; (404) 881-0144. *M*. Extra-popular Midtown brunch.

Dim Sum is Chinese brunch, a leisurely mid-Sunday eating experience where diners pick and choose among a wide variety of items. A number of Atlanta's Chinese restaurants serve dim sum. Our favorites include: **Hong Kong Harbour** (C4), 2184 Cheshire Bridge Rd., NE; (404) 325-7630, *I*. **Royal China** (B5), 3295 Chamblee-Dunwoody Rd., Chamblee; (770) 216-9933, *I*. **Oriental Pearl** (B5), 5399 New Peachtree Rd., Chamblee; (770) 986-9866, *I*.

1848 House (A1), 789 South Cobb Dr.; (770) 428-1848. *M*. Enjoy a contemporary Southern brunch to the sophisticated backdrop of live jazz music, all in an authentic 1848 Greek Revival mansion.

57th Fighter Group (B4), 3829 Clairmont Rd.; (770) 457-7757. M *to E*. The officer's club is open for an All-American brunch.

Lickskillet Farm, Old Roswell Rd. and Buckmill Rd., Roswell; (770) 475-6484. *M*. A popular brunch with a delicious fruit bar, homemade biscuits, and plenty more.

Ray's On The River (A2), 6700 Powers Ferry Rd.; (770) 955-1187. *M*. Nestled on the banks of the Chattahoochee. A popular spot for all. Varied and delicious spread. Sunday only.

Ritz Carlton Buckhead (B3), 3434 Peachtree Rd., NE; (404) 237-2700. *E*. Brunch in The Dining Room reigns supreme with Old Atlanta and New Buckhead. Brunch with true Continental flair.

The Sun Dial (J9), Westin Peachtree Hotel; (404) 589-7506. *E*. Begin your week right with brunch 73 stories high.

The Waverly Grill (B2), the Galleria, 2450 Galleria Pkwy.; (770) 953-4500. *E*. The Waverly, a Renaissance Hotel, serves brunch in the elegant tradition.

Winfield's (B2), 100 Galleria Pkwy.; (770) 955-5300. M. A handsome magnet for East Cobb County for brunch.

COFFEE OR TEA

Caffeine or free, America's favorite brews can both perk you up or calm you down and, say devotees of green tea, clear your system of toxins. Mostly, it's a comfort thing, which could eventually put therapists out of business. Atlanta is a sociable town and loves to meet and gossip. In the past few years, coffeehouses have proliferated in all areas. The chains, such as **Starbuck's** and **Caribou,** and the smaller but excellent **Aurora,** are represented in every shopping area, and most bookstores have a coffee bar either on the premises or next door. There are many independent coffee and teahouses, however, that lend special nuances to the bliss of one's favorite espresso or tisane. Some serve lunch; most have desserts or bagels; and many include live entertainment of the grassroots kind. We list a few of our favorites below. Bear in mind that new ones can appear overnight, and discovering your own favorite sipping spot is part of the fun.

Java Monkey Coffee (C4), 205 E. Ponce de Leon in Decatur; (404) 378-5002. *I.* Enter around the corner on Church Street in the heart of Decatur's burgeoning boutique and bistro area, but the coffee house was here first. Décor is grab bag, fourth-hand chic, comfort without putting on airs. Popular with writers, students from Agnes Scott and Emory, local shoppers and business folk, Java Monkey Coffee boasts of a clientele so loyal they're like family. The café serves light lunch and limited but good desserts; try "The Last Seduction." Live acoustic music on weekend nights and occasional poetry readings. A good hot-weather choice: luscious iced tea mixed with one of their exotic syrups. We recommend the passion fruit. Open daily; until 1 am on weekend nights.
Sacred Grounds (D4), 510 Flat Shoals Ave.; (404) 584-5541. *I.* One of the first "new" businesses in East Atlanta Village, Sacred Grounds draws customers from nearby renovation neighborhoods but is also popular with the literati and on weekends draws a citywide crowd. The shop uses organic beans from Olympia, Washington, and granulated cane juice for sweetener. Tasty pastry from their affiliated shop, Cake Walk. Yes, they serve tea, too. The décor of ecclesiastical antiques and 1950's kitsch, most of it for sale, lends a unique ambiance. Occasional art shows, acoustic music, and poetry readings.
Joe Muggs Newsstand (C3), 3275 Peachtree Rd.; (404) 364-9290. *I.* If you like to catch up on the news while you sip, this coffee

shop in Buckhead has over 4,000 magazines and newspapers to choose from, both national and beyond. Comfortable seating indoors, but the outdoor patio is popular with the gen-X crowd. A good selection of both coffees and teas. Scrumptious pastries, too. Try the lemon bars.

Krispy Kreme (C3), 295 Ponce de Leon Ave., (404) 876-7307. *I.* If you haven't joined the Krispy Kreme doughnut craze, now's your chance. Yes, you can get coffee, but that's really not the point. Watch those round bites of heaven come fresh off the bakery line, inhale the aroma, and you'll forget the calorie count. An Atlanta institution, this Krispy Kreme is open all day until 1 or 2 am, and the drive-through stays open 24 hours to satisfy those wee-hour cravings.

Outwrite Bookstore and Coffeehouse (H12), 991 Piedmont Ave., NE; (404) 607-0082. Catering to a primarily gay and lesbian clientele, Outwrite offers books, cards, coffee, pastries, and the occasional poetry reading and book signing for the literary set.

Ritz Carlton-Buckhead (B3), 3434 Peachtree Rd.; (404) 237-2700. *E.* For sheer elegance, indulge in high tea at this major hotel. Tapestries, upholstered arm chairs, white napery, fresh flowers. Strictly first class. Expensive but a royal treat.

San Francisco Coffee (C4), 1192 Highland Ave.; (404) 876-8816. *I.* Popular with denizens of the sophisticated Virginia-Highland area, San Francisco Coffee is a few steps from Camille's primo Italian restaurant, and other fine eating spots. A good place to finish off a meal with delicious dessert and brew. It has exposed brick walls and large picture windows for some interesting people watching. If you can't hold a pastry on top of lasagna, there's a good assortment of fine chocolate candy, by the piece, bar, or box.

Teavana (B3), 3500 Peachtree Rd., Suite 1370; (404) 261-3004. *I.* Explore the world of tea in this wonderful shop. They carry 90 kinds, including black, green, herbal, decaffeinated, flavored and scented, Oolongs, and white teas. The teas are stored in large tins, and management is expert at presenting each for you to see and sniff. Take your time selecting; the aromas are magnificent. No tea bags here. The brewing is part of the experience, and teapots of various size and design are also for sale. Comfortable tables and chairs, discreet music. The flagship has been so successful it has spawned two offspring—a plush location at Peachtree City and a small, mostly take-out store at Lenox Square. All teas are for sale in bulk, ranging in price from $2.75 for two oz. of a vanilla bean blend to $18 for two oz. of an organic white tea that's harvested but once a year. Caffeine or non, these brews are happily addictive.

BEYOND ATLANTA

Blue Willow Inn, 294 N. Cherokee Rd. (Ga. Hwy. 11), Social Circle, Ga. 30025; (770) 464-2131 or toll free (800) 552-8813. *I.* A famous buffet in a beautifully restored Southern home, Blue Willow Inn has been featured in *Southern Living* magazine. It serves lunch and dinner daily with both Southern and seafood buffets for dinner. Prices, under $20, include beverages and desserts, and you can go back for refills until you're too full to move. Children 4-11 eat at half price. The white-columned plantation home has been decorated with care and is adorned with special holiday trim during December. Take I-20 east to exit 98, turn left and travel four miles into Social Circle. Reservations recommended. Ask about group discounts.

Sprayberry's Barbecue, 1060 E. Hwy. 34 near Newnan; (770) 253-5080. *I.* Forget the calories and fat grams and chow down Southern style. Sprayberry's may remind you of church dinner on the grounds with a variety of barbecue plates and sandwiches, great fries, and home-made lemon icebox pie, among others. Generous portions. Family friendly. Look for their signs about 30 min. south of Atlanta on I-85. Open Mon-Sat 10:30 am-9 pm. Either before or after eating, drive into Newnan to see the lovely historic homes.

Yesterday Café, 120 Fairplay Rd., Rutledge, Ga. 30663; (706) 557-9337. *I to M.* Not quite an hour's drive east of Atlanta, Yesterday Café in the tiny hamlet of Rutledge is located in a renovated 1893 drugstore. Owners Terri and Alan Bragg preserved the original tiled floors and pressed tin ceiling and have lined the walls with vintage photographs of the local area. They serve New American cuisine, winning raves for shrimp, veal scaloppini, and Caribbean chicken salad with tropical dressing. Don't resist the homemade buttermilk pie. Take I-20 east to exit 105. Café is open daily for lunch; Tue-Sun for breakfast; and Thurs-Sat for dinner. Make reservations for five or more; otherwise simply show up and enjoy.

PERFORMING ARTS

The performing arts match the economic surges in Atlanta with equally vigorous expressions in music, the dance, and theater. From jazz to symphony, from ballet to street mime, from storefront drama to the proscenium stage, Atlantans turn out to see and hear classical and cyclical performances as well as those on the cutting edge of change in cultural expressions. Many cultural organizations sponsor exciting and memorable events that Atlantans are welcome to attend. Turn one of our listings into an evening of special meaning and enrichment; let Atlanta perform for you.

Dance

Atlanta Ballet, 1400 W. Peachtree St., NE; (404) 873-5811. This fine regional ballet company holds the honor of being the oldest continually performing ballet company in the United States. Born in 1929, the Atlanta Ballet repertory company, under the direction of Robert Barnett, has regularly scheduled performances in Atlanta and on tour. Expect innovation in presenting traditional programs at the Fox Theater (I10) and original productions at Robert Ferst Center for the Performing Arts (H10) on the Georgia Tech campus.

Atlanta Jazz Theatre, Inc., 5568 Chamblee-Dunwoody Rd., Dunwoody; (770) 393-9519. Energetic young troupe is the state of Georgia's official jazz dance company.

Ballethnic Dance Company (E2), 2587 Cheney St., East Point; (404) 762-1416. This exciting company is a classically trained, culturally diverse ballet company committed to performing classical ballet and blending that tradition with the art of ethnic dance. The company's "Urban Nutcracker" is a winter holidays tradition.

Decatur School of Ballet, 102 Church St., Decatur; (404) 378-3388.

Gwinnett Ballet Theatre, 2200 McGee Rd., SW, Lilburn; (770) 978-0188.

Lee Harper Studios, 380 E. Shadowlawn Ave.; (404) 364-9555. A

highly disciplined, modern dance troupe that offers stunning performances with Atlanta Opera and other venues. It has both an adult company and a children's company and offers classes to all ages.
Ruth Mitchell Dance Studio, 81 Church St., NE, Marietta; (770)
426-0007. The Ruth Mitchell Dance Company was founded more than
40 years ago and performs originally choreographed ballet and jazz
dancing.
Several Dancers Core, 133 Sycamore St., Decatur; (404) 373-4154.
A company of contemporary modern dance, Several Dancers Core
appears at the Fourteenth Street Playhouse and tours throughout the
Southeast and abroad. They have an active educational schedule,
including their "Rising Stars" program for at-risk children. As part of
their annual holidays celebration, they offer a dance presentation of
"Messiah."

Music

The Atlanta Symphony Orchestra (G11), the Robert W. Woodruff
Arts Center, 1280 Peachtree St., NE; (404) 733-4900. Tickets (404)
733-5000. Home for the Atlanta Symphony Orchestra is the Robert
W. Woodruff Arts Center, built in the 1960s as a memorial to 122
members of the Atlanta Arts Association who were killed in a plane
crash at Orly Airport, near Paris, France. The internationally
acclaimed orchestra won multiple Grammy awards under the legendary
Robert Shaw and his successor, Music Director Emeritus Yoel Levi.
Young, as orchestras go, the Atlanta Symphony will celebrate its 60th
anniversary in 2004. The typical season is full to overflowing with regular and special concerts, choral and dance joint events, with guest
conductors and musicians. Of particular note are the New Mornings
Coffee Series on selected Fridays, Casual Classics on Saturday afternoons, the SuperPOPS! Series, the Youth Orchestra, and, of course, the
Masterworks concerts. Special holiday events are always sell-outs.
Sometimes last-minute tickets can be obtained at a discount at the box
office. Group discounts are available in advance for 10 or more people.
The Atlanta Symphony Orchestra, one of the keystones of cultural
strength in the city, will bring you to your feet with its outstanding
music.

Masterworks Concerts. The Masterworks season begins in September
and lasts through May, the Symphony performing in Symphony Hall
on Thursday, Friday, and Saturday each week. Renowned guest soloists
add to the excitement. Pre-concert talks on Thursday nights by local
professors, music educators, and visiting musicians are a bonus for
Thursday night ticket holders. Fanfare, a cozy restaurant just steps away

from Symphony Hall, allows you to enjoy a delicious dinner or buffet prior to the concert without worrying about being late.

Holiday Concerts. In Symphony Hall. Concerts to honor Martin Luther King, Jr. Day are part of the Masterworks Series. Halloween and Thanksgiving are occasions for special musical events. The end-of-year holiday season brings Handel's *Messiah*, "Christmas with the ASO," conducted by William Fred Scott, a special "Kid's Holiday" program, "Gospel Christmas," and a New Year's Eve concert.

New Mornings Coffee Series and Casual Classics feature informal talks from the stage and a variety of favorite symphonic masterworks. New Mornings offers coffee and pastries prior to the 11 am program, and both four-program subscription series last about 1 hour and 15 minutes.

Atlanta Symphony Orchestra Chorus. The chorus, which earned international renown under the baton of the late Robert Shaw, performs periodically during the Masterworks Concert season, and often includes superb guest soloists. We recommend these exhilarating combination concerts.

Classic Chastain and *Country Chastain* concerts (B3). In the outdoor amphitheater in Atlanta's Chastain Park, the Symphony offers two summer seasons under the stars, featuring top names in pop and country music, plus selections by the Atlanta Symphony Orchestra. Rent a table or bring your own, open up a gourmet or down-home picnic in the amphitheater, and then settle back for a balmy evening of splendid music. Concerts are held on Wednesday, Friday and Saturday evenings.

Family Concerts. During the school year the Atlanta Symphony presents four Sunday afternoon concerts designed to entertain and enlighten a young audience. They often feature costumes, puppetry, and audience interaction.

The Atlanta Opera, 728 W. Peachtree St., NW; (404) 352-2584. This is a professional opera company which presents four productions each year, two in the fall and two in the spring. If they are performing during your stay in Atlanta, be sure to attend their performances at the Fox Theatre.

Philips Arena (J8), One Philips Dr.; (404) 249-6400. This multipurpose complex with state-of-the-art technology hosts some 200 events per year. Perhaps best known as home to major sports teams, it also presents performances as varied as Tina Turner and Luciano Pavarotti. Call the Arena for upcoming events.

Rialto Center for the Performing Arts (J9), 80 Forsyth St.; (404) 651-4727. A superb 900-seat theater in the historic Fairlie-Poplar district, the Rialto presents an eclectic season of dance and music, from jazz to rock to classical including a Chamber Music Series with the Lanier Trio.

Spivey Hall. (770) 961-3683. Located 20 min. from Downtown Atlanta at Clayton College and State University, Spivey Hall has been called "an acoustic gem" and "one of the top 10 small halls on the

Eastern seaboard" by National Public Radio. Mezzo-soprano Denyce Graves, Robert Shaw, and other notables have recorded CDs there, and concerts at Spivey are often broadcast on NPR's "Performance Today." The hall draws artists as diverse as jazz pianist Ellis Marsalis, Joshua Bell of "The Red Violin" fame, and Anonymous 4. It features a piano series, a jazz series, a guitar series, a choral series, and other fine entertainment. Take I-75 south to exit 233, turn left and drive to Clayton State Blvd. Connoisseurs of music, in whatever style, will never be disappointed at Spivey Hall.

Other groups performing regularly in the Atlanta area include the **Atlanta Chamber Players,** the **Atlanta Symphony Brass Quintet,** the **Atlanta Virtuosi Baroque Orchestra,** the **Callanwolde Concert Band,** and the **Georgian Chamber Players.** Local choruses include the **Atlanta Bach Choir,** the **Young Singers of Callanwolde, The Atlanta Singers,** and the **Atlanta Boy Choir.** Check local newspapers for current concerts. Also check with local churches, colleges, and universities for special music programs by faculty, students, and visiting musicians. See Students in the SPECIAL PEOPLE chapter.

Theater

Regional theater has grown from its early two or three root companies to clusters of small companies, some spinoffs, some specialists, all building a solid Atlanta theater community aware of its interdependence and dedicated to dramatic excellence. There is fire and sensitivity in this sector of Atlanta Resurgens.

Midtown and the Little Five Points area have become the "Theater Districts" in Atlanta, convenient to downtown visitors and to residents throughout the metro area.

Along with the recommended following companies check the weekly programs at the Fox Theatre, Fourteenth Street Playhouse, the Rialto, and the Atlanta Civic Center. Touring concerts, road companies, and other special shows are booked throughout the year. Call Ticketmaster, the central ticket office, at (404) 249-6400, or call (404) 873-1185 for current programs, times, and locations. AtlanTIX, located in Underground Atlanta, offers same-day, half-price tickets to various shows. Check Tue-Sun or call (770) 772-5572.

Academy Theatre (K2), 501 Means St., NW; (404) 525-4111. The Academy Theatre, which dates from the 1950s and was one of Atlanta's earliest professional theater companies, now offers staged readings of new plays, develops special touring plays for schools, and offers classes in playwriting and play development.

Agatha's: A Taste of Mystery (C3), 693 Peachtree St.; (404) 875-1610. At this unusual dinner theater, diners participate in mystery-solving with costumed actors and actresses. Each guest is given new identity papers at the door and spends the rest of dinner trying to figure out "who dunnit." Thurs-Sun evenings. Call for reservations.

Alliance Theatre (G11), the Robert W. Woodruff Arts Center, 1280 Peachtree St., NE; (404) 733-4700. The Alliance is Atlanta's most prestigious theater company. The full season, under the direction of Kenny Leon, consists of new and established plays, updated classics, and Shakespeare. Each play runs for about a month from October to May, generally to a full house. The proscenium theater with balcony and orchestra has a very large stage and a scenic design facility. You will enjoy the high standard of the Alliance Theatre.

Alliance Children's Theatre (G11), the Robert W. Woodruff Arts Center, 1280 Peachtree St., NE; (404) 733-4700. Adult actors and actresses present classic and contemporary drama for children.

Atlanta Broadway Series (C3), brings touring companies of popular Broadway hits to the Fox Theatre. Call (404) 817-8700 for ticket information.

The Center for Puppetry Arts (C3), 1404 Spring St., NW (at Eighteenth St.); (404) 873-3089 or (404) 873-3391. The center has become in 30 years the most comprehensive puppetry center in the nation. It offers a museum of the South's largest permanent collection of international puppets, a puppetry school, and the resident troupe, the Vagabond Marionettes. International puppeteers give regularly scheduled performances. Call for show times and museum times.

Dad's Garage Theatre (D4), 280 Elizabeth St.; (404) 523-3141. Improvisation is the thing. Dad's award-winning comedy improv show "TheatreSports" draws enthusiastic fans on Sat. nights. The company also produces new and unusual premiere plays.

Dave & Buster's Mystery Dinner Theater (A1), I-75 and Delk Rd.; (770) 951-5554. Enjoy a good meal and help solve a crime at the same time at this fun-filled Marietta dinner theater. Saturday evenings only.

Fourteenth Street Playhouse (G11), 173 14th St., NE; (404) 733-4750. A three-stage facility with several resident theatres, the 14th Street Playhouse also books touring shows, offering a diverse schedule of theatre, dance, and music.

Georgia Shakespeare Festival (B4), Oglethorpe University, 4484 Peachtree Rd., NE; (404) 264-0020. A not-for-profit repertory company, the Festival began in 1986 in a tent. In 1997 it moved into the new Conant Center, a 510-seat theater at Oglethorpe University Auditorium walls can be raised during pleasant weather to continue the open-air tradition. Pre-show picnicking is a Festival tradition, too. Bring your own picnic or order from the Festival caterer.

Fox Theatre, (I10), 660 Peachtree St., NE; (404) 249-6400. Don't miss an opportunity to visit the Fox Theatre and the Fox district as a banner experience. The Fox is a 1920s movie palace complete with Moorish and Egyptian-revival decor, a majestic original period organ, and stars a-twinkling on its interior ceilings. Across the street is the Georgian Terrace Hotel where Clark Gable, Vivien Leigh, and the rest of the *Gone with the Wind* cast stayed for the 1939 premier showing. The management of the Fox looked on with envy as they left for the Loew's theater—now the location of the Georgia-Pacific building—where the premiere took place.

Gainesville Theatre Alliance, Georgia Mountains Center, P.O. Box 1358, Gainesville, GA 30503; (770) 718-3624. For a fantastic evening away, visit the Georgia Mountains Center and attend one of the Gainesville Theatre Alliance's outstanding performances. Call for reservations.

Horizon Theater (C3), 1083 Austin Ave.; (404) 584-7450. This company's focus is on plays by internationally renowned playwrights whose works are seldom performed in the Southeast, with an emphasis on works by and/or about women. Located in artsy Little Five Points.

Jewish Theatre of the South (G11), 173 Fourteenth St., NE; (404) 368-SHOW. This professional theater, residing at the Fourteenth St. Playhouse, produces regional premieres and seldom produced plays with Jewish content.

Jomandi Productions (G11), 173 Fourteenth St., NE; (404) 876-6346. Four productions a year are presented by the innovative Jomandi troupe of black actors, the state's oldest and largest black professional theatre company. New works are company-developed and often feature world and regional premieres.

Neighborhood Playhouse (C5), 430 W. Trinity Place, Decatur; (404) 373-5311. This terrific neighborhood family theater offers a full season of big-name musicals and dramas. Senior discounts. Call for offerings and dates.

Onstage Atlanta (G11), 173 Fourteenth St., NE; (404) 897-1802. Producing live theatre in Atlanta since 1971, this small company offers comedies, dramas and musicals from Broadway, off-Broadway and regional theatres. It's also home of Abracadabra Children's Theatre.

Push Push Theater (C4), 1123 Zonolite Rd.; (404) 892-7876. An avant-garde theater group, this studio theater works with professional actors from various Atlanta theaters to develop new skills and directions. Produces a Spring Short Play Festival and a summer theatre camp for children.

Seven Stages (D4), 1105 Euclid Ave., NE; (404) 523-7647. In Little Five Points in Inman Park, this theater does original and avant-garde works as well as readings, international collaborations, and premieres.

Shakespeare Tavern (I10), 499 Peachtree St.; (404) 874-5299. This is the world's only Shakespeare Tavern, a place where you can eat, drink, and nourish your soul with British pub food, Irish beer, and Elizabethan drama. Come early to eat. Food service cuts off before the play begins.

Stage Door Players (A4), North DeKalb Cultural Center, 5339 Chamblee-Dunwoody Rd. in Dunwoody; (770) 396-1726. This neighborhood nonprofit theater group offers several quality productions each year.

Theater in the Square (A1), 11 Whitlock Ave., Marietta; (770) 422-8369. Some of the finest theatrical productions in the Atlanta area are staged at this 225-seat theater on Marietta's town square. The theater won the Georgia Governor's Award for the Arts for its first-class presentations of standard and new plays.

Theater of the Stars (I11). Performances are at the Fox Theatre. This Atlanta company has faithfully brought stars of the theater, film, and television to Atlanta audiences since the early 1950s. Presently, it seeks to preserve, create, or recreate the American musical. For individual performance tickets, call Ticketmaster, (404) 249-6400. For season ticket information, call (404) 252-8960.

Theatre Gael (G11), 173 Fourteenth St., NE; (404) 876-9762. An inter-Celtic arts organization dedicated to preserving and fostering the rich cultural heritage of Ireland, Scotland, and Wales, Theatre Gael produces the plays, poetry, music, and film of Celtic and Celtic-American artists.

The Theatrical Outfit (G11), 70 Fairlie St., NW; (404) 577-5255. Now performing at the Rialto, Theatrical Outfit has built a terrific ensemble of theatre artists for more than 20 years. It produces classical and contemporary works, emphasizing those indigenous to the Southern culture.

NIGHTLIFE

From Downtown to the far-flung suburbs, hundreds of nightclubs, bistros, supper clubs, singles bars, music halls, and hideaways present everything from jazz to salsa, comedy and magic acts, blues, Dixieland, rock, pop, oldies, Irish balladeers, big bands, and easy listening music. Most clubs are open until well after midnight, seven nights. Those with live entertainment usually have an admission charge.

Downtown and Midtown

A Point of View (J10), Atlanta Hilton Hotel, 255 Courtland St.; (404) 659-2000. Chic disco atop the hotel attracts locals and visiting firemen with its throbbing music and pulsating lights.

Champion's (J10), Marriott Marquis, 265 Peachtree Center Ave.; (404) 586-6017. A sports bar with 25 TVs, pool tables and sports-related games. Full menu and more than 40 different beers. Open daily, 11:30 am-2:00 am.

Churchill Grounds (I10), 660 Peachtree St.; (404) 876-3030. Next to the Fox Theater, this jazz club is the place to go for live international and local acts. Light menu and gourmet coffees. Full bar and cigar list.

The Cotton Club (J9), 1021 Peachtree St.; (404) 874-1993. Some of the hottest acts in reggae, salsa, pop, rock, and New Wave play this large, very lively club in the Peachtree-10th Street neighborhood.

The Country Place, Colony Square (J10), Peachtree and Fourteenth Sts.; (404) 881-0144. The gardenlike bar area of the popular midtown restaurant is a mingling place for Colony Square workers, and a nice place to relax after visiting the nearby High Museum of Art and Woodruff Arts Center.

Dailey's (J9), 17 International Blvd.; (404) 681-3303. The downstairs lounge area of this popular eatery features lively singers and pianists.

Fusion (C3), 550-C Amsterdam Ave., Midtown Outlets; (404) 872-6411. A Miami/New York-style night club with light shows and amazing sound system. Format varies to include energetic dance, alternative and hip hop. Opens at 10 pm.

Hard Rock Café (J9), 215 Peachtree St.; (404) 688-7625. Yes, this is *the* Hard Rock Café, just like the ones in all the other cool international entertainment centers. Rock in the megadecibels. And T-shirts, lest you forget.

The Masquerade (H11), 695 North Ave., NE; (404) 577-8178. You might say fallen angels fill this multi-level concert/disco venue. In "Heaven" there are live rock bands and dance music. "Purgatory" is pool tables, a game room, and a jukebox. "Hell" is (wouldn't you know it) a disco with jazz, spin techno, industrial, and old wave music.

Reggie's British Pub (J8), CNN Center; (404) 525-1437. Loyalty to the Crown and the British traditions of public house good fellowship prevail at this chummy pub, a bit of Old England transplanted in downtown Atlanta. Owner Reggie Mitchell recites Kipling, and relates his colorful stories of service in India, as you enjoy British ales and food and the full range of cocktails and wines. Piano.

Royal Peacock (J11), 186 1/2 Auburn Ave.; (404) 880-0745. Reggae, hip-hop, and international music in a room with a name that harks back to the days of "Sweet Auburn's" first flowering.

Underground Atlanta (D3), downtown Atlanta. Located in the heart of downtown Atlanta, Underground offers entertainment and dining for all tastes. Cuisine choices include seafood, Spanish Continental fare, Italian, barbecue, fondue, and American-style dining, as well as a host of fast-food restaurants. Entertainment options in Underground's clubs are many and varied. In addition, concerts and other entertainment are often offered in Underground's Fountain Square.

Buckhead, Sandy Springs, and Dunwoody

The Bar, Ritz-Carlton Buckhead Hotel (B3), 3434 Peachtree Rd.; (404) 237-2700. One of Atlanta's most beautiful and sophisticated rooms. Enjoy wines, cocktails, hors d'oeuvres, and the smooth sounds of progressive jazz in an ambience of rich mahogany paneling, a working fireplace, and 19th-century English hunting art.

C.J.'s Landing (B3), 270 Buckhead Ave., NE; (404) 237-7657. Live music inside and on the deck, and a reggae bar, too.

The Café Lounge (B3), Ritz-Carlton Buckhead Hotel, 3434 Peachtree Rd.; (404) 237-2700. The lounge area of Atlanta's most fashionable hotel features singers and pianists for your listening and dancing enjoyment.

Chameleon Club (B3), 3179 Peachtree Rd., NE; (404) 261-8004. The energy of live rock music draws patrons to this Buckhead club.

Chequers Seafood Grill (A4), 236 Perimeter Center Pkwy.; (770) 391-9383. Fresh mesquite-grilled seafood flown in daily with live jazz Tuesday through Saturday. Also a Sunday brunch with Dixieland jazz. A fun and exciting place.

Churchill Arms (B3), 3223 Cains Hill Pl.; (404) 233-5633. Buckhead's anglophiles pack this jolly pub for British ale, darts, and camaraderie around the sing-along piano.

Dante's Down the Hatch (B3), 3380 Peachtree Rd., NE; (404) 266-1600. For more than a decade, Dante's Down the Hatch has been an Atlanta showcase. The nautical nightclub is unique in manifold ways. The Paul Mitchell Trio, one of Atlanta's greats in jazz, plays on board the "sailing ship." Besides the reputation for terrific music, Dante prides himself on his fondue fare, service, wines, and whiskey, in surroundings that are thoroughly seaworthy. Jazz Mon-Sat from 9 pm. See DINING chapter.

Good Ol' Days Buckhead (B3), 3013 Peachtree Rd., NE; (404) 266-2597. Lively, casual, and venerable, the Good Ol' Days still packs 'em in for fun and live entertainment as it did nearly 20 years ago.

Havana (B3), 247 Buckhead Ave.; (404) 869-8484. A cigar bar, as the name suggests. Hand-rolled cigars and personal humidors lockers. Live Latin entertainment on weekends. Open daily until 4 am.

Jellyrolls (B3), 1295 E. Paces Ferry; (404) 261-6866. Come sing along. The piano players here know thousands of songs, from the 1940s to current hits. Open Wed and Thurs until 2 am; Fri and Sat until 3 am.

Johnny's Hideaway (B3), 3771 Roswell Rd.; (404) 233-8026. An Atlanta institution. Big band, swing, and disco music. A favorite of those over 40—but you'll find just as many patrons in their twenties and thirties simply because they like the music and "that kind of ballroom dancing."

LuLu's Baitshack (B3), 3057 Peachtree Rd., NE; (404) 262-5220. Buckhead center for authentic Delta-Cajun cuisine. If you dare, order their 96-ounce fishbowl drink and listen to live music on the 3000-sq.-ft. roof top deck.

Otto's (B3), 265 E. Paces Ferry Rd., NE; (404) 233-1133. Jazz, blues, and contemporary music keep Otto's near the top of the list of Buckhead's trendy night spots.

Peachtree Café (B3), 268 E. Paces Ferry Rd.; (404) 233-4402. The Yuppie set packs the bar and outdoor patio of this very chic Buckhead landmark. The café's attractive main dining room serves a trendy selection of seafood, chicken, pastas, and salads.

The Punch Line (A3), 280 Hildebrand Dr., off Roswell Rd., Sandy Springs; (404) 252-5233. Local and nationally known comedians keep the crowds in good spirits at Atlanta's most popular comedy club.

Rio Bravo Cantina (C3), 3172 Roswell Rd.; (404) 262-7431.

Strolling *mariachi* bands entertain diners and bar guests at this campy Tex-Mex cantina in the heart of Buckhead.

Virginia-Highland, Little Five Points, City of Decatur

Atkins Park Restaurant (C4), 794 N. Highland Ave.; (404) 876-7249. A great place to go for drinks and talk with old friends, and meet some brand new ones. The long Victorian bar is perpetually packed with Atlantans of all ages. The adjoining restaurant serves a trendy American/Continental menu.

Blind Willie's (C4), 828 N. Highland Ave.; (404) 873-2583. Along about midnight, purveyors of New Orleans-style blues send the crowds into a frenzy at this storefront bistro and café.

Dugan's (C3), 777 Ponce de Leon Ave.; (404) 885-1217. Amiable neighborhood pub has a large outdoor patio, usually packed with fun-seekers sampling 260 brands of beer, spicy Buffalo-style chicken wings, salads, and Mexican food.

Eddie's Attic (C4), 515-B North McDonough St., Decatur; (404) 377-4976. This popular club is a Decatur fixture and Atlanta's premier listening venue. It offers live acoustic music seven nights a week in a smoke-free music room. Local singer/songwriters as well as national touring acts perform here. Opens daily at 4 pm. Tasty menu and full bar.

Limerick Junction Pub (C4), 822 N. Highland Ave.; (404) 874-7147. A bit of old Erin in trendy Virginia-Highland, the pub has Guinness and Harp on tap, Irish stew, salads and sandwiches, and balladeers and musicians straight from the old country itself.

Manuel's Tavern (C4), 602 N. Highland Ave.; (404) 525-3447. For 30 years, Manuel's has been the number one watering hole for politicians, writers, students, and a cross-section of natives and visitors. Great drinks, great talk, great darts, and just about the best chili dogs in town.

Star Community Bar (D3), 437 Moreland Ave.; (404) 681-9018. A funky, some might say wild, spot in Little Five Points, where the clientele is part of the entertainment. Mostly live music, from rockabilly to swing. The Grace Vault, a shrine to Elvis, attracts diehard groupies. Open Mon-Thurs and Sat 3 pm-3 am; Fri 3 pm-4 am.

Twain's (C4), 211 E. Trinity in Decatur; (404) 373-0063. Atlanta's "best billiard experience" with good food, full bar, and 20 full-size pool tables. Open seven days until the wee hours. Trivia contests on Mondays.

Cobb County

Dave & Buster's (A2), I-75 and Delk Rd.; (770) 951-5554. You name it, chances are it's at Dave & Buster's—live music, a play-for-fun blackjack casino, virtual reality video games, even a murder mystery dinner theater.

Jocks and Jills (B2), 1 Galleria Pkwy.; (770) 952-8401. As with its other locations, this sports bar offers a lively spot to watch broadcast games while enjoying good food and ale. Open weekdays until 1 am; weekends till 2 am.

Mardi Gras (A2), 6300 Powers Ferry Rd.; (770) 955-1638. A gentleman's sports club offering premium spirits, wines, champagnes, and domestic beers. Cabaret-style performances. Watch major sports via satellite. Full-service kitchen. Open daily, noon- 4 am.

Ray's On The River (B2), 6700 Powers Ferry Rd., at the Chattahoochee River; (770) 955-1187. Live music, jazz singers for entertainment, and dancing.

Airport and Elsewhere

Bentley's Lounge (E2), Marriott Hotel Atlanta Airport, 4711 Best Rd., College Park; (404) 766-7900. Live music for dancing and listening in a campy room with an auto-oriented decor.

Concorde Bar and Grill (F2), Renaissance Atlanta Hotel-Concourse, One Hartsfield Centre Pkwy.; (404) 209-9999. Live jazz for easy listening in the bar of this first-class hotel.

Crowe's Nest MegaPlex (F2), 5495 Old National Hwy.; (404) 767-0123. Lively supper club and sports bar featuring live entertainment. Enjoy jazz, R&B, and Oldies. Open nightly 4 pm-4 am.

Gregory's Lounge (D1), Ramada Inn Six Flags, 4225 Fulton Industrial Blvd.; (404) 691-4100. Country music and dancing.

Lanierland Music Park, 6115 Jotemdown Rd., just off GA 400 in Cumming; (770) 887-7464. This music park is filled to its 5,000 capacity with two shows every Friday and Saturday night from May to October. The setting is a pasture. The biggies in country music from Johnny Cash to Loretta Lynn to Charlie Pride pull in the crowds from every county around.

Mama's Country Showcase (D6), 3952 Covington Hwy.; (404) 288-6262. This is the place to come for more than one kind of country fun. Listen to live acts, play blackjack and pool, dance on a 3,000-square-foot floor, and ride the mechanical bull.

Studebaker's Southside (E2), Ramada Renaissance Hotel, 4736 Best Rd., College Park; (404) 559-7329. DJs playing '70s and '80s music brighten the nights for guests of this deluxe airport area hotel.

Film

Atlanta has several theaters offering vintage and foreign films and also a number that offer almost current releases at budget prices, so you can see them on the big screen at video-store prices. Check the newspaper for showings, and also for other theaters with current releases.

LeFont Garden Hills Cinema (B3), 2835 Peachtree Rd. in Buckhead; (404) 266-2202.

LeFont Plaza (D4), 1049 Ponce de Leon Ave.; (404) 873-1939.

The Screening Room (C3), 2581 Piedmont Rd. in Lindbergh Plaza; (404) 231-1924.

Special films are shown at the following centers. Call for information:

Atlanta History Center (B3), 3101 Andrews Dr., NW; (404) 814-4000.

Atlanta-Fulton County Library (J9), One Margaret Mitchell Square, NE; (404) 730-1700. These are generally classics and educational films. Also at the Branch Libraries. Free.

Goethe Institute (G12), 400 Colony Square, NE, Fourteenth and Peachtree Sts.; (404) 892-2388. This is the German cultural center offering current and classic German films as well as lectures and special programs. Free.

High Museum of Art (G11), 1280 Peachtree St., NE; (404) 898-9540. Many of these films are shown free; others at bargain prices.

Many theaters offer half-price "twilight matinee" prices on their first show (the one that starts between 5 pm and 5:45 pm). There are also a number of theaters in Atlanta which show current and re-released films at surprisingly low prices for all shows, among them:

Brannon Square, Brannon Square in North Fulton; (770) 986-5050.

Lawrenceville, 501 West Pike St., Lawrenceville; (770) 986-5050.

Tower Place 6 (B3), Peachtree and Piedmont; (404) 816-4262.

SIGHTS

Atlanta's major attractions reflect the pluralistic character of the city. A building boom is being balanced more and more with preservation awareness, interfacing a futuristic city with scattered samples of nineteenth- and early twentieth-century Atlanta.

Consider some of the sights to be seen, all intriguing in their own right and held together as a catalog of attractions by a city that thrives on contrast and competition. Here are megastructures for the sophisticated traveler and urbanite. Here are an intown zoo with a tropical rain forest and a botanical garden bursting with thousands of varieties of flora and fauna from around the world. Here are recreational parks built on fun and fantasy and a historical society geared to keeping the traditions and artifacts. Consider a small Victorian cottage that housed the writer of the Uncle Remus tales—an earlier, more gentle way of explaining how things came to be then reflect on a high-tech broadcasting center. Visit an observatory to chart the Southern skies, and creek beds and battlefields to scour for arrowheads and Civil War relics. Visit the government, stately in its gold-domed splendor, and another district honoring civil rights—for all Americans.

From the heady rush of the glass elevators up the outside of the Westin Peachtree Plaza Hotel to your viewing station at the top, to the lateral movement in the downtown business district, Atlanta, the city reaching for her destiny, is the greatest sight to see. Enjoy the many faces of this vibrant city.

Sights designated by a *CH* indicate an admissions charge. Those designated by an *NCH* are free.

Ante-Bellum Plantation. See Stone Mountain Memorial Park below.

Atlanta Botanical Garden (C3), Piedmont Park at the Prado, NE; (404) 876-5859. *CH.* Situated on 60 acres in Piedmont Park, the botanical garden offers a conservatory with tropical plants and orchids, a vegetable garden for the urban gardener with displays of seasonal crops, a home-demonstration garden, and three specialized gardens— the Fragrance Garden, the Japanese Garden, and the Rose Garden. The Dorothy Chapman Fuqua Conservatory houses four exhibit areas: an

105

11,000-square-foot tropical rotunda, a 3,650-square-foot desert and Mediterranean house, a 600-square-foot special exhibit area, and a 650-square-foot orangerie. The Botanical Garden is a key to enjoying and understanding the verdant beauty of Atlanta. Its two wooded areas contain plants native to Georgia and one of the few remaining hardwood forests in Atlanta. The new Scottish Rite Children's Garden also delights adults. Programs, scheduled speakers, woodland tours, and ongoing classes and workshops are offered for both members and nonmembers; cultural and social events are presented throughout the year in these carefully groomed and colorful gardens. The Atlanta Botanical Garden is impressive, a quiet resting place, only five minutes from Downtown. Open Tue-Sun, 9 am-6 pm Oct.-Feb.; 9 am-7 pm, March-Sept. Closed Mondays and legal holidays.

Atlanta History Center (B3), 130 Paces Ferry Rd. in Buckhead; (404) 814-4000. CH. A half-day's visit to the historical society, with lunch at the Swan Coach House, is a delightful must for the visitor. The society maintains four historical buildings on its 33-acre property.

Atlanta History Museum is the newest structure. This $11 million facility captures Atlanta's history in exhibitions chronicling the city's growth, the Civil War's effect on Atlanta, the growth of black enterprise, Southern folk crafts, and traditional celebrations in the city's ethnic and immigrant communities. It's a great place to get the big picture of Atlanta's beginnings, the city's growth, and its people.

Walter McElreath Hall, the modern administration building, is named for the society's chief benefactor and houses the archives and library. Collections of photographs, manuscripts, and artifacts are on exhibit throughout the year and afford the visitor an important look into Atlanta's past. Films, seminars, and lectures are presented in the Woodruff Auditorium. Special programs and field trips are scheduled also. Call ahead for details.

The *Swan House,* fronting on Andrews Drive, is an elegant neo-Palladian mansion built in the 1920s by Atlanta's classical architect Philip Schutze, for Edward H. Inman, and is furnished with a spectacular collection of antiques from England and other parts of the world. This is one of the most beautiful residences in Atlanta and an excellent example of the Gatsby era in the South.

Swan Coach House, originally the servants' quarters, houses a luncheon restaurant, an art gallery, and gift shop.

The *Tullie Smith House* was moved from DeKalb County to a site behind the Swan House in the late 1960s and is an excellent example of a "plantation plain" Georgia farmhouse from 1845, with log barn, slave cabin, double corncrib outbuildings, gardens, and farm animals.

Tours of both the Swan House and Tullie Smith House are available on the half-hours, and there is a trail through the grounds. Offices and museum open Mon-Sat 10 am-5:30 pm; Sun noon-5:30 pm. Exhibits and tours start at 11 am till 4 pm Mon-Sat and 1:00-4:00 pm Sun.

Atlanta-Fulton County Public Library-Central (J9), One Margaret Mitchell Sq., NW (one block northwest of Central City Park, Downtown); (404) 730-1700. *NCH*. Marcel Breuer designed this library on the site of the old Carnegie Library. The building transforms one city block into an exciting consortium of Bauhaus geometrics, well worth a walk around the block. Inside, the structure holds more than a million volumes, the Margaret Mitchell collection of memorabilia, a children's reading and program room, 700 periodicals, a circulating collection of 10,000 video cassettes, a genealogy and Georgia history special collection, and a Learning Center with computers for public use. The Ready Reference line, (404) 730-4636, is a friendly, quick way to get answers to esoteric questions. The library offers a full program of lectures and art exhibits. Open Mon, Fri and Sat 9 am-6 pm; Tue-Thurs 9 am-8 pm; Sun 2-6 pm.

Auburn Avenue Research Library on African American History and Culture (K10), 101 Auburn Ave.; (404) 730-4001. *NCH*. Opened in 1994, this impressive facility houses invaluable documents and records, including the Sam Williams collection of black history, and also hosts exhibits and lectures. Open Mon-Thurs 10 am-8 pm; Fri-Sun noon-6 pm.

Bulloch Hall. See Historic Roswell below.

Carter Presidential Center (C4), 453 Freedom Pkwy.; (404) 420-5100. *CH*. Two miles east of Downtown, with the skyline as a dramatic backdrop, the Carter Center's four contemporary circular buildings are placed among 30 acres of trees, Japanese gardens, waterfalls, and lakes. Inside the buildings are thousands of documents, photos, gifts, and memorabilia of Jimmy Carter's White House years. The Center is really a tribute to all who have held the nation's highest office.

You may walk into a full-scale reproduction of the White House Oval Office. Photos follow Carter from his boyhood in Plains, Georgia, through his naval career, marriage, state politics, and the presidency. Gifts to the Carters range from splendid silver, crystal, and ivory from heads of state, to whimsical paintings and peanut carvings from admirers around the world. "Presidents," a 30-minute film, takes a fascinating look at the crises and triumphs that hallmarked past administrations.

You can enjoy a light lunch, with a view of the gardens, in the Center's restaurant, and buy a book or souvenir at the gift shop. The museum is open Mon-Sat 9 am-4:45 pm; Sun noon-4:45 pm.

Centennial Olympic Park (J8), Marietta St., NW at International Blvd.; (404) 233-4412. Open daily 7 am-11 pm. Built for the 1996 Summer Olympic Games, this 21-acre park is the largest inner-city park built in the last quarter century. A popular site is the Fountain of Rings, where free water shows occur daily at 12:30 pm, 3:30 pm, 6:30 pm, and 9 pm. There's also a free summer concert series. For schedule of events call the info hot line (404) 222-PARK.

Chateau Elan Winery, about 30 min. northeast of Atlanta. Take I-85 North to Exit 126. *CH.* Chateau Elan, a winery built in the style of a 16th-century royal retreat in southern France, occupies 3,100 acres in Barrow, Jackson, and Gwinnett counties and operates 361 days a year. The complex includes 60 acres of vineyards, a state-of-the-art winery, a golf course and club, a visitors center, an art gallery, restaurants, retail store, nature trails, and picnic areas. There are four tours daily, which include a tasting. Chateau Elan wines have won more than 60 medals for quality. For tour schedules and other information, call 1-800-233-WINE or (770) 932-0900.

Chattahoochee Nature Center, 9135 Willeo Rd. (in Roswell); (770) 992-2055. *CH.* The center includes 130 acres of preserved wetlands and woodlands, a bald eagle aviary, a raptor aviary, and other fascinating exhibits of reptile and animal wildlife native to the area. The shop sells field guides and wildlife publications. Two short but charming nature trails adjoin the center. A refreshing visit for children and adults, ideal for a picnic lunch. Mon-Sat 9 am-5 pm; Sun. noon-5 pm.

Chattahoochee River National Recreational Area. See SPORTS chapter, Hiking.

CNN Center (J8), 1 CNN Center; (404) 827-2300. Here CNN news is *really* live. The complex is one of Atlanta's megastructures housing a large atrium mall with shops and offices. The mall is connected to the Omni Hotel and to the Georgia World Congress Center and the Philips Arena, where the NBA Atlanta Hawks perform. The CNN megastructure should not be missed. A 45-min. walking tour includes an exhibit area, the Special Effects Studio, and the main newsroom.

Confederate and National Cemeteries, Goss St. off Powder Springs St., and Washington St. in Marietta. These two cemeteries are the burial grounds of soldiers killed during the Civil War. Both contain monuments and grave markers of historical interest.

Cyclorama (D3), 800 Cherokee Ave., SE (in Grant Park); (404) 658-7625. *CH.* The amazing 50-foot-high, 400-foot (15 x 122 meters) painting in the round, with three-dimensional figures, sound and light effects, and narration, depicts the 1864 Civil War Battle of Atlanta. You watch the battle from a revolving stage. The restoration of the original painting of 1886, the largest painting in the round in the world, combined with the renovation of the facility in which it is installed, makes this sight one of Atlanta's most memorable. If weather permits, visit the Cyclorama and then have a picnic lunch in Grant Park.

Dahlonega, Georgia, located in the North Georgia Mountains. Take Hwy. 400 to its end; turn left onto Hwy. 60 and follow it into Dahlonega. The site of the nation's first goldrush, 20 years before the 1849 gold rush to California, this old Southern town has undergone a charming restoration and is a unique attraction that should not be missed. Park and stroll around the courthouse square which features a gold museum, bricked sidewalks lined with massive trees, antique shops, boutiques selling handmade clothing, and bakeries. There are several good places to eat where one will find quick service and seating on porches overlooking the square. Within walking distance is the *Worley Homestead Bed and Breakfast Inn* featuring seven rooms furnished in antiques. This 1840s home has also been recently restored and the staff dresses in period costumes. It is located at 410 W. Main Street, Dahlonega, GA 30533; (706) 864-7002. There is also a wealth of antique stores in and around the town. For more information about Dahlonega, call the Chamber of Commerce at (706) 864-3513.

The History Center, 13 Wall St., Cartersville; (770) 382-3818. CH. A nominal fee gets you into this museum, which teaches local history through exhibits of artifacts and documents from Bartow County and northwest Georgia. Exhibits include old hand-stitched quilts, artifacts from famed Barnsley Gardens, an anvil on which Confederate arms were forged, and hundreds of other northwest Georgia relics. The museum also sponsors an oral history program, complete with a small recording studio. Take I-75 north to the Etowah Indian Mounds/Main St. exit. Go into town and turn right at the railroad tracks. The History Center is next to the Old Grand Theater.

Etowah Indian Mounds, RFD 1, Cartersville (north on I-75 40 miles to Cartersville, turn west on GA 61, and follow signs to Etowah Indian Mounds); (770) 387-3747. CH. Just an hour's drive from Atlanta, you will see the remains of the Etowah Indian culture that thrived on the banks of the Etowah River between A.D. 1000 and 1650. The three large mounds on a 50-acre plain were originally surrounded by a wooden palisade. The museum displays artifacts from this early North American civilization. Tue-Sat 9 am-5 pm, Sun 2-5:30 pm; closed Mon.

Federal Reserve Bank Monetary Museum (J8), 1000 Peachtree St. (H11) at 10th Street; (404) 521-8764. NCH. The museum houses a historical collection of monetary artifacts, from early trade beads and hides to gold bars and sheets of gold certificates and other paper money. Mon-Fri 9 am- 4 pm for self-guided tours. Advance appointments required for groups of ten or more. Guided tours by appointment for 12-year-olds and up.

Fernbank Museum of Natural History (C4), 767 Clifton Rd.; (404) 929-6300. CH. You're walking on fossils when you enter the lobby of this fascinating museum, and that's just the first of the excellent exhibits, both permanent and traveling, you'll find here. This magnificent facility is the first major natural history museum to be built in the United States in 50 years. Take "A Walk in Time Through Georgia" and watch the state's geological history come alive. And don't miss the IMAX theater, where you will be swept up into natural history movies shown on a spectacular four-story screen. If you're a gardener, or simply love beauty, stroll through the Robert L. Staton Rose Garden. Museum hours: Mon-Sat 10 am-5 pm; Sun noon-5 pm.

Fernbank Science Center (C4), 156 Heaton Park Dr., NE (near Artwood Rd., Decatur); (404) 378-4311. Another must-visit, for families especially, the Center, operated by the DeKalb County Board of Education, offers a variety of facilities and programs day and night. The 65-acre original *Fernbank Forest* has trails open Mon-Fri and Sun 2-5 pm, Sat 10 am-5 pm. The *Observatory* has the Southeast's largest telescope, open Thurs-Fri dark to 10:30 pm if the sky is clear, 8-9:30 pm if sky is cloudy, closed during inclement weather. The *Planetarium's* 70-foot-diameter dome features excellent programs including a children's holiday series. Shows are both afternoons and evenings. Call for times. Also included at the center are botanical gardens, a meteorological lab, and an electron-microscope lab. Free admission except for Planetarium. Botanical gardens are closed on Sundays.

Fox Theatre. See the chapter on PERFORMING ARTS.

Georgia Department of Archives (D3), 330 Capitol Ave., SW (near the Atlanta Stadium); (404) 656-2393. NCH. The archives building is the resting place for all the state's historical and genealogical records and maps. The lobby houses changing exhibits and original documents and artifacts. The archives collection includes gifts to the state of Georgia from other nations, such as France's gift to Georgia of historical French items as a token of appreciation following World War II and a statue of Confucius from the People's Republic of China given during the U.S. bicentennial celebration. Call for current exhibitions.

Georgia Dome (J8), 1 Georgia Dome Dr.; (404) 223-9200. The 70,000-seat domed stadium is home to the Atlanta Falcons and was a prime 1996 Olympic venue. The $210 million stadium is also the site for numerous other sports events, concerts, and assemblies. Take MARTA to get there.

Georgia State Capitol (K9), Capitol Square, SW; (404) 656-2000. NCH. Georgia was the 13th and last of the original colonies of the United States. The present state capitol building was built in 1889 and is headquarters for the Georgia governor, legislature, and secretary of state. The gold leaf on the dome was mined near Dahlonega in North Georgia and first brought to Atlanta in 1958 in mule-drawn carts. The Georgia Assembly meets from January to March; you can see the legislative process in action during this time.

The building also includes the *Georgia State Museum of Science and Industry*, the *Georgia Hall of Fame*, and the *Hall of Flags*—all well worth the visual instruction in the state's history, as is the tour of the capitol buildings, gardens, and statuary. Mon-Fri 8 am-5 pm; tours Mon-Fri, 10 and 11 am and 1 and 2 pm.

Georgia World Congress Center (J8), Marietta St., NW, at International Blvd. (next to Omni Hotel); (404) 223-4636. NCH. The center, officially named the George L. Smith II Georgia World Congress Center, is an enormous trade facility—352,000 square feet on a single floor, the largest of its kind in the U.S. The *Georgia Hall* has displays on historical Georgia, industrial and agricultural products, Coca-Cola, BellSouth, Lumus Industries, Georgia-Pacific and Georgia Ports, and special Georgia attractions.

Georgia's Stone Mountain Park (C6); (770) 498-5690. (Seven miles east of I-285 on U.S. 78, Stone Mountain Freeway.) CH. Stone Mountain, the largest granite outcropping in the world, can be seen from the city on the eastern horizon. The relief carving on its north side depicts Jefferson Davis, the Confederate president, and Robert E. Lee and Stonewall Jackson, the two Confederate generals. A 3,200-acre park surrounds this national phenomenon and massive sculpture, providing a full-day's entertainment out of doors.

The *Swiss Skylift* will take you to the top of the mountain; however, if you are feeling energetic, walk the 1.3 miles up its side.

The *Ante-bellum Plantation* will bring alive those days before the Civil War, having 19 authentically restored different buildings, including the manor home, overseer's house, slave cabins, and more.

The world's largest electronic *Carillon* is played Mon-Sat at noon, 4, and 7 pm; Sun 1, 3, 5, and 7 pm. It is a delightful experience to sit out and listen to it.

The *Laser Light and Sound Show* is displayed on the carved side of the mountain every night at 9:30 pm from May through Labor Day.

The *Scenic Railroad* takes you for a 30-min. ride around the base of the mountain, while the *Riverboat* cruises around the 365-acre lake. You can also rent a pedal boat, rowboat, or pontoon boat for an individual excursion.

Clayton House Craft Shop features the largest pottery collection in the Southeast, and works from more than 150 Georgia craftspeople.

If you still haven't seen and done enough, there are beaches, golf, tennis, batting cages, waterslides, canoeing, and an Ice Chalet with full skating facilities. Rent a bike to get around and explore the healthy way.

Picnicking and camping are available, as well as more formal overnight accommodations at the Stone Mountain Inn.

The park also hosts many annual festivals and gatherings, including the Highland Games and the Yellow Daisy Festival. It was also a venue for the 1996 Summer Olympic Games.

Confederate Memorial Carving, Stone Mountain

Open year-round except Christmas day. Most attractions and rides open at 10 am but closings vary. Special rates for groups over 25. Call for current hours and admission charges.

Governor's Mansion (B3), 391 W. Paces Ferry Rd., NW (in Buckhead); (404) 261-1776. *NCH.* The present mansion, built in 1968 by then-Georgia governor Lester Maddox, reflects the Greek Revival style of the antebellum South, with Federal period furnishings. The mansion has a featured location in one of Atlanta's most beautiful northside residential areas on West Paces Ferry Road. Include the Governor's Mansion in your day of touring the historical society in this elegant section of the city. Tours Tue, Wed, and Thurs 10-11:30 am.

Heritage Row (J8), 55 Upper Alabama St. (at Underground Atlanta); (404) 584-7879. Live the Battle of Atlanta in a hastily built bomb shelter. Stand inside a turn-of-the-century trolley car. Move through Atlanta's past and feel yourself become a part of her history in this fascinating exhibit. For a look at Atlanta's future, view a high-definition TV program. This is history you can see and touch.

Herndon House (D2), 587 University Place, NW; (404) 581-9813. This stunning 15-room Greek Revival mansion was built in 1910 by Alonzo E. Herndon, a former slave, who founded the Atlanta Life Insurance Company, the second-largest black-owned insurance company in the United States. The house displays its original furnishings and photographs.

Historic Roswell (25 miles north of Atlanta); (770) 640-3253. Browse among the antique shops and boutiques bordering the square. The Roswell Historical Society will arrange, one week in advance, group tours (minimum of 10) of this charming, small antebellum town. Regular tours for any number occur 10 am Wed and 1 pm Sat. The tour includes a visit to a private and occupied home in the area that is open to the public on a restricted schedule. *The Allenbrook House,* which houses the Roswell Historical Society, is open Mon-Fri 9 am-5 pm, Sat 10 am-4 pm, Sun noon-3 pm. *CH. Bulloch Hall,* the childhood home of President Teddy Roosevelt's mother, is open Wed 10 am-3 pm. Call for special programs and tours.

Johnny Mercer Room (J8), Library South Building, Georgia State University; (404) 651-2477. *NCH.* The Johnny Mercer Room pays homage to the Savannah native who gave the world "That Old Black Magic," "Moon River," and dozens and dozens of other wonderful tunes. Memorabilia, manuscripts, and first-edition sheet music were donated to GSU by Mercer's widow. To put you in the proper frame of mind, a vintage jukebox plays Mercer's classics. Open Mon-Fri 9 am-5 pm. Saturdays by appointment.

Kennesaw Civil War Museum, 2829 Cherokee St., Kennesaw (30 miles northwest of Atlanta); (770) 427-2117. *CH.* Both Civil War

buffs and train enthusiasts will enjoy this museum, which displays artifacts from the war period, the main attraction being the Confederate
locomotive *The General*. The Walt Disney film, *The Great Locomotive
Chase*, popularized and dramatized the skirmishes and chase in the historical incident associated with this train. The museum is expanding to
include the Glover Steam Locomotive exhibit and a new theater. Mon-
Sat 9:30 am-5:30 pm; Sun noon-5:30 pm. Winter hours are Mon-Sat 10
am-5 pm; Sun noon-5 pm.

   Kennesaw Mountain National Battlefield Park, GA 120 about 25
miles north of Atlanta; (770) 427-4686. *NCH.* This was a major Civil
War site in the Union movement from Chattanooga to Atlanta. Self-
guided tours of the battlefield are available. We suggest starting at the
visitors center and museum where a slide presentation will acquaint
you with the battle sequence. The park has two picnic areas, four hiking trails, and a free shuttle bus to the top of the mountain. Park open
daily until dusk. Visitor Center open Mon-Fri 8:30 am-5 pm; Sat-Sun
8:30 am-6 pm.

   Margaret Mitchell House, (H11), 990 Peachtree St., NE; (404)
249-7012. *CH.* This three-story Tudor Revival mansion, now listed on
the National Register, was home to Margaret Mitchell from 1925 to
1932. At that time it was a ten-unit apartment building, which
Mitchell called "the Dump." She wrote much of her novel *Gone with
the Wind* while living here. The adjacent Gone with the Wind Museum
contains memorabilia from the movie, including the famous Scarlett
portrait and film footage from the premiere. The house also serves as a
literary center for readings and other events. Open daily, 9 am-4 pm;
museum shop 9 am-5 pm. Free parking. One block from the Midtown
MARTA station.

   **Martin Luther King, Jr. Memorial, Historic District, and Center
for Social Change** (K11), Auburn Ave. at Boulevard, SE; (404) 524-
1956. *CH.* The five-block historic district is on the National Register
of Historic Districts and includes new and old buildings of importance
to the memory of one of Atlanta's renowned citizens, Nobel Prize winner and father of the Civil Rights Movement, Dr. Martin Luther King,
Jr. Dr. King's birthplace at 449 Auburn Avenue is open Mon-Fri 9 am-
8 pm. The Ebenezer Baptist Church at 407 Auburn Ave., where Dr.
King shared the pulpit with his father, is open Mon-Fri 10 am-4 pm, Sat
and Sun during summer. Dr. King's tomb is within the memorial park.
The district also includes an Interfaith Peace Chapel, a community
center, and the Center for Social Change, headed by Dr. King's widow,
Coretta Scott King. Tours Mon-Sun 9 am-8 pm.

   Michael C. Carlos Museum (C4), 571 S. Kilgo St., Emory
University; (404) 727-4282. *CH.* A trip here will introduce you to the
attractive Emory campus and the surrounding turn-of-the-century

neighborhood of Druid Hills. The museum hosts exquisite traveling exhibits of art from the past both near and distant. Permanent exhibits include art and archaeology from the ancient Mediterranean and Middle East as well as Asian, pre-Columbian, and Indian artifacts. Also prints, photos, paintings, and sculpture from the Middle Ages to the present. Advance reservation required for groups. Park on Oxford Rd. and have lunch in Emory Village at Everybody's, Cedar Tree, or any of the fine restaurants, all reasonably priced. Or eat at the museum café. The Carlos Museum is open Mon-Sat 10 am-5 pm, Sun noon-5 pm. Closed on major holidays.

Monastery of the Holy Spirit, 2625 Hwy. 212, SW, Conyers (from Downtown, take I-20 east for 27 miles to GA 138 exit, right 5 miles to GA 212, left 2 miles); (770) 483-8705. *NCH.* The monastery was built by the Trappist monks and is a self-sufficient, working religious community open to the public. The abbey is clean white gothic architecture, radiating with colored lights from the stained-glass windows and filled with plainsong during services. The grounds are immaculate—a picnic area by a small pond is ideal for lunch. The monastery welcomes visitors to its bonsai greenhouse and to its gift shop with pottery, handcrafts, and monastery bread available for purchase. Women are not allowed in the cloister, but are offered a slide presentation on the life of the Trappists. Open daily from dawn until dusk, although the Gift Shop and Bonsai greenhouse are open Mon-Fri only, 9:30 am-4:30 pm. Group tours must be prearranged. Call for tours and services open to the public. Leaving the city for a day trip to the Monastery will give you an appreciation for the spiritual and agricultural tradition still preserved in monastic life plus a side trip to the farmlands of North Georgia.

Oakland Cemetery (D3), 248 Oakland Ave., SE (at Martin Luther King, Jr. Dr.); (404) 688-2107. *NCH.* Oakland is Atlanta's oldest cemetery, established in 1850, and the burial ground for eminent Atlantans including *Gone with the Wind* author Margaret Mitchell and Atlanta's first mayor, Moses Formwalt. The tombstones reflect the multiple funeral styles of the late 19th century, and the office building is from circa 1899. A bell tolls at sundown each day to alert visitors to closing time. Cemetery is open daily from dawn to dusk. Visitor Center is open March-Oct., Mon-Fri 9 am-5 pm, Sat-Sun 1 pm-5 pm. Tours may be scheduled for groups of 10 or more, March-Oct.

Panola Mountain State Conservation Park (E5), 2600 GA Hwy. 155, Stockbridge; (770) 389-7801. *NCH.* About 25 miles southeast of downtown Atlanta, Panola Mountain is a peaceful 585-acre day-use park, where you may have a walk in the woods, a picnic, and wonder at a 100-acre granite outcropping sometimes dubbed "Little Stone Mountain." From the park's Nature Center, trails lead you through the hardwood and pine forests to an overlook on one of the mountain's major outcroppings. Park naturalists conduct weekend nature walks and lectures. Picnic tables, rest rooms, and soft drink machines are near the Nature Center. Open daily 8 am-sundown.

Peachtree Center (J9), Peachtree St. between Harris St. and International Blvd. Atlanta's Peachtree Center is a showcase for the urban development and design concepts of Atlanta's international architect John Portman. This is a downtown center still expanding from its original core development at the Merchandise Mart and the Hyatt Regency Atlanta Hotel. The spectacular atrium hotel with its capsule elevators is the prototype and trademark for other Portman hotels. The center is located on the highest point of the Peachtree ridge, a few blocks north of Five Points. The complex includes office towers, plazas for people watching on Peachtree Street, a shopping mall, the Merchandise Mart, the Apparel Mart, the Gift Mart, Inforum, the Peachtree Plaza Hotel, the Marriott Marquis, the Hyatt Regency Atlanta Hotel, and ample parking lots, all connected by pedestrian bridges. Peachtree Center is a hub of commercial and retail activity, a meeting place for Atlantans, a convention center, and an area for sophisticated dining and entertaining from Japanese to continental cuisine.

Rhodes Hall (C3), 1516 Peachtree St., NW; (404) 885-7800. CH. Home of the Georgia Trust for Historic Preservation, this granite neo-Romanesque structure was the elegant home of one of Atlanta's wealthy families. The heirs of Amos G. Rhodes deeded the property to the State of Georgia, and from 1930 to 1965 Rhodes Hall was the primary archives building. The house is maintained in its original state with period furnishings and an exhibit hall. It was listed on the National Register of Historic Places in 1974. Tours are given Mon-Fri 11 am-4 pm and Sun noon-3 pm. The Georgia Trust for Historic Preservation is open Mon- Fri 9 am-5 pm.

Road to Tara Museum and Gift Shop 104 N. Main St., Jonesboro; (770) 210-1017. *Gone with the Wind* lovers can sink their teeth into this. Take a look at the first copy of Margaret Mitchell's famed book to come off the presses or a replica of the late Atlanta author's typewriter. There's a Civil War gallery, a movie memorabilia gallery, a Margaret Mitchell Memorial gallery. There's even a vintage 1870 carriage like the replicas used in the 1939 movie. In the mini-theater you can see short films on GWTW-related subjects. Located 15 miles south of downtown Atlanta in Clayton County. Open Mon-Sat 10-6; Sun 1-6.

SciTrek, the Science and Technology Museum of Atlanta, 395 Piedmont Ave., NE; (404) 522-5500. Part of the Atlanta Civic Center complex, this museum is devoted exclusively to physical science and technology. Visitors can tour the Hall of Mechanics, the Hall of Light,

Kidspace, and the Hall of Electricity. People of all ages will delight in the "interactive" exhibits which provide users with opportunities to learn basic principles of physical science. One of only three museums of its kind in the country. Open Tue-Sun 10 am-5 pm.

Six Flags Over Georgia (C1); (770) 948-9290. (Off I-20 Six Flags exit, 10 miles west of Downtown.) *CH*. This recreational park is named for the six flags that have flown over Georgia—from Spain, France, England, Georgia, the Confederacy, and the U.S. The 331 acres of rolling hills and ponds are packed with breathtaking rides, spectacular shows, concessions, restaurants, and resting places.

The "Land of Screams and Dreams" lives up to its reputation with the world's only triple-loop roller coaster, appropriately named the "Mind Bender." The names of other rides like the "Looping Starship," the "Great American Scream Machine," and "Thunder River" speak for themselves.

You will find Six Flags a clean, well-managed, and cheerful place. The season runs from mid-March to mid-November. The park is open daily during the summer; weekends only from mid-March to mid-May and from Labor Day to November. Call for current times. One-price ticket is good for all rides and shows, including repeats.

Stone Mountain Village (C6). If you're visiting Stone Mountain park, be sure to include a visit to historic Stone Mountain Village, a restored small town at the base of the mountain, filled with wonderful shops, crafts, and antiques.

Swan Coach House. See Atlanta History Center above.

Swan House. See Atlanta History Center above.

Sweetwater Creek State Park (C10), Mt. Vernon Rd., Lithia Springs, 25 miles west of downtown Atlanta; (770) 732-5871. *NCH*. The ghostly ruins of the New Manchester Mfg. Co. stand by the churning rapids of Sweetwater Creek, from which it drew the power to produce uniforms for the Confederate Army. After torching the brick building during the Battle of Atlanta campaign, Gen. William T. Sherman's troops set the fashion for today's visitors—they kicked off their shoes and waded into the creek's swift, cool waters.

Five miles of nature trails lead you through the surrounding woodlands, alongside the creek. A 250-acre reservoir is stocked with bass, catfish, and bream, which you may catch, fry in a pan and serve on one of the park's picnic tables. Open daily 8 am-sundown.

Tullie Smith House. See Atlanta History Center above.

Underground Atlanta (D3), downtown Atlanta. Located at Atlanta's historic birthplace, the Zero Mile Post, Underground Atlanta covers six city blocks and 12 acres in the heart of Atlanta between the governmental and financial centers of the city. This fascinating historic district was created in the 1920s when viaducts elevated the street system, leaving a "city beneath the streets." Today, this area offers an array of fine shops, great restaurants, and topflight entertainment. Shop on Fashion Row for an excellent selection in men's and women's apparel, or visit any of the many restaurants and nightclubs in Kenny's Alley. Humbug Square Street Market, at Lower Alabama Street and Pryor Street, is filled with street vendors selling their wares from antique trucks and pushcarts. This exciting shopping and entertainment complex offers something for everyone.

White Water Park (A1), 250 N. Cobb Pkwy., Marietta; (770) 424-9283. CH. Located just off I-75 at Exit 265, this exciting Atlanta park offers a variety of water attractions, including a 40-foot water wheel, a wave pool (the Atlanta Ocean) that creates 4-foot waves, a continuous flowing river called "The Little Hooch," and thousands of feet of water flumes. The park also features a children's participation area with more than 25 activities with water guns, waterslides, and tube rides. There are locker and shower facilities for your convenience, as well as restaurants and picnic areas.

William Weinman Mineral Center and Museum (A1), 30 minutes north of Atlanta in Cartersville at the corner of I-75 and U.S. 441; (770) 386-0576. CH. Gems, minerals, and fossils from all over the world in an impressive marble building featuring a mock cavern and audiovisual room. Georgia gems and minerals are strongly represented. Tue-Sat 10 am-4:30 pm; Sun 1-4:30 pm.

World of Coca-Cola Pavillion (D3), 55 Martin Luther King, Jr. Drive (at Underground); (404) 676-5151. The story of Atlanta's famed Coca-Cola beverage, past, present, and future, comes alive through fascinating exhibits and an eye-popping collection of memorabilia. Enjoy classic radio and TV ads for the world-famous soft drink, view a fanciful representation of the bottling process, and visit a spectacular soda fountain of the future.

Wren's Nest (D3), 1050 Ralph David Abernathy Blvd., SW (near Lawton St.); (404) 753-7735. CH. A national historic landmark, the home of Joel Chandler Harris, Georgia author of the Uncle Remus stories, is preserved in its original Victorian cottage style with the addition of Uncle Remus memorabilia. Special storytelling sessions. The house is located in West End. Tue-Sat 10 am-4 pm; Sun 1-4 pm.

Yellow River Wildlife Game Ranch (C6), 4525 U.S. 78, Lilburn; (770) 972-6643. CH. Just off very busy U.S. 78, three miles east of Stone Mountain Park, the game ranch is a 24-acre home for dozens of free-roaming deer, foxes, wolves, pigs, porcupines, huggable bunny rabbits, donkeys, goats, mountain lions, a skunk named "William T. Sherman," and a spring-forecasting groundhog named "Robert E. Lee."

You're no sooner on the tree-shaded walking trail than whole families of deer amble up for handouts of bread and crackers. Small children get a kick out of the "Bunnie Burrows," an enclosure where rabbits of all sizes and colors enjoy being petted and hand-fed raw carrots and celery.

What's purportedly the largest herd of American buffalo east of the Mississippi roams a back meadow. Black bears, bobcats, mountain lions, foxes, and wolves are secured in open-air enclosures.

You may reserve Yellow River's "Birthday House" for your youngster's special day, or for a family reunion or other group activity. Open daily Memorial Day-Labor Day 9:30 am-dusk, rest of the year 9:30 am-6 pm.

Zoo Atlanta, Grant Park, 800 Cherokee Ave., SE, off I-20 East; (404) 624-5600. CH. The big attraction these days at Zoo Atlanta is the giant pandas exhibit. Lun Lun and Yang Yang arrived from China in Nov. 1999 for a ten-year visit, making Zoo Atlanta one of only two U.S. zoos exhibiting giant pandas. More than 250 other species also reside at Zoo Atlanta, including Chilean flamingos, polar bears, sea lions, Vietnamese pot-bellied pigs, monkeys, elephants, zebras, giraffes, tropical birds, and one of the world's largest reptile exhibits. The $4.5 million, five-acre Ford African Rain Forest is a natural habitat for gorillas. Many of the zoo's animals are featured in regularly scheduled shows. Adjacent to the Cyclorama and Grant Park picnic areas, the zoo is open daily except Thanksgiving, Christmas, and New Year's Day. There's no extra charge for the panda exhibit, but a limited number of panda tickets are issued each day, so try to arrive early. The zoo reports that Lun Lun and Yang Yang are most playful in the afternoon. Other attractions include the Norfolk Southern Zoo Express Train, the Publix Petting Zoo, a café, and a gift shop.

VISUAL ARTS

Atlanta's emergence as a regional visual arts center is evidenced by the increasing development of its major museum, the High Museum, and by the expansion and depth of its gallery system.

MUSEUMS

APEX (African American Panoramic Experience) (J10), 135 Auburn Ave.; (404) 521-2739. An excellent museum that features art and history exhibits depicting the cultural heritage of African-Americans and their contributions and achievements in American history. Permanent exhibits include "Auburn Avenue," a history of Auburn Avenue and the achievements of its residents, including a continuous video, "Sweet Auburn, Street of Pride." Also features works by many South African artists. The museum's archives are available for geneological research. Open Tue-Sat 10 am-5 pm; summer Sundays 1-5 pm.

Atlanta Contemporary Arts Center (I8), 535 Means St., NW (off Marietta St.); (404) 688-1970. The Contemporary, formerly called Nexus, showcases cutting-edge and contemporary art works from the region and nation. This nonprofit, multidisciplinary facility also includes studios and Nexus Press, one of the country's two presses that publish artists' books. These are not "art books," but books created by artists themselves. 11 am-5 pm Tue-Sat.

Atlanta-Fulton Public Library (J9), One Margaret Mitchell Square at Carnegie and Forsyth Sts.; (404) 730-1700. The library's art galleries are located on the ground and lower levels. *Gone with the Wind* fans must stop in to see the permanent Margaret Mitchell collection, which contains a number of the writer's personal belongings, the typewriter on which she wrote her famous book, and other movie memorabilia. In addition, the library hosts exhibits of regional and national artists' works, including drawings, paintings, sculpture, and weaving. Open Mon, Fri, Sat 9 am-6 pm; Tue, Wed, and Thu 9 am-8 pm; and Sun 2-6 pm.

Atlanta International Museum of Art and Design (J9), Marquis Two Tower, 285 Peachtree Center Ave. Garden Level; (404) 688-2467. A small, private, downtown museum gallery with an international

120

emphasis, showing art and handicrafts from over the world. There is also a small museum gift shop. 11 am-5 pm Tue-Sat.

Michael C. Carlos Museum, (C4), 561 S. Kilgo St., on the Emory University campus; (404) 727-4282. Emphasis here is on the past, ancient and more recent. Touring exhibits have included Renaissance and Impressionist painters. The museum has an excellent collection of Pre-Columbian and Egyptian art and artifacts. The latter includes an authentic mummy and sarcophagus—guaranteed to get the kids' attention. Open Mon-Sat 10 am-5 pm; noon-5 pm Sun.

Clark Atlanta University Art Galleries (D3), in Trevor Arnett Hall, Greensferry and James P. Brawley Dr., SW; (404) 880-6102. This permanent African-American art collection is the largest in the nation featuring paintings, sculpture, and graphics by black artists including Charles White, Elizabeth Catlett, John Wilson, Calvin Burnett, and Jacob Lawrence. Permanent historical African art collection and a contemporary European art collection. Also featured in the library is the Hale Woodruff Art of the Negro murals. Call for hours.

Hammonds House Galleries and Resource Center (D2), 503 Peeples St., SW; (404) 752-8730. Located on the 130-year-old Victorian estate of Dr. Otis Hammonds, the Hammonds House Galleries houses a superb collection of African, Haitian, and African American art. The facility sponsors a variety of educational/informational formats, including tours, lectures, cultural programs, forums, and video presentations. 10 am-6 pm Tue-Fri; 1-5 pm Sat & Sun.

The **High Museum of Art** (C3), Woodruff Arts Center, 1280 Peachtree St., NE; (404) 733-4437. The High Museum is Atlanta's major visual-arts museum and is the oldest member of the Atlanta Arts Alliance. The museum was first proposed in 1905 by the newborn Atlanta Art Association and became a reality in 1926 when Mrs. Joseph High donated her home as a museum. In 1968 the present Woodruff Arts Center building incorporated the former museum site, and now the museum, designed by architect Richard Meier, occupies a separate site next to the Arts Center. A gleaming post-modern asymmetrical structure, the High Museum of Art is a unique architectural and cultural landmark for the city.

The museum collection includes works from early Renaissance to modern, with emphasis on European and American works from the late 19th and 20th centuries. The museum is noted for its strong contemporary painting and print collection. The equally strong photography collection focuses on late 19th- and 20th-century masters. The African Gallery offers theme-centered exhibitions from the African collection throughout the year. Also, the decorative arts are featured in the Decorative Arts Gallery in a continuing series of displays. The Junior Arts Center leases a permanent exhibition for children. The High

Museum program of regular events includes lectures, films, tours, festivals, and special educational courses. Conclude your visit at the excellent Museum Shop. For the weekly schedule of events, call the Public Information number, (404) 733-4444. Museum hours, Tue-Sat 10 am-5 pm; Sun noon-5 pm.

High Museum of Art Folk Art and Photography Galleries (D3), 30 John Wesley Dobbs Ave., in Georgia Pacific Center; (404) 733-4437. A branch of the High Museum of Art, this gallery has rotating exhibits featuring regional and national folk and photographic artists. Free entertainment daily. Open Mon-Fri 11 am-6 pm. Free.

Marietta/Cobb Museum of Art (A1), 30 Atlanta St., NE Marietta; (770) 528-1444. Cobb County's gem of a fine arts museum. Call for hours.

Oglethorpe University Museum (B4), 4484 Peachtree Rd., NE; (404) 364-8555. One of Atlanta's best kept secrets, this small museum three miles north of Lenox Square offers superb exhibits free to the public. Ample free parking. Excellent gift shop. Open Tues-Sun noon-5 pm.

Spelman College Museum of Fine Arts (D3), Cosby Academic Center, Spelman College, 350 Spelman Lane, SW (Downtown); (404) 681-3643. The Spelman collection includes African, Caribbean, and contemporary American art. Open Tue-Fri 10 am-5 pm.

William Breman Jewish Heritage Museum (C3), The Selig Center, 1440 Spring St., NW; (404) 873-1661. The largest museum of its kind in the Southeast, this facility gives a unique glimpse of Atlanta, with special emphasis on the Atlanta Jewish experience. Volunteers donated a wealth of photographs, documents, and memorabilia. The museum's core galleries present "Absence of Humanity: The Holocaust Years" and "Creating Community: The Jews of Atlanta from 1845 to the Present." It also has a gallery for special exhibitions, a genealogy center, a library, and a gift shop. Open Mon-Thurs 10 am-5 pm, Fri 10 am-3 pm, Sun 1 pm-5 pm.

GALLERIES

Atlanta's gallery scene has grown tremendously in size, sophistication, and substance in the last two decades, paralleling the growth of the city's business community.

Although the listing below is not comprehensive, we recommend to you, as a casual viewer or serious collector, the following galleries for their excellence in quality, uniqueness of concept, and established professionalism.

Abstein Gallery (G11), 558 14th St., NW (Midtown); (404) 872-8020. Original art in all media by Atlanta and Southeastern artists,

Leila Kepert Yarborough, Betty Loehle, Michael Crouse, and others. Mon-Fri 8:30 am-5:30 pm; Sat 10 am-4 pm.

The Allen Gallery (C3), 116 Bennett St., NW, at The Stalls; (404) 352-9646. Specializing in British art of the 19th and 20th centuries, Allen offers all original oil paintings, watercolors, and drawings. Also features Continental art from the same periods. Call for information on special showings. Open Mon-Sat 10 am-5 pm.

Ann Jacob Gallery (B3), 3261 Roswell Rd., NE; (404) 262-3399. Contemporary sculpture featuring Pomodoro, Consagra, Calder, Berrocal. Paintings, tapestries, art glass, collectibles, antiquities, and African and Asian art collection. Mon-Sat 10 am-5:30 pm.

Artist's Atelier of Atlanta (C3), 800 Miami Cir., Suite 200; (404) 231-5999. This is studio, classroom, and gallery for about 20 artists. Contemporary and expressionistic work in most media. The gallery also presents a miniature show, tiny paintings and sculpture. Open Mon-Fri 10 am-5 pm, Sat noon-4 pm.

Atlanta Art Gallery (B3), 262 E. Paces Ferry Rd., NE; (404) 261-1233. This convenient Buckhead gallery deals in 19th- and 20th-century drawings, paintings, and sculpture by both American and European artists. 10 am-5 pm Mon-Fri; 11 am-4 pm Sat.

Atlanta College of Art Gallery (C3), 1280 Peachtree St., NE (Midtown); (404) 733-5008. Nonprofit gallery specializing in painting, sculpture, photography, and crafts by regional and national artists, and students. Tues, Wed and Sat 10 am-5 pm; Thur-Fri 10 am-9:30 pm; Sun noon-5 pm. Call for summer hours and about the annual student art sale.

By Hand South (C4), 112 E. Ponce de Leon Ave., Decatur; (404) 378-0118. Contemporary crafts by top local and national artists—woodworking, pottery, weaving, jewelry. By Hand has been named one of the Top 100 Retailers of American Craft, based on a poll by *NICHE* magazine of 20,000 professional craft artists in the U.S. and Canada. 10 am-6 pm Mon-Fri; 10 am-5 pm Sat; noon-5 pm Sun.

Cafe Tu Tu Tango (B3), 220 Pharr Rd.; (404) 841-6222. A popular Buckhead eatery where local artists create beautiful—well, sometimes weird—art while you eat. A place to get a unique souvenir of Atlanta at bargain prices. Open daily 11:30 am until late at night.

Callanwolde Gallery (C4), 980 Briarcliff Rd., NE (near Virginia Ave.); (404) 872-5338. DeKalb County operates this center in the restored Candler mansion, offering classes and programs for the public in the visual, literary, and performing arts. The center is the headquarters for a dance group, concert band, theater group, the Callanwolde Young Singers, and small musical ensembles. Special events include the Callanwolde Fall Festival and Christmas at Callanwolde. Call for times of specific programs. The art gallery is open Mon-Fri 10 am-8 pm; Sat 10 am-3 pm. Free.

Chastain Arts Center Gallery (B3), 135 W. Wieuca Rd., NW (in Chastain Park); (404) 252-2927. The Chastain Center is known for its extensive selection of classes in visual arts and handcrafts for adults and children. Sessions last ten weeks. Mon-Thu 9 am-10 pm; Fri-Sat 9 am-5 pm. Ask about weekend and one-day workshops. The center houses the Chastain Gallery which shows local, regional, and national artists. Gallery open Tue-Sat 1-5 pm.

D. Miles Gallery (C4), 120 Sycamore Place, Decatur; (404) 378-9011. The outside looks like an old automotive shop, but it houses a 600-sq. ft. gallery and a hive of individual artists working in acrylic, oil, watercolor, pottery, glass, and mixed media. Exhibits by both resident artists and other contemporary artists from the area. Visitors may watch artists at work and may purchase work from the studios or gallery. Open Tue-Fri noon-6 pm, Sat noon-4 pm.

Dalton Galleries (C4), Dana Fine Arts Building, Agnes Scott College, 141 E. College Ave. (Decatur); (404) 471-6366. Changing exhibits such as Southeast fiber exhibits, black art, and American art. Open during the school year, Mon-Fri 10 am-4:30 pm; Sat-Sun, 2 pm-4:30 pm.

Fay Gold Gallery (B3), 247 Buckhead Ave., NE; (404) 233-3843. Features paintings, prints, photography, and sculpture by contemporary American artists, including Robert Rauschenberg, Alex Katz, and George Segal. Mon-Sat 10 am-5:30 pm.

The Fräbel Gallery, Inc. (C3), 695 Antone St. off Northside Dr.; (404) 351-9794. Featuring the original and signed crystal sculptures of Hans Fräbel and the Hans Fräbel Studio of Atlanta. Mon-Fri 9 am-5pm; Sat 9am-3 pm.

Georgia State University Gallery (K9), Art and Music Building, 10 Ivy St. (Downtown); (404) 651-0489. Changing exhibits of nationally known artists in all medias with accompanying lectures and workshops. Call for current exhibits and lectures. Mon-Fri 9 am-7 pm.

Robert Ferst Center Galleries (H9), 349 Ferst Dr., NW, on the Georgia Tech campus; (404) 894-9600. Contemporary American artists in photography, painting, sculpture, fiber arts, and prints. Eclectic exhibits in all media by student and national artists. Galleries are open one hour before live performances in the adjacent theater. Call for times.

Greggie Fine Art (A3), 6025 Sandy Springs Cir., (404) 843-1868. A wonderful collection of fine, uncommon old master original paintings. Other items include rarities from the 16th century to the present. Greggie hosts varying exhibits throughout the year in addition to its permanent collection. Open Mon-Fri 9 am-5 pm. Other hours by appointment.

Heath Gallery (B3), 56 26th St. NW; (404) 873-5990. American art of the 1960s, 1970s, and 1980s. Tue-Sat 11 am-5 pm.

Ray Ketcham Gallery (B3), (404) 255-8745. Established more than 30 years in Atlanta, the Ray Ketcham Gallery includes in its collection works by 19th- and 20th-century European and American painters. Call for an appointment and directions.

Knoke Galleries (B3), 5325 Roswell Rd., NE; (404) 252-0485. The Knoke houses one of the largest galleries of American paintings south of New York. Mon-Fri 10 am-6:30 pm, Sat 10 am-5:30 pm.

Lagerquist Gallery (B3), 3235 Paces Ferry Pl., NW (Buckhead); (404) 261-8273. American artists including Dale Rayburn, Burke, Winterle, Loehle, Carpenter, Ramsey. Tue-Sat 10 am-5 pm.

Madison-Morgan Cultural Center, 434 S. Main St., Madison; 706-342-4743. This fine regional center is well worth a day's visit in Madison for its reputable art shows, theater, and music programs. Open Tue-Sat 10am-4:30 pm, Sun 1 pm-4:30 pm. Call for hours of evening performances.

Modern Primitive Gallery (C4), 1402 N. Highland Ave., NE; (404) 892-0556. The Modern Primitive Gallery specializes in works by established and rising regional folk artists. Call for hours.

O'Karma Jones (G11), 450 14th St., NW; (404) 874-9461. Started in 1952, this gallery may be the oldest in Atlanta. Here you'll find a selection of antique and contemporary paintings, antique botanicals, and English sporting engravings. Mon Fri 8:30 am-5 pm.; Sat 9 am-1 pm.

Out of the Woods (C3), 22 Bennett St., NW; (404) 351-0446. This remarkable and delightful assemblage of fine crafts and original art confines itself to ancient and contemporary handmade ethnic items of cultural significance. 10:30 am-5 pm Mon-Fri; Sat 11 am-5 pm.

Ray's Indian Originals (C5), 90 N. Avondale Rd., Avondale Estates; (404) 292-4999. Native American art and artifacts are shown by appointment.

Regency Fine Art (A5), 6458 Dawson Blvd., Doraville; (770) 840-7701. From Dali to Delacroix, Neiman to Erte, you'll find it at this Gwinnett County gallery. Mon-Fri 9 am-6 pm, Sat 10 am-6 pm, Sun noon-6 pm.

Right Brain Art Gallery (C4), 664 N. Highland Ave.; (404) 872-2696. This gallery exhibits contemporary paintings, ceramics, sculpture, and original children's book illustrations. Tue-Sat noon-5pm or by appointment.

Shade Gallery (D4), 465-A Flat Shoals Ave.; (404) 577-3338. This tiny gallery in East Atlanta Village specializes in authentic Southern folk art. You'll find work by Howard Finster and the like, but the most fun is "discovering" an obscure folk artist's unique spin on this world and the next. Call for hours.

The Signature Shop & Gallery (B3), 3267 Roswell Rd., NW (Buckhead); (404) 237-4426. Premier contemporary American crafts in all metals, glass, fiber, ceramics, wood, and weaving. Tue-Sat 10 am-5:30 pm, or by appointment.

Swan Coach House Gallery (B3), 3130 Slaton Dr., NW; (404) 266-0057. Local and regional artists are displayed in this charming restaurant setting on the grounds of the Atlanta History Center. Mon-Sat 10 am-4 pm.

Unitarian Universalist Art Gallery (B4), 1911 Cliff Valley Way, NE (off I-85); (404) 634-5134. Monthly shows of local and regional artists, in all media. Mon-Fri 9 am-5 pm; Sun 9:30 am-1 pm.

SELECTED ARTISTS' STUDIOS

The following studios of some of Atlanta's most established and respected artists in various media are recommended to the visitor or resident with serious art interest, art collectors, and those in the professional arts.

Hans Fräbel Studio (C3), 695 Antone St., NW; (404) 351-9794. Glass artist Hans Fräbel's work is world-renowned. He came to Atlanta from East Germany many years ago, where he was trained at the Jena Glassworks. With work in the Smithsonian and White House collections, he is accepted today as one of the world's foremost flamework glass sculptors. A visit to his studio is an opportunity to watch him and his trained associates at work, or if you wish to commission a custom-designed glass sculpture for your home or business. Open 9 am-5 pm Mon-Fri, but arrive before 3:00 to see glass artists' demonstrations. Also open Sat 9 am-3 pm.

Lyn Sterling Montagne Home Studio (L10), 476 Bryan St., in Grant Park; (404) 577-6007. Lyn Sterling Montagne is a prominent Atlanta weaver who specializes in custom-designed rugs woven of wool, cotton, or sisal. Call for an appointment to see this well-known weaver's work.

TULA Showrooms and Studios (C3), 75 Bennett St., NW; (404) 351-3551. The works of local and national artists are on display in TULA's 11 galleries and some 17 local artists maintain studios in this converted warehouse. Artists keep their own individual hours, but the best times to visit are Tuesday through Saturday from noon to 5 pm.

Jack Warner Home Studio (C4), 1264 Cumberland Rd., NE; (404) 872-5777. Jack Warner is a nationally-known woodturner and writes a syndicated woodworking column. His works juxtapose wood's rough, spiky burl with satiny smooth surface finishes. Call for an appointment to see his work.

SHOPPING

You have come to *the* place to shop in the Southeast, a retail wonderworld of everything from haute couture and antiquities to trendy camp and bargains galore. Atlanta's shopping trade is in full gear at all times with sales and incentives constantly enticing the spoiled natives, Southern pilgrims, and domestic and international visitors.

Buckhead, Downtown, the metro malls, and minicenters offer a variety of shopping experiences. A birthday or anniversary coming up in your family? Thinking about the next holiday season, a house gift, a business purchase, an addition to your private collection, a hard-to-find accessory for your home, a unique antique, or a spontaneous splurge on yourself? They are all here in Atlanta. We will help you match the Atlanta merchant to your shopping need.

SHOPPING DISTRICTS

Downtown

The downtown shopping area was the first shopping center of the city. Many suburban mall stores began as branches of main stores that were located downtown. Macy's, a large and prominent department store, has been downtown for decades, originally as the locally-owned Davison Paxon Company, or Davison's. Rich's downtown store, founded just after the Civil War, closed in the early 1990s. Rich's Store for Homes building, and the glass bridge that linked it to the main store, were torn down to make way for a federal office building. One corner of the main store was incorporated into the newer building, and its decorative caryatids are visible from the Five Points MARTA station. The Buckhead store at Lenox Square is now the chain's Atlanta headquarters. Both Rich's and Macy's are household words in Atlanta. Since the regional malls tend to be crowded, we recommend Macy's downtown store, as well as The Gap, Brooks Brothers, the shops of Peachtree Center, and the many shops of Underground Atlanta for an unencumbered and friendly shopping spree. Underground is particularly fertile shopping terrain. Its 12 acres comprise the best of old and new Atlanta in an exciting complex of fine shops, restaurants, entertainment, and plenty of venues for souvenirs of Atlanta.

Macy's (J9), 180 Peachtree St., NW; (404) 221-7221.
Underground Atlanta (J8), 50 Alabama St., SW; (404) 523-2311.

Buckhead

This district lies about eight miles north of Downtown, straight out on Peachtree Street. The character of this village outside original Atlanta is still maintained in the cozy homes-turned-shops along Pharr Road, East Paces Ferry Road, and other once-residential streets between Peachtree and Piedmont. Buckhead is a center for antique and boutique shopping and services. Minicenters, too, such as Cates Plaza, Andrews Square, and Peachtree Battle Shopping Center, are crammed with different and exciting stores.

Lenox Square and Phipps Plaza

About two miles beyond Buckhead proper, two well-established malls on Peachtree Street offer you some of the most fertile shopping grounds in the South and in the nation.

Lenox Square is a pioneer mall built in the early 1950s and is still exploring new shopping frontiers with its three-story redevelopment of the Plaza area. Lenox is a blend of Southern comfort and cosmopolitan flair. Rich's, Macy's, and Neiman-Marcus stake out three corners, and filling in between the finest shops in the United States and Europe, quality restaurants featuring Continental fare, fast-food houses, movie theaters, and superb community programs draw the crowds through the greenhouse spaces at this remarkable shopping center.

Phipps Plaza is sometimes referred to as the New York of the South, a large center with New York's Saks Fifth Avenue and Lord and Taylor as anchors, along with a new Parisian department store, and Tiffany's right in the middle. Points in between include first-class boutiques and specialty shops such as Abercrombie & Fitch and Gucci movie theaters, and restaurants.

Lenox Square (B3), 3393 Peachtree Rd., NE; (404) 233-6767.
Phipps Plaza (B3), 3500 Peachtree Rd., NE; (404) 261-7910 or
(404) 262-0992. Generally open from 10 am to 9:30 pm Mon-Sat,
afternoons on Sun.

Suburban Malls

As Atlanta has expanded so have her shopping needs in the outlying communities. Most malls listed below have a covered, skylit interi-
or with a host of shops, restaurants, and large, encircling parking lots.
Their main "anchor" stores come from a list that includes Rich's,
Macy's, Parisian, J. C. Penney, Nordstrom, and Sears. The following is
a list of major regional malls:

Cumberland Mall (B2), 2860 Cobb Pkwy., NW; (770) 435-2206.
Greenbriar Mall (E2), 2841 Greenbriar Pkwy., SW (at GA 166);
(404) 344-6611.
Gwinnett Place, 2100 Pleasant Hill Rd., Duluth; (770) 476-5160.
Mall of Georgia, 3333 Buford Dr., NE, Buford; (678) 482-8788.
North DeKalb Mall (C5), 2050 Lawrenceville Hwy. (at N. Druid
Hills); (404) 320-7960.
Northlake Mall (B5), 4800 Briarcliff Rd. at LaVista Rd., NE; (770)
938-3564.
North Point Mall, 1000 North Point Circle, Alpharetta; (770) 740-
9273.
Perimeter Mall (A4), 4400 Ashford-Dunwoody Rd. (at I-285);
(770) 394-4270.
Shannon Southpark Mall (F1), 1000 Shannon Southpark, Union
City; (770) 964-2200.
South DeKalb Mall (D5), 2801 Candler Rd. at I-20; (404) 241-
2431.
Southlake Mall (F4), 1000 Southlake Mall (I-75 at Morrow-
Jonesboro exit); (770) 961-1050.
Town Center at Cobb, I-75 at 400 Ernest Barrett Pkwy., Kennesaw;
(770) 424-9486.

Minicenters

Atlanta's growth has also spawned a number of intriguing small
shopping areas filling in between the major districts above, Downtown,
Buckhead, Lenox-Phipps, and the malls on the Perimeter.

Around Lenox (B3), an independent center of variety shops, next to Lenox Square.

Bennett Street (C3), west off Peachtree at Mick's Restaurant (2110 Peachtree Rd.). The place for "in" art and interior design items—antiques, Oriental rugs, art, art crafts, gifts, and more.

Colony Square (G12), at Peachtree and Fourteenth Sts. has a charming shopping and meeting area around its tree-studded mall.

East Village Square (B3), corner of Buckhead and Grandview Aves., Buckhead. A three-story complex filled with small boutiques and art galleries, all connected by a three-level gourmet coffee and exotic dessert shop. An exciting place to browse and shop.

Galleria Specialty Mall (B2), Galleria Pkwy., U.S. 41 and I-285. Taking its lead from the Houston Galleria, the Galleria Specialty Mall incorporates retail space intermingled with restaurants under an airy skylight. The tempo is upscale.

Little Five Points (D4), in Inman Park at Moreland and McLendon Avenues. Poets, punkers, rockers, and wannabes go after ethnic art, vintage clothing, books, gifts, and New Age paraphernalia.

Loehmann's Plazas (B2), 2460 Cobb Pkwy., SE, Smyrna; (C4), 2480 Briarcliff Rd.; (A3), 8610 Roswell Rd., NE, Dunwoody. Minimalls of discount high-fashion and other shops. The perfect spot for the well-off shopper with frugal instincts and the spartan shopper with champagne tastes.

Marietta Square (A1). This historic area in the heart of Old Marietta has proved a magnet for interesting restaurants and shops.

Merchant's Walk (A1), 1325 Johnson Ferry Rd., NE, Marietta. A restored town square, Merchant's Walk's storefronts are filled with attractive gifts.

Miami Circle (B3). Turn right off Piedmont just north of Lindbergh Plaza to find one of Atlanta's fave antiques and interiors havens. Here's where the pro interior designers shop for fine furnishings and antiques at good prices.

Northlake Festival (B5), LaVista Rd. at I-285. Located directly across from Northlake Mall, this minicenter contains a host of specialty stores and restaurants. Crafts, sporting equipment, clothing, and furniture can all be found here.

Park Place (A4), 4505 Ashford-Dunwoody Rd. Located across from Perimeter Mall, Park Place is for chic, sophisticated clientele looking for the latest "in" things.

Stone Mountain Village (C6), Main St., Stone Mountain. An historic district with an irresistible row of antique shops, gift shops, and craft galleries.

Vinings Jubilee (B2), Paces Ferry Rd., NW at Vinings. Once a sleepy old-style village on Paces Ferry Road and now in the heart of a thriving business and commercial area, Vinings Village provides lots of good browsing and buying for the antique-seeker. You'll find a variety of specialty and custom shops as well as fine eating. The atmosphere is charming and relaxing.

Virginia-Highland (C4), intersection of Virginia Ave. and N. Highland Ave. This village in the city contains a variety of small shops filled with interesting and unusual items, as well as a number of pubs and eateries. Great for browsing and buying that one-of-a-kind gift.

ANTIQUES

Connoisseurs of fine things and antique-hounds will find their dream pieces and little surprises here in Atlanta. Since the antique-shopping areas define themselves, we suggest the following districts and then a selected list of scattered independent shops. Flea markets, which have many fine antique shops, are listed under a separate section.

Buckhead

Bennett Street. See MINICENTERS above.

Beverly Bremer Silver Shop (B3), 3164-A Peachtree Rd., NE; (404) 261-4009. This is a sterling shop for sterling silver offering matching flatware service.

Burroughs Wellington Antiques (C3), 631 Miami Circle, NE; (404) 264-1616. Terrific selection of genuine Chinese porcelain and decorative oil paintings in addition to antique furniture.

Canterbury Antiques (C3), 660 Miami Cir., NE; (404) 231-4048. Deals in European stripped pine and mahogany furniture.

Deanne D. Levison American Antiques (C3), 2300 Peachtree Rd., NW; (404) 351-3435. This small shop specializes in period American antiques, with an early American selection, pure and exquisite.

Joseph Konrad Antiques (C3), 693 Miami Cir., NE; (404) 261-3224. Beautiful selection of antique furniture and accessories, including mirrors, sconces, brackets, chandeliers, and much more.

Williams Antiques (C3), 699 Miami Circle, NE; (404) 231-9818. Here are 28,000 square feet of eighteenth- and nineteenth-century antiques as well as handcrafted custom reproductions. This unusually large collection is often the target of area moviemakers who rent pieces to round out a period setting.

Decatur Area

All Things Vintage (C4), 340 Church St.; (404) 373-5523. Here you'll find an eclectic assortment of jewelry, folk art, antiques, and collectibles. Mr. Bookman provides a free search for rare books. Located just a few steps from the Decatur MARTA station.

Miss Ann's (C4), 111 Clairmont Ave.; (404) 378-7354. A delightful mix of antiques and collectibles draws people back again and again to this small shop just a few steps from the courthouse square.

Old Mill Antiques (C5), 3252 N. Decatur Rd., Scottdale. A collection of six stores offering great collectibles and antiques, everything from vintage clothing to dolls, Victorian furniture, and books. Hours for each store vary, but you can usually browse Mon-Sat 10 am-5 pm.

Rue de Leon (C4), 131 E. Ponce de Leon; (404) 373-6200. You'd never guess that the graceful Provençal building on the corner of E. Ponce de Leon and Church St. used to be a service station. After transforming the building, owner Catherine Krell filled it with lovely antiques and gifts with strong connections to France where she has family ties. From lavender soaps to fine old porcelain to antique armoires, there's something for every budget and occasion. A lovely selection.

SoRare (C4), 407 W. Ponce de Leon Ave.; (404) 377-0102. The playful exterior of this house-turned-shop hints at the delightful collection inside. Women's vintage clothes mix with antiques and unique items. Find something here to surprise yourself.

Chamblee

Broad Street Antique Mall (A5), 3550 Broad St., Chamblee; (770) 458-6316. Choices here are wide in areas from primitives to fine dark wood furniture as well as in accessories.

Chamblee Antique Dealers Assoc. (A4), 5486 Peachtree Rd.; (770) 458-1614. You can spend a full day in this conglomerate of antique stores sharing the same location.

Eugenia's Place (A5), 5370 Peachtree Rd., Chamblee; (770) 458-1677. This unique shop specializes in antique hardware for doors, furniture, bath, and kitchen. Also chandeliers and sconces.

Great Gatsby's (B4), 5070 Peachtree Industrial Blvd., Chamblee; (770) 457-1905. An "architectural antique" treasure house, packed with stained-glass windows, fireplace mantels, doors, hardware, and much more. Auctions regularly.

Other Antique Shops

The Antique Center of Roswell, 39 Hill St., Roswell. A collection of antique shops, conveniently located together. A haven for the antique-lover. Browse in shop after shop of antique furniture and other collectibles.

Antiques on the Square (A1), 146 South Park Square, NE, Marietta; (770) 429-0434. This is a fun assemblage of antiques and early collectibles that will delight browsers.

Architectural Accents (C3), 2711 Piedmont Rd.; (404) 266-8700. Antiques, custom mantelpieces, interior and exterior lighting fixtures, and an incredible collection of brass hardware. Stripping and re-engineering services available.

Atlanta Antiques Exchange (C3), 1185 Howell Mill Rd., NW; (404) 351-0727. This emporium sparkles with a vast collection of 18th- and 19th-century English and Chinese porcelains, furniture, and objets d'art.

Crabapple. Visit this historic town north of Atlanta where small antique shops are clustered along the street. All kinds of treasures for all kinds of collectors. We particularly like Camille's inside *Shops of the Gin*, (770) 475-3647. Camille specializes in English nineteenth century transferware and Edwardian Scottish linens as well as fine decorative accessories. For decades, Crabapple has also hosted an antique festival twice a year that draws 100 dealers from across the U.S. and 10,000 visitors. Go north on GA 400. Take Exit 4B, Holcomb Bridge Road. Turn right at the sixth traffic light on Crabapple Road. Go about 3.5 miles.

Gold's Antiques and Auction Gallery (D2), 1149 Lee St.; (404) 753-1493. This active antiques showroom and auction gallery has been selling off fine furnishings, rugs, bronzes, and porcelains since 1967. It's a landmark among antiquers.

Irish Country Pine (A3), 8877 Roswell Rd., Dunwoody; (770) 992-1412. Stripped pine antiques from Ireland are displayed in a homey setting.

Lakewood Antiques Market (E3), 2000 Lakewood Ave., SW, at the Lakewood Fairgrounds; (404) 622-4488. This show, the second weekend of every month, is a collector's bonanza. Antique lovers bring their pickups and load up.

Red Baron's Antiques (A3), 6450 Roswell Rd., NW; (404) 252-3770. More than 30,000 square feet of lighting fixtures, fine furniture, collectibles, stained glass, and more. Fascinating and fun.

Remember When Collectibles (C6), 6570 Memorial Dr., Stone Mountain; (770) 879-7878. This is the place for collectors of Coca-Cola memorabilia. You'll also find antique Coke machines, juke boxes, pin-

19th-century structures in historic Crabapple

Courtesy Sweet Apple Cottage

ball machines, and slot machines. A fun and educational treat.

Roswell Clock and Antique Company, 955 Canton St., Roswell; (770) 992-5232. This terrific shop displays a selection of fine antique clocks along with antique furniture for homes and offices. You might say it's a great place to pass the time. It's certainly a fun place to browse.

Tara Antiques (C4), 2325 Cheshire Bridge Rd. at LaVista Rd.; (404) 325-4600. More than 100 dealers show their collections at this in-town center. You'll find everything from furniture to jewelry. Open seven days, 11 am-7 pm.

The Wrecking Bar (D4), 292 Moreland Ave., NE; (404) 525-0468. This fascinating business, in a gracefully columned house on the edge of Inman Park, was begun in 1969 by early Inman Park residents to supply authentic stained and beveled glass windows, heavy walnut paneled doors, antique porch posts and railings, and other trophies for neighborhood restorationists. Today's antique architectural components come from all over the world. They're cleaned, restored, and ready to install.

ART SUPPLIES

Any and every art supply needed by the commercial and amateur artist can be found at the centers below.

Binders (B3), 2581 Piedmont Rd., NE; (404) 233-5423. (A3), 206 Johnson Ferry Rd., NW; (404) 252-1203. 2320 Pleasant Hill Rd., Duluth; (770) 497-9919.

DeKalb Art Supply (C4), 3922 N. Druid Hills Rd., Decatur; (404) 633-7311.

Dick Blick Art Materials, 1117 Alpharetta St., Roswell; (770) 939-5719. (B6), 6330 Lawrenceville Hwy., Tucker; (770) 939-5719. 2615 George Busbee Pkwy., Kennesaw; (770) 514-8456.

Pearl (B3), 3756 Roswell Rd., (404) 233-9400. Pearl offers a giant selection from every major brand. Find supplies here for both fine art and technical and graphic art, as well as craft supplies. Open seven days.

Sam Flax Art & Design (C3), 1460 Northside Dr.; (404) 352-7200.

BOOKS

It is impossible to list all the excellent bookstores in Atlanta, even those carrying this book. We have chosen to list only those that deal in antique and unique books. If you are a resident, seek out your neighborhood bookstore. It's a pleasure to browse and pass the time.

Barnes & Noble, B. Dalton, Borders, and **Waldenbooks** are national chains with multiple stores in the Atlanta area malls. **Chapter 11,** with 13 stores is an established local chain. **Borders Books** is a familiar destination for Buckhead bibliophiles. Old-book collectors will be pleased with the American Association of University Women's annual used-book sale, which fills Lenox Square from one end to the other in September, and with the Brandeis Book Sale, which fills a huge tent with delightful used books for sale every May. Check your Yellow Pages for additional bookstores in your area.

A Cappella Books (D4), 1133 Euclid Ave. in Little Five Points; (404) 681-5128.

Atlanta Vintage Books (B4), 3660 Clairmont Rd., Chamblee; (770) 457-2919.

C. Dickens Out-of-Print & Collectible Books (C3), Lenox Square; (404) 231-3825.

Charing Cross Road Booksellers, 3000 Old Alabama, Alpharetta; (770) 667-8319.

Memorable Books (C6), 5380 Manor Dr., Stone Mountain; (770) 469-5911.

Science Fiction & Mystery Bookshop (C4), 2000-F Cheshire Bridge Rd.; (404) 634-3226.

Old New York Book Shop, (770) 393-2997. By appointment only.

Yesteryear Book Shop (C3), 3201 Maple Dr.; (404) 237-0163.

CD'S, TAPES AND RECORDS

Camelot Music (B3), Lenox Square; (404) 261-7422. Located at several other malls. Records, tapes, video discs and games, sales and rental of video movies.

Tower Records (B3), 3400 Around Lenox Dr., NE; (404) 264-1217. A huge collection of CD's, tapes, videos and books. Friendly staff is great with music trivia and research. Can't think of the title to that favorite song back when? This is the place to go.

Wherehouse Music. Multiple locations in the metro area, including (B4), 3061 Buford Hwy., NE; (404) 633-2539. No matter where you are, you're always close to a Wherehouse store.

Wax 'n' Facts (D4), 432 Moreland Ave., NE; (404) 525-2275. We're talking records here. Pre-owned and collectible. Nostalgia city.

Wuxtry (C4), 2096 N. Decatur Rd.; (404) 329-0020. A large collection of collectible records and a staff that appreciates them.

CLOTHING

Women, men, and children find Atlanta a mecca for clothes shopping. With the largest apparel mart in the Southeast, Atlanta is a regional distribution center and fashion frontier, as well as a mecca for the well-dressed consumer.

Women's Clothing

Atlanta women have had two alternative sources for apparel shopping—the large, established clothing and department stores and the small, specialty clothiers. The first group includes Atlanta's favorites—**Rich's, Macy's,** and **Muses,** at Lenox Square and other malls (Macy's has a downtown store as well); **Neiman-Marcus** at Lenox Square; **Lord and Taylor** and **Saks Fifth Avenue** at Phipps Plaza; and **Parisian** at Phipps Plaza, Northlake, and Town Center. **Nordstrom** has also joined the lineup at Perimeter Mall and Mall of Georgia.

The apparel boutiques that carry fashions from the world's most lustrous designers include **Betsey Johnson, Laura Ashley,** and **Ann Taylor** at Lenox Square. Phipps Plaza showcases **Adrienne Vittadini, Gucci, Abercrombie & Fitch, Lillie Rubin, Inc.,** and **Tootsies.**

Fine quality informal wear for day and night is offered at Lenox Square and other locations by **Casual Corner** and in Buckhead at the **Snappy Turtle.**

For clothing exclusively for the large woman try **Added Dimensions** at Perimeter Mall or **Anna's Wardrobe** in Decatur, and for that All-American commodity, blue jeans, you'll find a mind-boggling selection from Levis to designer types at **The Gap** and **The Limited** at most malls. Finally, for lovers of camp, vintage, and secondhand clothes see **Stefan's, Days Gone By, The Junkman's Daughter** in Inman Park, or **Wear It Again.**

Atlanta's shopping districts have innumerable other stores to meet women's fashion needs and financial requirements. The businesswoman, the homemaker, the socialite, the retired woman, and the young teenager will each find the outfit of her choice in the bustling malls, in mini-centers, or in individual boutiques. Atlanta is a fashion-conscious, image-creating city, where women shop to look their very best.

Listed below are the shops starred in our text plus a few favorites located throughout the city to introduce shoppers to the many options available in women's clothing.

Ann Taylor (B3), 3393 Peachtree Rd., NE; (404) 264-0450. (A4), 4400 Ashford-Dunwoody Rd., NE; (770) 671-8874. Fine career dressing with youth and verve is what you'll find at these two Ann Taylor stores.

Backstreet Boutique (B3), 3655 Roswell Rd., NE; (404) 262-7783. Delightful duds that are very, very now decorate this trendy shop with a long Buckhead history.

Cotton Patch (A4), 4505 Ashford-Dunwoody Rd.; (770) 395-6988. This Park Place women's store specializes in private label fashions that are constructed from designer patterns. Also carries shoes and accessories.

Fashionably Tall (C4), 2480 Briarcliff Rd., NE; (404) 633-6544. If you're 5'8" or over, this store is just for you. Here you'll find well-designed clothes that suit your lifestyle.

Fredericks of Hollywood (B5), 4800 Briarcliff Rd., NE; (770) 934-8819. Yes, it's *the* Fredericks of Hollywood, and yes, you'll find everything you expect here and more. Sexy underwear, slinky outerwear. The forerunner to Victoria's Secret.

Mooncake (C4), 1019 Virginia Ave., NE; (404) 892-8043. These delightful fashions have a decidedly retro feeling. Don't miss the delicate cotton nightdresses that call to mind Victorian wedding nights.

Stefan's (C4), 1160 Euclid Ave., NE; (404) 688-4929. Vintage clothing for fun and elegance.

Talbots (B3), 2391 Peachtree Rd.; (404) 261-9222. For the classic look, always in style.

Men's Clothing

Men's dress in Atlanta has traditionally been conservative, even during the 1960s-70s advent of new casual styles and leisure suits. The tassled loafer is said to have never been obsolete in Atlanta even during those former decades of changing fashions.

At Lenox Square you can shop at a large cluster of fine men's stores—**Rich's, Macy's, Neiman-Marcus,** and the smaller men's clothiers: **Britches of Georgetowne, Bernini, H. Stockton,** and **Brooks Brothers.** Directly across from Lenox Square you will find **Joseph A. Banks,** and at Phipps Plaza the esteemed **Saks Fifth Avenue** and **Lord and Taylor** offer their fine lines as well as **Abercrombie & Fitch. Guffeys,** and **H. Stockton,** two small excellent Atlanta establishments, offer personal attention along with fine selections of traditional men's wear. For clothing for the great outdoors visit **Britches Great Outdoors, High Country, Blue Ridge Mountain Sports** and **REI (Recreational Equipment, Inc.).** For large men **Hyroops** will combine fashion authority with a large physique. Men of all sizes can be fitted for custom suits and shirts at **Bespoke Apparel** and **Hong Kong Tailors.**

Listed below are the men's shops in our text which are not located in the larger shopping malls.

Joseph A. Banks Clothiers (B3), 3384 Peachtree Rd., NE; (404) 262-7100.

Bespoke Apparel, Inc. (B5), 3180 Presidential Dr., NE; (770) 587-5100.

The Executive Shop (J9), 48 Marietta St., NW; (404) 577-2898.

Guffey's of Atlanta (C3), Tower Place, 3340 Peachtree Rd.; (404) 231-0044. (B2), Galleria, One Galleria Pkwy.; (770) 955-0500.

Hong Kong Tailors (A6), 5378 Buford Highway, Doraville; (770) 458-8682. Here is the place to create a custom suit or wardrobe that's elegant and just your style.

The Rogue (B3), 284 Buckhead Ave., NE; (404) 233-2646.

Children's Clothing

The major department stores, **Rich's** and **Macy's,** have clothed Atlanta children for festive occasions and everyday wear since the 1920s. **Saks** and **Lord and Taylor** have children's departments of the first rank. Smaller children's shops with exceptional children's clothes include **Chocolate Soup** and **The Children's & Prep Shop.** The gift shop at the **Swan Coach House** of the Atlanta Historical Society offers lovely handmade apparel for infants.

Jack & Jill (B2), 322 N. Main St., Alpharetta; (770) 475-2288. Clothes for infants to pre-teens. Special-occasion clothing for christenings, bar and bas mitzvahs.

The Children's & Prep Shop (C3), Peachtree Battle Shopping Center, 2385 Peachtree Rd.; (404) 365-8496.

Chocolate Soup (A3), Abernathy Square Shopping Center; (404) 303-9047.

The Gap Kids (B2), 4400 Ashford-Dunwoody Rd., NE; (770) 392-9155. (B3) 3393 Peachtree Rd., NE; (404) 264-1883.

Kangaroo Pouch (B3), 56 E. Andrews Dr.; (404) 231-1616. Traditional European fashions for infants to preteens.

Lemonade (C4), 248 W. Ponce de Leon Ave., Decatur; (404) 371-8346. Clothes and accessories for the newborn up to 10 years. Delightful gifts and handpainted furniture.

Oilily (B3), 3393 Peachtree Rd., Lenox Square; (404) 816-6556. Bright colors, unique patterns, from this Dutch company that offers everything from dresses and pants to backpacks and eyeglasses.

Swan Coach House (B3), 3130 Slaton Dr., NW; (404) 261-0636.

COINS AND STAMPS

Trading, gift giving, collecting, investing? Atlanta is a superb market in which to do all four.

Al Adams Rare Coins, Inc., (770) 740-1774. Estates and collections appraised and purchased.

Cherokee Rare Coins, 11940 Alpharetta Hwy.; (770) 751-1000. Many gold, silver, and platinum coins bought and sold. Rare and high-quality U.S. coins. Also paper money. Appraisals.

Georgia Coin and Jewelry Company (B3), 550 Pharr Rd., NE; (404) 816-5800. Georgia's oldest, this company has been a tradition since 1947.

Hancock & Harwell (B3), 3155 Roswell Rd., NE; (404) 261-6566. Rare coins, silver, gold, platinum—Bob Harwell and Jack Hancock have been serving Atlanta investors and collectors since 1976.

Larry Jackson Numismatics (A3), 5299 Roswell Rd., NE; (404) 256-3667. Rare coins bought, sold, and appraised by rare coin experts with over 30 years' experience in the field.

World Numismatics (C5), 3835 N. Druid Hills Rd. at North DeKalb Mall; (404) 636-8819. In business since 1959, this company deals in gold, silver, platinum, and palladium coins, and in stamps and baseball cards. A nationwide teletype service gives instant coin quotes.

CRAFTS

Babyland General Hospital, 19 Underwood St., Cleveland, GA 30528; 1-(706) 865-2171. Soft-sculpture, life-size babies are delivered by skilled crafts people at this old city hospital. Signed and unsigned editions are available at many Atlanta "adoption centers." Visit the showroom in Cleveland, one and a half hours north of Atlanta, or call to find the adoption center closest to you. A unique craft product and fantasy experience.

Bead Lady Gallery (C3), 620 Medlock Rd., Decatur; (404) 329-1988. An exquisite selection of beads, beadworking equipment. Also classes and a friendly atmosphere.

By Hand South (C3), 112 East Ponce de Leon Ave., Decatur; (404) 378-0118. A wonderful collection of art crafts in ceramics, glass, wood, jewelry, and fiber. Named a Top 100 Retailer of American Craft by *NICHE* magazine. A great place to browse and buy.

Coomers—The Original Crafters Mall (C5), 1825 Rockbridge Rd., SW, Stone Mountain; (770) 879-9244. A selection of crafts and craft dealers all in one location.

Michael's Arts & Crafts. Many metro locations, including (A4), 1155 Mt. Vernon Hwy., Dunwoody; (770) 394-4988. Offers supplies to create your own craft items. Most merchandise at discount prices.

Out of the Woods (C3), 22 Bennett St., NW; (404) 351-0446. Fine crafts and original art with emphasis on Southwestern and Native American works.

Sidewalk Studio (C4), 996 Virginia Ave., NE; (404) 872-0147. A wide selection of crafts by local artists in this convenient Virginia-Highland gallery.

The Signature Shop and Galleries, Inc. (B3), 3267 Roswell Rd., NE; (404) 237-4426. The most sophisticated crafted works of art in the Southeast. This long-established gallery includes the finest in ceramics, fiber, metals, and glass.

Silver Wings and Golden Needles (E2), 5611 Riverdale Rd., College Park; (770) 991-2225. Arts and crafts supplies, classes, needlework, folk art, seasonal crafts, floral designs.

FACTORY OUTLETS AND DISCOUNT STORES

Loehmann's Plazas (C4), 2480 Briarcliff Rd., NE; (404) 633-4156. (A3), 8610 Roswell Rd.; (770) 998-2095. Numerous designer outlets in one convenient location. Clothing for men, women, and children as well as gifts, textiles, and more.

Midtown Outlets (C3), 500 Amsterdam Ave., NE; (770) 451-0318. Once a warehouse district backing up to Piedmont Park, this area has been reborn as a neighborhood retail center. Discounted designer shoes, clothing, furniture, and more.

North Georgia Premium Outlet Center, 800 Hwy 400 S, Dawsonville; (706) 216-3609. More than 140 designer and name-brand outlet stores welcome the serious bargain hunter, including Off 5th Saks Fifth Avenue Outlet, Calvin Klein, Gap Outlet, Williams-Sonoma, etc. Discounts from 25 to 75 percent. Take GA 400 north to Dawsonville; about 35 min. from Atlanta.

Outlets, Ltd., 3750 Venture Dr., Duluth, off I-85, N. Exit 104; (770) 622-9000. Discount shopping for all needs.

Plaza Fiesta (B5), 4166 Buford Hwy., NE; (404) 982-0670. This mall contains more than 40 restaurants and outlets including Burlington's and Marshalls. Other stores feature shoes, books, linens, housewares, and much more.

Women's Clothing Outlets ─────────────

Banker's Note (C3), 2581 Piedmont Rd., NE; (404) 233-5233. Three other locations.

The Clothes Bin (C3), 2351 Peachtree Rd., NE; (404) 262-9742.

Dan Howard Maternity Factory Outlet (A3), 6631 Roswell Rd., Sandy Springs; (404) 252-1155. (B5), 4135 LaVista Rd., Tucker; (770) 270-5747.

Syms (A6), 5775 Jimmy Carter Blvd., Norcross; (770) 368-0200.

Men's Clothing Outlets

K & G Associates (C2), 1750 Ellsworth Industrial Dr.; (404) 352-3471.

Syms (A6), 5775 Jimmy Carter Blvd., Norcross; (770) 368-0200.

Zeeman's (C5), 4879 Memorial Dr., Stone Mountain; (404) 296-1401. (F4), 1311-A Morrow Industrial Blvd., Morrow; (770) 968-3966. (D1), 4515 Fulton Industrial Blvd.; (404) 696-1680. Men's, boys', and formal wear.

Children's Clothing Outlets

Baby Depot (E2), 2841 Greenbriar Pkwy., SW, at Burlington Coat Factory; (404) 349-6300. (A1), 1255 Roswell Rd., Marietta; (770) 971-6540. Several other locations.

Carter's Outlet, 216 Main St., Barnesville, about one hour south of Atlanta on I-75; (770) 358-1263. Also at North Georgia Premium Outlets, about 35 min. north of Atlanta. Take Ga. 400 north to Dawsonville.

Children's Wear Outlet (D5), 3527 Memorial Dr., Decatur; (404) 289-4128.

Shoes

A.J.S. Shoe Warehouse (C2), 1788 Ellsworth Industrial Blvd., NW; (404) 355-1760. Designer shoes, boots, handbags for women.

Bennie's (C3), 2581 Piedmont Rd.; (404) 262-1966. (B1), 2441 Cobb Pkwy., SW, Smyrna; (770) 955-1972. (A5), 5192 Brooks Hollow Pkwy., Norcross; (770) 447-1577. All major brand names men's shoes.

Foot Locker. Many locations, including (A4), Perimeter Mall, Dunwoody; (770) 393-4447. Sports shoes for men, women.

Friedman's Shoes (B3), 4340 Roswell Rd., NW; (404) 843-2414. Men's and women's shoes. Also at (J9), 209 Mitchell St., SW; (404) 524-1311, men's shoes only, and (J9), 223 Mitchell St., SW; (404) 523-1134, ladies' shoes only.

Payless ShoeSource. Many locations, including (J9), 55 Peachtree St., NW; (404) 659-5200.

S & H Shoe Warehouse (C2), 1240 Old Chattahoochee Ave. at

Ellsworth Avenue; (404) 350-0861. Thousands of famous-name shoes for women.

Shoemakers' Warehouse (C3), 500 Amsterdam Ave.; (404) 881-9301. Shoemakers' offers better and designer shoes and accessories at terrific prices.

FABRICS AND LINENS

Calico Corners Fabrics (B3), 4256 Roswell Rd., NW; (404) 252-7443. (B3), 2950 Paces Ferry Rd.; (678) 305-0506. Upholstery, drapery, slipcovers, and fine decorator seconds.

Classic Linens (B3), 3168 Peachtree Rd., NE; (404) 841-6520. Irish table and bed linens. European linens and down.

Curran Designer Fabrics (C3), 737 Miami Cir., NE; (404) 237-4246. Designer upholstery and fabrics.

Forsyth's (C2), 1190 Foster St., NW; (404) 351-6050. Thousands of bolts of designer fabrics. Also drapery rods and ties, furniture.

Hancock Fabrics. Many locations, including (C3), 2625 Piedmont Rd., NE; (404) 266-0517. For everyday fabric shopping, Hancock has it.

Lewis Textiles (C2), 912 Huff Rd., NW; (404) 351-4833. Designer dress fabrics, upholstery, remnants, trims.

The Linen Loft (C4), 2915 N. Druid Hills Rd., NE; (404) 633-9354. A large selection of bedspreads with coordinating window treatments from many famous manufacturers. Also sheets, towels. Seven other locations.

Linens 'n' Things. Three locations, including (A3), 1171 Hammond Dr., NE; (770) 698-0374. Towels, sheets, bedspreads, comforters, bath and table accessories at discount prices.

Pierre Deux (B3), 3500 Peachtree Rd., NE; (404) 869-7790. French fabrics and accessories.

FLEA MARKETS

Atlanta is a mecca for the flea-market aficionado. Whether you are searching for junk or jewels, check out one of these Atlanta area markets. There are many others but just not enough space to list them all.

A Flea-Antique II (C4), 1853 Cheshire Bridge Rd., NE; (404) 872-4342. Antiques, collectibles, statuary, and unique findings.

Caché Antiques (C4), 1845 Cheshire Bridge Rd., NE; (404) 815-0880. Small but eclectic assortment of treasures.

Georgia Antique Center & International Market (A5), 6624 I-85 N. Access Rd. between I-285 and Jimmy Carter Blvd.; (770) 446-9292. Antiques, brass, jewelry, crafts.
Kudzu Flea Market (C5), 2874 E. Ponce de Leon Ave., Decatur; (404) 373-6498. A small flea market with lots of offbeat collectibles.
Scavenger Hunt (B4), 3438 Clairmont Rd., NE; (404) 634-4948. Lots of collectibles, antiques, and oddities. Open seven days 10 am-7 pm.
Tara Antiques (C4). See Other Antique Shops.

FLORISTS

When the occasion calls for flowers or plants, see the following selected florists in Atlanta. Most have FTD (Florist Telegraph Delivery) service and local delivery.

Botany Bay (A3), 6074 Roswell Rd., NE; (404) 255-3340. Cut flowers and floral arrangements are combined with houseplants here.
Maude Baker Florist (C4), 609 Church St., Decatur; (404) 373-5791. Flowers, balloons, gourmet baskets since 1947.
Flowers from Holland (B3), Lenox Square, 3393 Peachtree Rd.; (404) 305-1842. The new spare look in florists with cut flowers arranged in modern cylinders, priced by the flower—more like a street market inside.
Gresham's Florist (J9), 260 Peachtree St., NW; (404) 522-3215. Since 1913 Gresham's has brought flowers to Atlantans and sent flowers from Atlanta's homes and Atlanta's visitors.
Harpers Canary Cottage Flowers (C3), 4280 Peachtree Rd., NE; (404) 237-2886. Three generations have served Atlanta since 1921.
Weinstock's Flowers (B3), 5290 Roswell Rd., NW; (404) 255-1611. Weinstock's began their florist business in 1917, another fine established Atlanta company.

FOOD

Shopping for food can be a tasty addition to the total shopping experience. Here are some appetizing suggestions for gifts of food or immediate consumption.

Bakeries ———

Cloudts' Bakery, (A6), 3920 Peachtree Industrial Blvd., Duluth;

(770) 623-4146. Freshly baked pastries, cookies, breads on premises. Wedding and custom cakes. Since 1931.

Southern Sweets (C4), 186 Rio Circle, Decatur; (404) 373-8752. This bakery is near the DeKalb Farmers Market, a lovely coincidence for dessert shoppers. Better than Mom used to make.

The German Bakery (C4), 2914 White Blvd., Decatur; (404) 296-4336. These folks have been turning out great German breads and cakes, deli and gourmet foods since 1963.

Henri's Bakery (B3), 61 Irby Ave., NE; (404) 237-0202. (A3), 6289 Roswell Rd.; (404) 256-7934. A superior local bakery, a tradition in Atlanta for more than 50 years, Henri's is also a fine delicatessen and meeting place in the heart of Buckhead.

Outrageous Cakes (B3), 524 E. Paces Ferry Rd., NE; (770) 216-9767. Edible works of art, as delicious as they are beautiful.

Palace Bakery (B4), 2881 N. Druid Hills Rd. (Toco Hills Shopping Center); (404) 315-9017. New York-style cakes and pastries.

Pastries A-Go-Go (C4), 250 West Ponce de Leon Ave., Decatur; (404) 373-3423. Flaky croissants, scrumptious pies and cakes. Special requests are welcome.

Pepperidge Farm Thrift Store (A5), 6725 Jimmy Carter Blvd., NW; (770) 446-2669. This national chain will sell you quality breads at considerable discounts, especially good for bulk buying.

Rhodes Bakery (C4), 1783 Cheshire Bridge Rd., NE; (404) 876-3783. Breads, cakes, cookies since 1930. An Atlanta tradition.

Health Food Stores

Health food establishments have come into their own during the last two decades, offering a variety of products from grains and vitamins to equipment and cosmetics.

Bill Stanton's Health Market (B3), 2581 Piedmont Rd., NE; (404) 814-9935. Discount prices and expert nutritional guidance.

The Good Earth. Two Atlanta locations, including (B3), 211 Pharr Rd., NE; (404) 266-2919. A complete health food store with vitamins at big discounts.

Life's Essentials Market (D2), 2329 Cascade Rd., SW; (404) 753-2269. Organic foods and extensive selection of herbs. Imported African and Caribbean products.

Rainbow Grocery (D4), 2118 N. Decatur Rd., NE; (404) 636-5553. Organic produce, vitamins, books, a deli, and a natural foods restaurant make this a popular Emory-area gathering place.

Sevananda Natural Foods (D3), 467 Moreland Ave., SE; (404) 681-2831. This community-owned grocery in Little Five Points carries organic produce, vitamins, health food products, and what is probably the area's most complete selection of bulk herbs.

Unity Natural Food Markets (B3), 2955 Peachtree Rd.; (404) 261-8776. Good selection of health and healthy foods.

International and Gourmet Foods

Treasures of specialty foods are hidden in Atlanta's neighborhood pockets, shopping centers, and along the commuter highways. Follow us to an assortment of international foods, fish, meats, and cheese, an offering that expands with Atlanta's increasingly international population.

Callaway Gardens Country Store (E2), 210 Peachtree St.; (404) 524-1151. (J8), World Congress Center; (404) 588-1545. This famous mid-Georgia resort also produces a lengthy selection of canned goods and preserves, hams and slab bacon, grits and grains, and country folk crafts. Try the muscadine sauce made from one of Georgia's varietal grapes.

Coffee Plantation (C4), 2205 LaVista Rd., NE; (404) 636-1038. (A3), 4920 Roswell Rd., NW; (404) 252-4686. This gourmet coffee roaster specializes in the finest coffees from around the world. Roasted fresh each day, the coffees in this shop are unique and delicious. Complete selection of coffee accessories, including the finest grinders and brewers and other hard-to-find items. Second location on Roswell Road.

DeKalb Farmers Market (C5), 3000 E. Ponce de Leon Ave., Decatur; (404) 377-6400. See Markets.

E. Forty-eighth Street Market (A4), Williamsburg at Dunwoody Shopping Center, 2462 Jett Ferry Rd. at Mount Vernon Hwy.; (770) 392-1499. Mama mia! A bonafide New York/Italian deli-grocery in the heart of suburban Dunwoody, E. Forty-eighth Street gleams with such delicious treats as eggplant parmigiana sandwiches to go, veal meatballs, freshly made lasagne, baked ziti, sun-dried tomatoes, breads, sausages, peppers, and a host of other wonders. Open Mon-Fri, 10 am-7 pm.; Sat, 10 am-6 pm.

EatZi's Market & Bakery (B3). See Dining chapter.

Happy Herman's. Several locations, including (C3), 2297 Cheshire Bridge Rd., NE; (404) 321-3012. One of Atlanta's most reputable delicatessens, Happy Herman's stocks everything from soup to nuts, lox to tenderloin, and wines and beer from the world over.

Harry's Farmer's Market. See Markets.

Honey Baked Ham Company. Many metro locations, including (C4), 2909 Buford Hwy., NE; (404) 633-8562. For easy serving and delicious sweet ham, try this company's spiral-sliced honey-baked ham. For gift shopping, (880) 367-2426.

Metro Market (C4), corner of W. Ponce de Leon Ave. and Commerce, in Decatur; (404) 371-9121. An offshoot of The Food Business, a popular Decatur restaurant on the square, Metro Market is a New York-style market with a gourmet bakery and take-out meals, as well as a fine selection of produce, meats, wines, and other essentials for the good life.

Nayarat Mex American Food (D3), 568 Boulevard, SE; (404) 622-2187. (F1), 6715 Roosevelt Hwy., Union City; (770) 969-0308.

Nippin Daido Japanese Grocery (B5), 2390 Chamblee-Tucker Rd., Chamblee; (770) 455-3846. Everything you need to cook Japanese.

Proof of the Pudding (C3), 2033 Monroe Dr., NE; (404) 892-2359. Gourmet meals to go, jars of spices, coffees and teas, and shelves filled with gourmet delectables make this attractive shop and catering company a constant stopping-off place for Atlantans.

Quality Kosher Emporium (B4), 2153 Briarcliff Rd., NE; (404) 636-1114. This small friendly deli specializes in everything from A to Z in kosher foods and products.

Sausage World, 5363 Lawrenceville Hwy., Lilburn; (770) 925-4493. Specializing in Italian and ethnic-type meats that are all natural, preservative free, and relatively lean. Also prepares hot sandwiches.

Markets

Atlanta State Farmers Market (F3), 16 Forest Pkwy., Forest Park; (404) 366-6910. Wholesale and retail. Plan a full day, and can and preserve right there on the premises. Call for dates for canning.

DeKalb Farmers Market (C4), 3000 E. Ponce de Leon Ave., Decatur; (404) 377-6400. A banquet for the senses, this mammoth bazaar is like the great, colorful indoor markets of Europe and Latin America. More than 100,000 square feet of air-conditioned space is piled high with fruits and vegetables from around the world; herbs and spices; cheeses, breads, sausages, fresh seafoods and meats; coffees, teas, and condiments; deli items and pastries; fresh flowers; and much, much more. The market is one of Atlanta's most international attractions, worthwhile even if you think you're not in a shopping frame of mind. Open daily, 10 am-9 pm. Cash, checks; no credit cards.

Harry's Farmer's Market (A4), 1180 Upper Hembree Rd., off U.S. 19, Alpharetta; (770) 664-6300. 2025 Satellite Rd., NW, Duluth; (770) 416-6900. Atlanta's budding chain of international food bazaars started in Alpharetta with a 75,000-square-foot extravaganza of food and wines from around the world, where your wondering eyes will behold everything from live eels and lobsters to abalone, purple basil, pasilla peppers, olive oils, hundreds of cheeses and sausages, fresh-cut flowers, and Belgian chocolates. The Duluth store is a delightful replica of the first. Open Tue-Sat, 9 am-9 pm.; Sun, 10 am-7 pm. Cash, checks accepted; no credit cards.

Sweet Auburn Curb Market (K10), 209 Edgewood Ave., SE; (404) 659-1665. Situated in the Sweet Auburn historic district, this municipal market will introduce you to the "soul food" of Southern greens, chitlins, tripe, and pork. Enjoy the colorful signs and succulent food, especially on Friday and Saturday when folks come to market.

FURNITURE MAKERS

If you are furniture shopping, take advantage of the varied selections below.

Brumby Chair Company (A1), 37 W. Park Square, NE, Marietta; (770) 425-1875. The Brumby rockers were first designed and constructed by the Brumby family of Marietta in the 1870s with cane seats and backs and extra large arms, and were as sturdy as the red oak from northern Appalachia from which they were made. These rockers are still crafted for rocking on the porch in the summer and by the hearth in the winter and are now part of the White House collection of American furniture.

Chicken Lips (A4), 5484 Chamblee Dunwoody Rd.; (770) 395-1234. Like its name, the company produces delightful custom-painted furniture for children. They'll custom-paint your existing furniture, too.

Field Furniture (A1), 1260 N. Cobb Pkwy., Marietta; (770) 422-8585. At this custom furniture dealer, choose frames for sofas, chairs, loveseats, and ottomans, select a fabric from more than 200 designs, and have your furniture made to order.

Furniture Craftsmen (A1), 1700 White Cir., Marietta; (770) 427-4205. This large shop carries traditional furniture, colonial and eighteenth-century, including its own reproductions.

Homescape Artisans (C4), 2000 Cheshire Bridge Rd.; (404) 321-4141. Custom made furniture with exquisite hand painting. They do metal working for banisters, fire screens, and such and will paint original murals for a child's room.

Wood N Choices (A6), 6438 Dawson Blvd., Norcross; (770) 417-1233. Offering a full line of unfinished furniture, from contemporary to traditional to country colonial styles. All fine wood, custom finished. Beautiful selection of upholstery fabrics. Located in the Roswell Exchange.

Palace Forge (C3), 652 Miami Circle, NE; (404) 237-3825. Handmade wrought iron furniture and heavy glass table tops.

Trinity Furniture Shop (D6), 7260 Center St., Lithonia; (770) 482-1133. Reproductions made to order, restorations of antiques.

GIFT SHOPS AND GREETING CARDS

There are many fun-filled gift shops in the city, many in the suburbs and the malls. Our selections highlight some of the best.

Artlite (C3), 1851 Piedmont Rd.; (404) 875-7271. If your giftee loves fine writing instruments, browse through one of Atlanta's largest collections, including Montblanc, Cross, and Parker pens. Artlite also carries many accessories for his or her office.

The Brookstone Company (A4), Perimeter Mall; (404) 394-6700. This store will warm the hearts of the whole family with its happy combination of tools, household gifts, and personal items.

Crystal Blue (D4), 1168 Euclid Ave., NE; (404) 522-4605. Jewelry, crystals, New Age gifts. Atlanta's first New Age store.

Domestic Instincts (C4), 416 Church St., Decatur; (404) 377-9188. Combine avant-garde with beauty and a sense of humor, and you have a good description of this wonderful store. Unique—yes, really—home accessories and gift items.

Fitz & Floyd (J9), 230 Spring St., NW; (404) 688-9557. Fantastic selections of fine china, ceramic gifts, and other home accessories.

Glass, Etc. (B5), 4135 LaVista Rd., Tucker; (770) 493-7936. Glass and collectibles.

High Museum of Art Gift Shop (G11), Atlanta Memorial Arts Center, 1280 Peachtree St., NE; (404) 898-1155. Unusual and interesting greeting cards and notes are sold as well as local and international crafts, gifts and clothing, art magazines, and books. Discounts for members of the museum.

The Inner Child (C4), 308 West Ponce de Leon Ave., Decatur; (404) 377-7775. For the child in your life or the child in you, this specialty toy store has something to intrigue and stimulate. Called "the best toy store for thinking kids" by *Atlanta* magazine.

Paper Parlour (B5), 3363 Buford Hwy., NE; (404) 728-0100. Six thousand square feet of paper, balloons, plastic cups, pens with Day-Glo ink, Halloween costumes, and funny hats. Anything and everything you would need for a theme party. A terrific place to do your party shopping.

Tijara (D3), 992 Ralph D. Abernathy Blvd., SW; (404) 753-7824. This West End store carries African clothing and jewelry, perfumes, incense, as well as T-shirts and cards.

Traditionally Georgia (C6), 979 Main St., Stone Mountain; (770) 682-0032. Georgia memorabilia, gift baskets, collectibles.

HOME INTERIORS

The Brass Butler (B2), 585 Cobb Pkwy. South, Suite J, Marietta; (770) 426-8024. Offers polishing, lacquering, and repairs to brass, copper, and silver. Also sells a full scope of brass items, including beds, candlesticks, all lighting fixtures, and outdoor lighting.

Brownlee's Furniture, 309 Maltbie St., NW, Lawrenceville; (770) 963-6435. A huge stock of furniture, all at discount prices. Custom upholstering. Many well-known furniture lines.

Classic Home Furnishings (A3), 1205 Johnson Ferry Rd., NE, Marietta; (770) 973-7011. Beautiful selection of sofas, loveseats, sleepers, sectionals, and chairs. Styles to complement any decor, including 18th century, English, Italian, French, and much more. Choose from hundreds of fabrics.

Diversified Cabinet Distributors (A6), 5250 Brook Hollow Pkwy., NW, Norcross; (770) 447-6363. Top-quality cabinets for kitchen and bath can be ordered at discount prices. Staff will also help with kitchen design. A "must" visit for anyone remodeling a kitchen.

Home Concepts (A6), 6440 Dawson Blvd., Norcross; (770) 448-8425. Furnishings for home and office. A large selection of futons, futon frames and covers.

Home Depot Expo Atlanta (A4), 1201 Hammond Dr.; (770) 913-0111. One of the really great ideas! A one-stop shop for anyone who's building or remodeling a home. Forget the usual Home Depot plywood and nails. This is the fun stuff. Plumbing fixtures, cabinets, wallpaper, tile, lighting, windows, doors, lots more. Expert advice is also available.

House of Denmark (A6), 6248 Dawson Blvd., Norcross; (770) 449-5740. Fine furnishings of elegantly simple Danish designs. For home or office.

House Parts (D3), 479 Whitehall St., SW; (404) 577-5584. A treasure trove of "artifactory," House Parts reproduces artifacts and architectural detail, including garden statuary, columns, and table bases.

Huff (B3), 3178 Peachtree Rd., NE; (404) 261-7636. Contemporary furnishings, custom design service. One of the area's largest contemporary design showrooms.

Lamps 'N Things (A1), 1205 Johnson Ferry Rd., NE, Marietta; (770) 971-0874. Located in the Fountains of Olde Towne shopping center, Lamps 'N Things offers a wide variety of lamps and other home accessories. Great selection of framed pictures and mirrors to complement any home decor.

Legatto (C3), 2140 Peachtree Rd., NW; (404) 355-4305. Fine leather furniture.

Marcella Fine Rugs (J8), 240 Peachtree St., NW; (404) 523-1894. One of Atlanta's oldest and most established firms, Marcella offers a splendid selection of Oriental and other fine rugs at fabulous prices.

Matthews' (B2), 1240 W. Paces Ferry Rd., NW; (404) 237-8271. Matthews' offers fine 18th-century reproductions in mahogany and cherry in their elegant northside showroom.

Parr's, 512 N. Main St., Alpharetta; (770) 664-6291. 3086 Hwy. 29, Lilburn; (770) 923-3153. The best names in patio furniture can be found in these large showroom spaces at substantial discounts.

Peachtree Doors and Windows (A5), 4350 Peachtree Industrial Blvd, NW, Norcross; (770) 497-2000. This Atlanta company's fine windows and doors are displayed in a tasteful showroom. Design assistance is available. There's also an adjacent warehouse where "seconds" are available at substantial savings.

Pier 1. Many locations, including (B4) 3435 Lenox Rd., NE; (404) 233-1080. Design-savvy furnishings at affordable prices. Wicker and rattan, lamps, rugs, tabletop, gifts.

Pineapple House (A5), 2131 Plasters Bridge Rd., NE, Norcross; (404) 897-5551. Carries full line of fabrics, wallcoverings, carpets, draperies, and accessories. Full-time professional interior designers, upholsterers, and furniture makers.

Plantation Shutters (A5), 4373 Shallowford Industrial Pkwy., NE, Marietta; (770) 592-9934. Interior shutters for fine home decor and advice on proper selection.

Progressive Lighting (C6), 5094 Hwy. 78 E. Stone Mountain; (770) 979-4100. A fabulous selection of lighting fixtures to meet all your lighting needs. Also offers furniture accessories. Seven other locations.

Seventy-Ninth Street Gallery (C3), 2829 Peachtree Rd.; (404) 231-2108. A fantastic rug shop specializing in antique Herig and Serapis, dhurries, needlepoints, and Turkish and Romanian kilims. A must for serious rug shoppers who are looking for an elegant and beautiful addition to their homes.

Sofas & Chairs (B4), 3089 Peachtree Rd., NE; (404) 262-7376. Terrific selection of sophisticated and comfortable sofas, loveseats, and chairs. More than 3,000 fabrics to choose from. Reasonably priced.

Wicker Warehouse Outlet (A6), 963 N. Burnt Hickory Rd., Douglasville; (770) 942-3992. Fine furniture for an elegant yet comfortable Southern lifestyle. Specializing in wicker and rattan.

JEWELRY

Atlanta's established jewelers are joined by a group of relative newcomers to assure you a comprehensive jewelry selection. The Buckhead and Lenox area is emerging as the diamond and gem center of the city.

Bailey Banks & Biddle Jewelers (B3), Lenox Square; (404) 237-9247. The Atlanta BB&B stores continue the tradition of fine jewelry begun in 1832. Also in Northlake, Perimeter, Shannon, Gwinnett Place, and Town Center malls.

Beadazzles (A3), 290 Hilderbrand Dr.; (404) 843-8606. Create your own jewelry for all your fashion needs at this unique shop. Large selection of beads and rhinestones.

Brown & Co. (A3), 674 Holcomb Bridge Rd., Roswell; (770) 993-1080. Fine china and crystal, Rolex watches.

C. Alexander (A4), 5482 Chamblee-Dunwoody Rd.; (770) 551-8564. Custom-designed jewelry. Fine diamonds and gem stones.

Geode Ltd. Jewelry Designs (B3), Lenox Square; (404) 261-9346. For gold and silver jewelry designed by local and national craftspeople come to Geode's for chic care and service in Lenox.

Jewelry Artisans (A3), 6690 Roswell Rd., Ste 510; (404) 255-6268. Design your own jewelry or have your jewelry repaired at this unique shop. Choose from a complete selection of gemstones. Or stop ring twisting with their patented feature which permits rings to open wide and slip over knuckles.

Knox Jewelers (C3), 180 Allen Rd., NE; (404) 252-2256. Knox Jewelers specialize in custom design, pure and simple.

Maier and Berkeley Jewelers (B3), 3225 Peachtree Rd.; (404) 261-4911. Also in the following malls: Cumberland, Lenox Square, Perimeter, and North Point. Jewelers for more than 100 years. Excellent selection of diamonds and precious stones, gold and silver jewelry, silver, china, and crystal.

Skippy Musket (B3), Phipps Plaza; (404) 233-3462. Antique and estate jewelry. Here is another source of pleasure for your treasure hunt.

Tiffany and Company (B3), Phipps Plaza; (404) 261-0074. One of the world's greatest jewelers with more than 140 years experience, Tiffany's has swiftly become an Atlanta tradition, too.

LEATHER

Bally of Switzerland (B3), Lenox Square; (404) 231-0327. If you prefer classic style over trendy, shop Bally for luxury shoes, luggage and more.

Gucci (B3), Phipps Plaza; (404) 233-4899. The Italian designer's premier works are on display for Atlantans to purchase, from soft leather goods to silken scarves.

Legatto, 2140 Peachtree Rd., NW; (404) 355-4305. Fine European leather furniture.

Mori Luggage and Gifts.. Eleven metro locations, including (B3), Lenox Square; (404) 231-2146. This shop has a very wide spectrum of leather accessories in an equally wide price range.

OFFICE SUPPLIES

Anderson Office Supply (C3), 640 Tenth St., NW; (404) 897-1818. This is a complete office outfitter, with printing and prompt delivery. Second store at (A5) 1776 Northeast Expressway; (404) 633-6315.

Artlite Office Supply Co. (C3), 1851 Piedmont Rd., NE; (404) 875-7271. Artlite is a full-service supplier, including furniture, free delivery, and copy service. See the historic Artlite pen collection. Open Mon-Sat.

Staples/Ivan Allen (J10), 221 Peachtree Center Ave.; (404) 332-3000. Complete office service from design to supplies. Several other Staples locations.

Office Depot. Several locations, including (C3), 2581 Piedmont Rd.; (404) 261-4111. A warehouse of office supplies, all at discount prices.

Office Max. Several locations, including 2300 Pleasant Hill Rd., Duluth; (770) 476-0823. Office supplies discounted in a warehouse-type setting.

PHOTOGRAPHIC SUPPLIES

Most CVS and Eckerd pharmacies have photo centers, but the following retail stores provide full customer service including equipment sales, repairs, and developing for both shutterbugs and professional photographers.

Camera Bug (C4), 1799 Briarcliff Rd.; (404) 873-4513. Cameras, equipment, one-hour lab. Telescopes, binoculars.

Camera Country USA (A3), 270 Hildebrand Dr., NE; (404) 256-2595. Excellent personal attention for camera buffs. A full line of cameras and video cameras. Same day developing service.

Collectable Cameras/Colcam (C5), 3110 E. Ponce de Leon Ave., Scottdale; (404) 373-9911. This unusual shop buys and sells antique, collectible, and modern photographic equipment.

Image Photo (C3), 1000 Piedmont Ave., NE; (404) 875-9334. Individual service in a non-chain store. Fast processing, computer scanning, digital services. Open seven days.

Showcase (C4), 2323 Cheshire Bridge Rd., corner Cheshire Bridge and LaVista Rds.; (404) 256-2595. Complete camera specialty store with darkroom equipment and supplies. Friendly service.

Wolf Camera (C3), 150 14th St.; (404) 875-0071. Main showroom. More than 40 additional locations in the Atlanta area. One of the South's largest photographic dealers, with a full line of video equipment.

SHOES

Atlanta has many shoe stores of excellence for men, women, and children. We list a few below because of their unusual appeal.

Bally of Switzerland (B3), Lenox Square; (404) 231-0327. This men's shop filled with Bally's elegant Continental footwear, leather briefcases, and wallets is one of Atlanta's most exclusive stores.

Birkenstock Specialty Store (B3), 322 E. Paces Ferry Rd., NE; (404) 239-9358. If you like to pamper your feet, here's the place. Huge selection, some direct from Germany. Repair service, too, if you can't bear to part with your favorite Birkenstock sandals.

Pappagallo at Vinings (B2), 4300 Paces Ferry Rd., NW; (770) 333-0705. Those cute Pappagallo shoes for women are just waiting for you at the Pappagallo shop in historic Vinings Jubilee.

Red Wing Shoes. Four metro locations, including (A1), 2437 Cobb Pkwy., SE, Marietta; (770) 955-1437. Work and casual boots and shoes for men and women.

The Sport Shoe (C6), 5244 Memorial Dr., Stone Mountain; (404) 296-4367. A terrific outlet for sports shoes. Twenty Atlanta locations. Call (770) 279-7494 for the store nearest you.

Vogue Shoes (D3), 93 Broad St., SW; (404) 523-4814. Larger size ladies' designer shoes. One and a half blocks from the Five Points MARTA station.

SKIN CARE

Esthetiques-Electrolysis & Skin Care Clinic (A3), Mt. Vernon Rd., Dunwoody; (770) 671-0510. Food and skin allergy identification, nutritional counseling. This health-conscious clinic also specializes in treating sun-damaged skin.

Natural Body. Three locations including (C4), 1403 N. Highland Ave., (404) 876-9642. An all-natural bath, body and skin care store. Offers products and gifts. Day spa specialties in aromatherapy, body treatments and facials.

Repose, 8610 Roswell Rd.; (770) 587-0480. Located in Loehmann's Plaza, Repose is a full-service skin-care salon providing facials, full-body massages, manicures, pedicures, and hair removal. A luxurious way to spend the afternoon!

Spa/Sydell (B3), 3060 Peachtree Rd., NW; (404) 237-2505. Four other locations. Relax and be pampered with a stimulating massage of the face and upper body, skin analysis, skin-type treatment, professional makeup application, and much, much more.

SPORTS EQUIPMENT

With Atlanta's temperate climate, outdoor sports activity maintains a year-long momentum. If your tennis racquet breaks while visiting the city or you have a sudden urge to buy some new camping equipment, scan the list below for some of the best places to shop.

Abercrombie & Fitch (B3), Phipps Plaza; (404) 233-8522. This nationally known name in sporting goods offers the unusual and unique in equipment and gifts.

Atlanta Fly Fishing Outfitters (A4), 11060 Alpharetta Hwy., Roswell; (770) 649-9866. Everything for the fly fisherman—or fisherwoman. Tackle, clothing, classes, gifts.

The Fish Hawk (B3), 279 Buckhead Ave., NE; (404) 237-3473. For anglers who take their sport seriously—from the lightest freshwater to the heaviest saltwater.

High Country (B3), 3906 Roswell Rd., NE; (404) 841-0999. Also in Perimeter Mall, (770) 391-9657. Camping equipment, backpacks, canoes, kayaks, and outdoor clothing are High Country's major offerings.

Orvis Atlanta (B3), 3255 Peachtree Rd., NE; (404) 841-0093. Fly-fishing tackle, schools and private instruction. Also carries hunting equipment and apparel, men's and women's clothing, gifts and more. For the rare Atlanta cold snap, check out the array of warm socks.

Phidippides Sports Center (C3), 1544 Piedmont Ave., NE; (404) 875-4268. Phidippides, the great Greek marathon runner, is honored in this specialist running center. For running shoes and clothes, expert advice, and up-to-date data on Atlanta's running courses, clinics, and programs, come to Phidippides.

Play It Again Sports. Many locations, including (B3), 4279 Roswell Rd., NE; (404) 257-0229. This chain of stores buys, sells, and trades new and used sporting equipment.

REI-Recreational Equipment, Inc. (B4), 1800 NE Expressway; (404) 633-6508. Huge selection for outdoor and sporting activities. Canoes, tents, boots and more. Test yourself on their climbing wall. They also offer bike service and repair.

Rocky Mountain Snow Ski Shop (B3), 5323 Roswell Rd.; (404) 252-3216. Skis, boots, ski wear; call for ski rentals.

Soccer Alley (B3), 3265 Roswell Rd.; (404) 266-0762. (A4), 890-C Atlanta St., Roswell; (770) 992-1010. Salem Square, Conyers: (770) 922-2599. Uniforms, shoes, equipment, videos, and gifts for soccer, the largest children's sport in the USA.

TOYS

F. A. O. Schwarz (B3), Lenox Square; (404) 814-1675. The Atlanta branch of this famous New York children's toy store is conveniently located in Lenox Square.

Gandy Dancers Toy and Hobby Shop (A4), 5438 Peachtree Industrial Blvd., Chamblee; (770) 451-0278. From Lionel trains to Lincoln logs, you'll find it at this fascinating toy store.

The Inner Child (C4), 308 West Ponce de Leon Ave., Decatur; (404) 377-7775. Stimulating, inventive toys for all ages. Thomas the Train to Estes Rockets, wooden dollhouses, Breyer horses, games, crafts, and more. *Atlanta* magazine called it "the best toy store for thinking kids."

The Toy School (A3), 5517 Chamblee-Dunwoody Rd., Dunwoody; (770) 399-5350. An extensive selection of learning toys and games, also lots of children's books.

Toys 'R' Us. Eight locations, including (B1), 2997 Cobb Pkwy., NW, Smyrna; (770) 951-8052. This fantasy chain store for children has a prime and extensive selection of toys.

SPORTS

SPORTS TO SEE

When the word came down, "It's Atlanta!" for the 1996 Summer Olympic Games, a large percentage of Atlantans found the news not at all surprising. They took it as the way things were supposed to be. Atlanta has always been a sports-loving town. Since the 1960s, the city has endorsed major league sports, with two of the professional teams owned by ace sportsman and America's Cup winner Ted Turner. The Atlanta Braves, Turner's baseball team, highlighted the 1974 season with Hank Aaron's record-breaking 715th home-run hit. In the 1990s they won eight straight Division championships and carried home the National League Pennant five times. The other Ted Turner team, a favorite of Atlantans, is the Atlanta Hawks, who won their NBA division title in 1994. The Atlanta Falcons have had a solid following year after year on the football field. And the city's newest professional sports team, the Atlanta Thrashers, has brought ice hockey to Atlanta. Both the Thrashers and the Hawks play at the new Philips Arena.

Atlanta is also the center of major professional golf and tennis tournaments, motor-racing spectaculars, a steeplechase, and polo matches. Visitors from towns and cities all over the Southeast gravitate to the city to join Atlantans in one of their favorite pastimes, spectator sports—on the gridiron, or on the diamond, the links or the courts, the raceways or in the rolling countryside.

College Football

College football is dear to the hearts of Atlantans and is played in the heart of the city, on Grant Field inside Bobby Dodd Stadium at Georgia Tech. Culminating this keen interest in college football is the Peach Bowl, an annual postseason college football game, generally held on New Year's Eve, at the Georgia Dome. Tickets and information (404) 894-5447.

Georgia Dome

Courtesy Atlanta Convention and Visitors Bureau

A favorite rivalry between Morris Brown and Morehouse colleges, both part of Atlanta University, is played out in October. Information (404) 681-2800.

Golf

Golf tournaments occur every year in the Atlanta area. Both the LPGA and the PGA hold tournaments prior to the Masters in nearby Augusta. Other championship and specialty tournaments are held at various metro area courses, such as East Lake Golf Course and Eagle's Landing in Stockbridge. Check with individual venues or the PGA for schedules.

Major Leagues

The **Atlanta Braves,** National Baseball League. Games from April through October, at Turner Field. Ticket and game information (404) 249-6400 or (404) 577-9100. Fans will also enjoy the Ivan Allen Jr. Braves Museum and Hall of Fame, (404) 614-2311.

The **Atlanta Falcons,** National Football League. Eight regular home games beginning in the fall, one or two preseason games, at the Georgia Dome. Ticket and game information (404) 249-6400. Shuttle buses make transportation to the game an easy and fun Sunday party time.

The **Atlanta Hawks,** National Basketball Association. Games from October through March at Philips Arena. Ticket and game information (404) 827-DUNK or (800) 326-4000. Stroll the HawkWalk and grab a meal at one of the restaurants there or shop at Team Gear for souvenirs.

The **Atlanta Thrashers** National Hockey League. Games begin in late fall and run through spring at the Philips Arena. The Thrashers play 41 games on their home ice. Ticket and game information, (404) 584-PUCK.

Motor Racing

Stock car racing is a friendly and casual social event in the South. Driver and movie star Paul Newman occasionally turns up in Atlanta to add a bit of glamour to this down-to-earth sport.

The **Atlanta Motor Speedway** (25 miles south of Atlanta, I-75 to exit 235, south on U.S. 19 and U.S. 41, in Hampton, GA). CH. Events include the Purolator 500 in March, the Auto Fair in June, and the Hooters 500 in November. Tickets and information (770) 946-3931.

Road Atlanta (50 miles northeast of Atlanta, I-85 to GA 53, near Gainesville, GA). *CH.* Events include the AMA Championship Cup—Motorcycle in June and August, International Motor Sports Association GT series, and the SCCA Trans Am Championship in August. Call (770) 967-6143.

Tennis

Major tennis tournaments held in Atlanta include the Atlanta Tennis Challenge held every spring. Past champions of this exciting tournament include Ivan Lendl, John McEnroe, and Boris Becker. Call (770) 395-3500 for additional information. The Stone Mountain Tennis Center, built for the 1996 Summer Olympic Games, has 15,000 sq. ft. of covered exhibition space. It's 16 mi. east of downtown Atlanta on Hwy. 78. For information on events, call (770) 498-5728.

SPORTS TO DO

Visitors can share the active lives Atlantans lead. Perhaps you have thought of a golf game in the afternoon with a client or tennis/racquetball with your associate, a health club to continue your workouts, a convenient track to run on, some scenic jogging routes, disco roller-skating at night, ice-skating, or biking through Atlanta's famous intown and suburban neighborhoods. Maybe you want to spend the day rafting down the Chattahoochee River or fishing, sailing, or boating at Lake Lanier or Lake Allatoona. Here's how, whether you are solo, with a partner, your family, or a group.

Bicycling

Skate Escape (C3), 1086 Piedmont Ave., NE; (404) 892-1292. One-speed and tandem rental bikes available for biking in Piedmont Park in Midtown.

The Southern Bicycle League. Regularly scheduled guided tours and rides of varying distances throughout the hilly city and environs; bring your own bike. (770) 594-8350.

Stone Mountain Park (C6); (770) 498-5690, ext. 301. Rental bikes for men, women, and children available daily from June through August, on weekends from March through November. Three-speed, tandem bikes, and baby seats also available.

Bowling

Bowling is a longtime popular indoor sport in the South. To find out how you can get involved in bowling in Atlanta, get in touch with the **Greater Atlanta Bowling Association** (E3), 2555 Cumberland Pkwy., SE; (770) 319-1623, or the **Greater Atlanta Women's Bowling Association** (D4), 1244 Clairmont Rd., Decatur; (404) 320-7024.

Brunswick Cedar Creek Lanes (A1), 2749 Delk Rd., SE, Marietta; (770) 988-8813.

Express Bowling Lanes (C3), 1936 Piedmont Cir., NE; (404) 874-5703.

Brunswick Roswell Lanes, 785 Old Roswell Rd., Roswell; (770) 998-9437.

Forest Park Lanes (E3), 4839 Jonesboro Rd.; (404) 366-2810.

Glenwood Lanes (D5), 4161 Glenwood Rd., Decatur; (404) 284-1010.

Northeast Plaza Fun Bowl (B4), 3285 Buford Hwy., NE; (404) 636-7548.

Golf

Atlantans and Georgians enjoy golf year round. Golf courses generally do not close except for occasional ice storms or maintenance. Call for starting times, rental clubs, carts, and information. All courses 18 holes except where designated.

City Public Courses

Alfred Tup Holmes (D2), 2300 Wilson Dr., SW; (404) 753-6158.

Bobby Jones (C3), 384 Woodward Way, NW; (404) 355-1009.

Browns Mill (E3), 480 Cleveland Ave., SE; (404) 366-3573.

Candler Park (C4), 585 Candler Park Dr., NE; (404) 371-1260. Nine holes only.

North Fulton (B3), 216 W. Wieuca Rd., NW; (404) 255-0723.

Other Public Courses

Georgia's Stone Mountain Park (C6), Stone Mountain; (770) 498-5690. Designed by the renowned golf course architect Robert Trent Jones; 36 holes. Top-rated by *Golf Digest*.

Sugar Creek Golf Course & Tennis Center (C5), 2706 Bouldercrest Rd., SE, Decatur; (404) 241-7671.

Health Clubs

The national chain health clubs and exercise centers are everywhere in Atlanta. Check the Yellow Pages if you desire one of these. We list some preferred clubs.

Athletic Club Northeast (C4), 1515 Sheridan Dr., NE; (404) 325-2700. Offers aerobics, tennis, racquetball, and indoor and outdoor pools. Call for membership information.

Australian Body Works, many locations, including (A3), 5956 Roswell Rd., NW, Sandy Springs; (404) 255-8889.

Bally Total Fitness Centers. One of the nation's leading fitness center chains, Bally has nine Atlanta locations, most with racquetball courts. Call (800) 695-8111 for the club nearest you.

CNN Center Athletic Club (J8), CNN Center; (404) 577-6800. A full-service fitness center. Includes indoor lap pool and track; aerobic studios; squash court; Nautilus machines; racquetball courts; fitness testing and prescriptions; steam, whirlpool, sauna, and massage. Bar and lounge area. Corporate memberships available.

Concourse Athletic Club (A4), 8 Concourse Pkwy., NE; (770) 698-2000. Complete strength training equipment, Stairmasters, indoor pool, many other amenities.

Crunch Fitness, six locations, including (A1), Club Cobb, 1775 Water Place, NW, Marietta; (770) 952-2120. Exercise physiology, medical and nutritional departments, plus strength training, racquetball, aerobics, massage.

Main Event Fitness Club (A2), 2000 Powers Ferry Rd., Marietta; (770) 951-2120. This fantastic club offers indoor and outdoor aerobics, an outdoor track, an indoor lap pool, racquetball, massage, childcare, nutrition classes, and a rooftop track. Also has full range of workout equipment and aerobics classes.

Peachtree Health Club (J10), Peachtree at International Blvd.; (404) 525-1210. A full range of fitness workout equipment and other amenities. A sister club of the Downtown Athletic Club with all the same equipment.

Ravinia Athletic Club (A4), 2 Ravinia Dr.; (770) 392-7301. A private club, the Ravinia is an athletic dining facility, offering fine dining in addition to its athletic programs. The facility features three racquetball courts; two squash courts; steam, sauna, whirlpool, and massage; more than 30 aerobics classes per week; a four-lane, 25-yard lap pool; a basketball court; an array of Nautilus and Kaiser equipment; free weights; treadmills, bicycles, rowers, and Stairmasters; personalized training; and wellness programming, including nutrition classes. Associated with CCA. Call for membership information.

Wildwood Athletic Club, (A1), 2300 Windy Ridge Pkwy., Marietta; (770) 953-2120. A 26,000-square-foot facility featuring an indoor track; 3,000 square feet of aerobics space; a combination of Nautilus, Paramount, and free weight equipment; lifecycles, rowers, Stairmasters, and Gravitron; 25-yard indoor lap pool; whirlpool, sauna, and personalized training.

YMCA (J9), Downtown Branch, 100 Edgewood Ave., NE; (404) 588-9622. Other locations:

South DeKalb YMCA, (D5), 2565 Snapfinger Rd., Decatur; (770) 987-3500.

Southeast YMCA, (D4), 1765 Memorial Dr., SE; (404) 373-6561.

Southwest YMCA, (D2), 2220 Campbellton Rd., SW; (404) 753-4169.

Decatur-DeKalb YMCA, (C4), 1100 Clairmont Ave., Decatur; (404) 377-0241

Centennial Place Family YMCA, (J9), 555 Luckie St., NW; (404) 724-9622.

Ashford-Dunwoody YMCA, (A4), 3692 Ashford-Dunwoody Rd., NE; (770) 451-9622.

J.M. Tull/Gwinnett County YMCA, 750 Johnson Rd., Lawrenceville; (770) 963-1313.

West Gwinnett YMCA, (A6), 3945 Holcomb Bridge Rd., Norcross; (770) 246-9622.

South Metro YMCA, (F4), 144 Smith St., Jonesboro; (770) 471-1764.

Fayetteville YMCA, 215 Hulet Rd., Fayetteville; (770) 719-9622.

North Metro YMCA, 411 Rouse Lane, Roswell; (404) 588-9622.

Northside YMCA, (B3), 3424 Roswell Rd., NW; (404) 261-3111.

Butler Street YMCA, (K10), 22 Butler St., NE; (404) 659-8085.

Cobb County YMCA, (A1), 1055 E. Piedmont Rd., NE, Marietta; (770) 977-5991.

Call for current offerings.

Hiking/Walking

Hiking and walking in and around Atlanta can be planned as a leisurely outing or a course of strenuous activity. Twenty miles of greenway trails wind through the city. The PATH Foundation is working to extend the system to 60 miles. Call (404) 875-7284 for information. Some less urban walking areas are also conveniently located. Here are a few.

Chattahoochee River National Recreational Area (A2); (770) 399-8070. A relatively undisturbed and beautiful national river area in the heart of metro Atlanta. A day-use park open seven days a week. Trail maps of hiking areas and information available from the Information Center at U.S. 41 and the Chattahoochee River (one mile west of I-75 north, near the Perimeter I-285). Perfect for a picnic lunch and short hike.

Fernbank Science Center (C4), 156 Heaton Park Dr., NE; (404) 378-4311. Two-mile nature trail through 65 wooded areas, with shrubs and trees labeled. Maps available at the Forest Gate behind the center. The route also includes a paved trail with occasional benches for a leisurely outing. Open daily 2-5 pm; Sat 10 am-5 pm.

Georgia's Stone Mountain Park (C6), (7 miles east of I-285 on U.S. 78); (770) 498-5600. Nature trails and a 1.3-mile hike to the top of the granite mountain for a wonderful view of the whole park and nearby Atlanta.

Kennesaw Mountain National Battlefield Park (GA 120 about 25 miles north of Atlanta); (770) 427-4686. Four hiking trails and an historic Civil War mountain to climb.

Horseback Riding

The Atlanta area is beautiful horse country, with outstanding trails. The area has more than 20 excellent stables, which offer riding lessons in Western, saddle seat, and hunt seat, as well as boarding facilities. Only a few of these have horse rentals, which we list below.

Briarcliff Stables, 885 Mullinax Rd., Alpharetta; (770) 475-4761.

Chastain Horse Park, Chastain Park (B3), 4371 Powers Ferry Rd.; (404) 252-0115.

Clayton Springs Farms, 4940 Steele Rd.; (770) 968-0934.

Crawford Center for Therapeutic Horsemanship, Chastain Park (B3), 4371 Powers Ferry Rd.; (404) 257-1470.

Linda's Riding School, 3475 Daniels Bridge Rd., Conyers; (770) 922-0184.

Ice Skating

The Ice Forum, three metro locations, including the Atlanta Thrashers' practice facility at 2300 Satellite Blvd., NW, in Duluth; (770) 813-1010. Public and private lessons, figure skating, special events.

Parkaire Olympic Ice Arena (A3), 4880 Lower Roswell Rd., NE, Marietta; (770) 973-0753. Located behind the Kroger store.

Racquetball

Bally Total Fitness & Racquet Clubs. See Health Clubs.
Crunch Fitness. See Health Clubs.

Rifle Ranges

These places welcome out-of-towners.

Callaway Gardens Gun Club, Pine Mountain (1.5 hours drive on I-85 south of Atlanta). The club is open Wed-Sun year-round for skeet and trap shooting. Special economy rates apply on Saturdays for gun rental and ammunition. Call (706) 663-5129 or 1-800-282-8181.
DeKalb Public Firing Range (D6), 3905 N. Goddard Rd., Lithonia; (770) 484-3046. Open to the public Thurs-Sat 10 am-5:20 pm.
Ed's Gun and Tackle Shop, 2727 Canton Rd., NE, Marietta; (770) 425-8461.
Master Gunman (C6), 1900 Rockbridge Rd., Stone Mountain; (770) 469-0933.

Roller-Skating

Roller-skating has been popular in this area of the South with each generation learning on the city sidewalks and most recently rolling on bright skates in the roller rinks. Rollerblades have updated the sport.

All American Skating Center (C6), 5400 Bermuda Rd., Stone Mountain; (770) 469-9775.
Rainbow Roller Rink, 5480 Browns Mill Rd., Lithonia; (770) 981-3121.
Roswell Roller Rink (A3), 780 Old Roswell Rd., Roswell; (770) 998-9700. Open seven days a week.

Running

Runners are quickly reminded that Atlanta is a city of hills and dales, ups and downs, so pace yourself to accommodate the terrain and enjoy the scenic routes.

The Atlanta Track Club, 3097 E. Shadowlawn Ave., NE; (404) 231-9064. Cosponsors with the *Atlanta Journal Constitution* of Atlanta's Peachtree Road Race on the Fourth of July. In this event, 55,000 runners compete, making it the largest road race in the U.S. Every day of the year runners can be seen on the streets and in the parks. The Track Club also has a race hotline that lists upcoming races. Call (404) 262-RACE.

Other running clubs include the Buckhead Road Runners Club, (404) 816-6299; Atlanta Singles Running Organization, (404) 675-3824; and Chattahoochee Road Runners, (770) 427-4471.

Chattahoochee River National Recreational Area (A2); (770) 952-4419. A relatively undisturbed and beautiful national river area in the heart of metro Atlanta. Open during the day, seven days a week. Trail maps of hiking/running areas and other information available from the Information Center at U.S. 41 and the Chattahoochee River (one mile west of I-75 north, near the Perimeter I-285).

Fleet Feet Sports, specializes in athletic equipment for runners, walkers and triathletes. (A3), 224B Johnson Ferry Rd.; (404) 255-3338.

Phidippedes. See Sports Equipment.

Tennis

Atlanta is a tennis town. Bring your racquet and play tennis year round on its numerous courts, both public and private.

Atlanta Lawn Tennis Association (ALTA) (A3), 6840 Peachtree Dunwoody Rd., NE; (770) 399-5788. This is the largest local tennis organization in the world, with nearly 75,000 members. Sponsors matches for men, women, and juniors year round and publishes a magazine.

Public and City Municipal Courts

The following fine Atlanta tennis centers offer excellent facilities and lessons and are staffed with a tennis professional. CH.

Bitsy Grant (C3), 2125 Northside Dr., NW; (404) 609-7193. The city's major tennis center.

DeKalb Tennis Center (C4), 1400 McConnell Dr., Decatur; (404) 325-2520.

Stone Mountain Tennis Center (C6); (770) 498-5728.

Piedmont Park (C3), Piedmont at 12th St., NE; (404) 853-3461.
Washington Park Tennis Center (D3), 1125 Lena St., SW; (404) 658-6229.

For other city courts call (404) 817-6788.
For Fulton County courts call (404) 730-6200.
For DeKalb County courts call (404) 371-2631.
For Cobb County courts call (770) 528-8800.
For Gwinnett County courts call (770) 822-8840.

Walking. See Hiking.

Water Sports

Atlanta has two large man-made recreational lakes within 35 miles of its city limits (approximately 45 minutes driving time), plus several others to the south and east.

Lake Sidney Lanier, named after the 19th-century Georgia poet, is northeast of the city. This is the most popular lake in the nation that is supervised by the U.S. Army Corps of Engineers, with 15 million visitors annually.

Lake Allatoona, also an Army Corps of Engineers lake, is 30 miles northwest of Atlanta. Located on the western shore of the lake is an excellent Georgia state park, Red Top Mountain, with full recreational amenities.

These two large bodies of water provide flood control for the area, power generation, conservation, and extensive recreational facilities for water sports. For further information and maps call:

Lake Lanier Resource Manager (770) 945-9531.
Lake Allatoona Resource Manager (770) 382-4700.

The **Chattahoochee River** is the third major area for water sports in Atlanta. The river continues from the Buford Dam at Lake Lanier through the north and northwest sections of metro Atlanta. In 1978 the Chattahoochee River National Recreation Area was established, providing protection for this great river which flows from the Georgia mountains to the Gulf of Mexico. Atlantans draw not only their city water from the river but draw many pleasurable hours sporting in the waters of the Chattahoochee and relaxing on its banks. The river is rated a Class I and II waterway and attracts canoe, kayak and rafting fans.

Canoeing

Blue Ridge Mountain Sports, Lenox Square, NE; (404) 266-8372. Canoe and camping equipment rental, clinics in canoeing and kayaking, also rock climbing and backpacking. Canoe and hiking trips.

Georgia Canoeing Association, P.O. Box 7023, Atlanta, GA 3035; (770) 421-9729. For open canoe, deck canoe, and kayak clinics and organized group trips on Georgia's beautiful white-water and flat-water rivers, this is an outstanding association for membership.

Lake Lanier Islands, Lake Lanier (I-85 north to GA 365, follow signs); (770) 932-7200. Canoe and kayak rental at the beach, May through September.

White Water Learning Center of GA, 3437 Rockhaven Cir., NE; (404) 231-0042. Group and private instruction in kayaking and canoeing. The Center offers rentals, river trips and kayaking day camps. ACA certified.

Fishing

The Chattahoochee River, Lake Lanier, and Lake Allatoona are fished mainly for trout, bream, bass, and crappie. The devout fly fisherman can be seen tubing the river or casting into the shoals for the elusive trout, and fishing boats, trailed from the city to the lakes each weekend, wander in and around the coves and points on the lakes' shores. Fishing is permitted from all shorelines unless otherwise designated. A Georgia fishing license is required for freshwater fishing. Licenses are sold at Oshman's Sporting Goods, the Fish Hawk, and Reeder and McGaughey.

Doug Youngblood's Fish Lanier Guide Services, Lake Lanier Islands. Year-round fishing boat rental, bait sales, and tackle rental for both large and small groups. Driver's license required. Call (770) 945-0797.

Little River Landing, Lake Allatoona, 6986 Bells Ferry Rd., Woodstock; (770) 345-6200.

For further information and maps on fishing in the Atlanta area and in the state of Georgia, contact the Georgia Game and Fish Division, 205 Butler St., SE, Atlanta, (770) 414-3333; or the Fish Hawk, 279 Buckhead Ave., NE, Atlanta, (404) 237-3473.

Motor Boating

Lake Lanier Islands, (770) 932-7255. Pontoon boat rental, March through November, houseboat rental all year.

Rafting

Rafting on the Chattahoochee is a popular weekend recreation for Atlantans. The water is very cold, even in mid summer.

Chattahoochee Outdoor Center (A4), 1990 Island Ford Pkwy., Dunwoody; (770) 395-6851. The COC makes raft rental, transportation, and food service easy and enjoyable from May through Labor Day. Shuttle buses retrieve rafters and rafts at take-out points. The COC works with the National Park Service to create an urban outfitter post that serves the public with careful professionalism.

High Country Outfitters (A3), Perimeter Mall; (770) 391-9657. Sales, rentals, and clinics for water craft enthusiasts.

Rowing

The **Atlanta Rowing Club**, 500 Azalea Dr., Roswell; (770) 993-1879. This water-loving group hosts regattas on the Chattahoochee and has sculling and rigging clinics.

Sailing

Lanier Sailing Academy, Ltd., Lake Lanier Islands. Sailboat rentals include Sunfish, Hobie Cats, small and large day-sailers, and cruising auxiliary sailboats. Deposit required; advance reservations necessary. Write Lanier Sailing Academy, Ltd., 6920 Holiday Rd., Z Dock Buford, GA 30518. Or call (770) 945-8810.

Scuba

Scuba lessons are offered at several metro-Atlanta locations. Beginner and advanced lessons are available as are different types of certification. Three options for certification are listed below; both require out-of-town trips at the end of the lessons in order to be certified for open-water diving.

Divers Supply (A5), 4315 NE Expressway Access Rd., Doraville; (770) 939-3483.

Undersea Adventures, 2064 Briarcliff Rd., NE; (404) 321-4006.

YMCA Scuba Program Headquarters, 5825-2a Live Oak Pkwy., NE, Norcross; (770) 662-5172.

Swimming

Swimming pools are available at most hotels. City of Atlanta pools are located in three different quadrants of the city. Call (404) 817-6767 for other city locations.

Rafting on the Chattahoochee   *Courtesy Atlanta Convention and Visitors Bureau*

M. L. King Natatorium (K11), 70 Boulevard, NE; (404) 658-7330.
Chastain Memorial Park (B3), 235 W. Wieuca Rd., NW; (404) 255-0863.
John A. White (D2), 1101 Cascade Cir., SW; (404) 755-5546.
Piedmont Park (C3), 1085 Piedmont Ave. at 14th St., NE; (404) 892-0117.

The YMCAs in metro Atlanta have fine swimming facilities and programs. Most also have an infant aquatics class. Call the Northside Family YMCA at (404) 261-3111 for a reference to the Y in your area.

Bally Total Fitness Centers, listed under Health Clubs, have indoor pools.

Man-made swimming beaches are located at:
Callaway Gardens, I-85 to I-185 South to 27 South. See EXCURSIONS.
Georgia's Stone Mountain Park (C6) (seven miles east of I-285 on U.S. 78, Stone Mountain Freeway). See SIGHTS chapter.
Lake Lanier Islands, Lake Lanier (I-85 north to GA 365, follow signs). Bathhouses on the beach, waterslide.
Red Top Mountain State Park, Lake Allatoona. (I-75 north to Northside Dr. exit, left at light, continue north on U.S. 41 to exit 123, which goes to Red Top Mountain State Park.)

Water Skiing

If you have the equipment, there are many fine lakes. Call the State Parks Department, (770) 868-6263.

Downhill Skiing, Team Sports, and Car Rallies

Downhill Skiing

Atlanta Ski Club, 6255 Barfield Rd., NE; (404) 301-1460. More than 10,000 strong, this is the largest ski club in the country, offering social gatherings year round and group trips in winter to ski resorts from the Rockies, to Canada, to Europe. For ski lessons, call (404) 255-2356.

Polo

This thrilling sport combines speed, skill, grace, and danger and has been equated with chess for its finesse. The Atlanta area has some active polo clubs.

The Scuppernong Polo Club plays every Saturday at 2 pm in Cherokee County. Call (770) 252-5712 for further information. Another active club is Vinings Polo, in Vinings, (404) 355-1451. They play at a member's farm, so bring your own folding chair.

Rugby

Rugby is relatively new to Atlanta, but it is now played with gusto by a number of area teams.

The **Atlanta Renegades Rugby Club** plays in the Buckhead area. Call (770) 908-3999 for further information on playing schedules.

Soccer

Soccer is now well established in Atlanta as a recreational sport and as an integral part of the athletic curriculum of the schools.

Georgia Soccer Foundation, Inc. (A4), 3684 Stewart Rd., Doraville, has information regarding leagues and schedules of games. Call (770) 452-0505.

Softball

Every warm weekend you will see softball played in all the Atlanta parks.

City of Atlanta, Supervisor of Athletics, for information on leagues, schedules and locations of adult softball, youth baseball, youth basketball, football, and track call (404) 817-6767.

Sports Car Rallies

Sports car enthusiasts should call the Sports Car Club of America, (770) 455-7222. Monthly road rallies (except December).

Further Information ───────────────

For custom-designed sports programs for companies and conventions we recommend:

Corporate Sports Unlimited, 6400 Highland Pkwy., SE, Smyrna; (770) 432-0100. A professional staff provides the facilities, transportation, equipment, and food for corporate and convention sports activities. Specialty is a Super Sports Day. All sports included.

Further information on outdoor-recreation programs within Atlanta and the state of Georgia:

Georgia Conservancy, Inc., 1776 Peachtree St., NW; (404) 876-2900. The Conservancy is an advocacy organization sponsoring special field trips and hikes in ecologically sensitive or historically significant areas.

State of Georgia Department of Natural Resources, (770) 868-6263, provides information on state parks, hiking, camping, hunting, and fishing as well as licensing requirements.

U.S. Forest Service, (404) 347-4243, provides hiking and camping information on the Chattahoochee National Forest and the Appalachian Trail, which begins in the North Georgia Mountains.

SPECIAL EVENTS

The Atlanta calendar is overflowing with exciting events for the whole year, but some are special annual events around which Atlanta traditions are formed and celebrated. They are as seasonally anticipated as the dogwood blossoms in spring and the changing of the fall colors. These two beautiful seasons in particular generate innumerable home tours, garden tours, arts fairs, folk festivals, and sporting events. Of special note are the outstanding Atlanta Symphony free concerts during the summer months. Bring your picnic supper and enjoy a warm summer evening of fine music under the stars.

We are selecting annual highlights, those peak experiences that claim a hold on Atlanta's own citizens year after year. Be aware that special events stay in the same season but will shift sometimes from month to month during the change of years.

Atlanta's exceptionally good weather makes it a festive town. Every month, there are special events and gatherings that are open to the public and too new, or too numerous, to mention here. Many black-tie and casual parties and events are also held to benefit charitable organizations. These exciting and often unusual events can be expensive but are memorable and well worthwhile. Too numerous to list, these events are announced in Atlanta's leading publications.

January

Atlanta Boat Show (I11), Georgia World Congress Center; (404) 223-4636. The Boat Show is a late winter magnet for all the sailors and boatmen yearning for the next spring sail or pleasure trip on the nearby lakes, rivers, and the further waters of the Atlantic or Gulf. Every sort of boat is on display, with lucky draws and prizes for a chosen few. A full week of the nautical world.

King Week; (404) 331-3920. A week-long event commemorating the life and achievements of Martin Luther King, Jr. Includes a number of seminars, lectures, and awards ceremonies as well as gala events. Concludes on the national holiday with a Parade and March of Celebration. An outstanding tribute to the life of Dr. King held annually at the Martin Luther King, Jr. Center for Nonviolent Social Change on Auburn Avenue.

February

Annual Children's Festival (G11), Atlanta Memorial Arts Center, 1280 Peachtree St., NE; (404) 733-4231. Since 1985 the Children's Festival has attracted kids from Atlanta, with the Atlanta Symphony programs, high school jazz bands, a performance of the Alliance Children's Theatre, clogging, art exhibits, face painting, and sundry other forms of celebrating young life.

Goodwill Book Sale (B5), Northlake Mall, Lavista Rd. at I-285; (770) 938-5483. More than 250,000 used books.

Southeastern Flower Show (C3), at Atlanta Expo Center, 3650 Jonesboro Rd., SE, sponsored by the Atlanta Botanical Garden; (404) 876-5858. Originally the Camellia and Fine Arts Show, this delightful exhibition features the pride of flower growers and the work of local landscape artists, making February a month to celebrate natural and man-made manifestations of the beautiful.

March

Atlanta Passion Play (D3), Atlanta Civic Center. This production has become part of Atlanta's annual pre-Easter calendar. Call (404) 347-8400.

Six Flags Over Georgia Opening (D2), 7561 Six Flags Pkwy., SW, Austell; (770) 948-9290. West of Atlanta off I-20, the popular family amusement park opens weekends March till Memorial Day, then daily through the summer. See SIGHTS.

St. Patrick's Day Parade (C3, D3). The Irish have their way and their day down Peachtree Street, sporting the green with floats and bands and lots of Irish chatter, jokes, green beer, and good will.

April

Ansley Park Tour of Homes (C3). This charming early 20th-century suburb opens its homes and gardens to visitors during the height of the spring brilliance. Ansley Park is an attractive neighborhood of curving streets, gentle hills, and interior parks, between the Arts Center and Piedmont Park. Watch local listings for additional information.

Atlanta Braves Home Opener (D3), Turner Field; (404) 249-6400. Atlanta's stellar professional baseball team kicks off its home season. A great way to have a great time. A great place to spot celebrities.
Atlanta Dogwood Festival; (404) 266-7568. The triumphant blossoming of the dogwood heralds in the rites of spring. Atlanta's splendid festival features house-and-garden tours, exhibits, art shows, a grand parade, hot air balloon races, and a gala ball to honor the Dogwood Queen and her court. The city is awash with pink and white dogwood blossoms, a wonderland setting for these city-wide festivities.
BellSouth Classic (A1). This exciting PGA tournament is held each spring prior to the Masters in Augusta.
The Foxhall Cup. A three-day National Championship equestrian event, held in Douglas County, 15 miles west of Hartsfield Airport. A global competition, the steeplechase brings together distinguished horses and riders, while spectators lunch on grassy knolls and enjoy watching each other's gourmet picnics, complete with dinner-party trappings, right down to silver candelabra propped on car hoods. Dress includes everything from British tweeds to morning coats and long dresses. April or early May. Tickets must be purchased beforehand. Call for information.
Easter Sunrise Services (C6), Stone Mountain Park; (770) 498-5600. Sunrise services are held from the top and at the base of the mountain—a spectacular beginning to Resurrection Day.
Druid Hills Tour of Homes (C4). These spacious Emory-area homes, in a graceful neighborhood designed by Frederick Law Olmsted, formed the setting for the play and movie *Driving Miss Daisy*. Residents welcome visitors amid an extravagance of dogwood and azalea blossoms.
The Georgia Renaissance Festival, eight miles south of Hartsfield International Airport; (770) 964-8575. Festival-goers are invited to participate in events and experience life in the 14th century. Festival features strolling jugglers, magicians, mimes, bards, singers, dancers, gypsies, and of course, Shakespearean plays. Huge arts and crafts market, too. Held weekends from April through June.
Inman Park Festival and Tour (D4). This historic district's nationally recognized tour of homes opens its restored turn-of-the-century houses to the public. The festival includes a children's fair, bazaar, art show, music, and street circus. Watch local listings for additional information.
Midtown Tour of Homes (C3). The Midtown area is bounded by Ponce de Leon and 10th Street, Monroe Drive and Peachtree Street, and the tours include a variety of architectural styles from the late 19th century to today's condominium. Watch local listings for additional information.

Sweet Auburn Festival (J10), Auburn Avenue, downtown. Once black Atlanta's bustling commercial main street, Auburn Avenue celebrates its past and its future with entertainment, rides, arts and crafts exhibits, food, and fun for the whole family.

A Taste of Atlanta; (404) 248-1315. The largest outdoor food festival in the state of Georgia. A three-day event, the festival features 40 fine Atlanta restaurants. Attendees can sample the restaurants' specialties for less than $5. Also a fine arts and crafts show as well as nonstop entertainment. Proceeds go to the National Kidney Foundation of Georgia. Admission charged.

May

Atlanta Jazz Festival (L10), Grant Park and other venues, presents some of the nation's top jazz artists in a series of free concerts.

Atlanta Storytelling Festival (B3), Atlanta History Center, 130 West Paces Ferry Rd., NW; (404) 814-4000. The nation's top storytellers gather to enchant children of all ages in this weekend event.

The Decorators' Show House. Each year the Junior Committee of the Atlanta Symphony procures a fine old house for three weeks, and Atlanta's exciting decorators design and accessorize individual rooms. A chance to see current interior design trends and gather ideas for your own home, as well as seeing one of the city's lovely old houses.

DeKalb Sheriff's Posse Rodeo (C6), Stone Mountain Park. This annual rodeo has been going on some 30 years, with riders and acts to delight young and old.

Stone Mountain Lasershow (C6), Stone Mountain Park. The Stone Mountain carving provides the backdrop for the spectacular nightly show of color and light that has become a summertime Atlanta tradition.

June

Chastain Park Concerts (B3), Atlanta Symphony Orchestra. See PERFORMING ARTS chapter.

Dahlonega Bluegrass Festival, Hwy. 60 S., Dahlonega; (706) 864-2257. Held the fourth weekend in June, come hear the nation's top bluegrass bands. Camping facilities available.

Fox Film Festival (I10), 660 Peachtree St., NE; (404) 881-2100. During the summer, the fabulous Fox Theatre sponsors a series of 12 screen classics. For an extra treat, the Mighty Moeller organ is played prior to the screenings.

Piedmont Park Free Concerts (C3), Atlanta Symphony Orchestra. See PERFORMING ARTS chapter.

Virginia Highland Summerfest; (404) 222-8244. Held on North Highland and Virginia Avenues from Ponce de Leon to Amsterdam, this street celebration is an exciting event. Live music issues from three stages set up at various points while jugglers and street musicians entertain sidewalk sale shoppers. There is also a walking tour of homes. Proceeds go the Virginia Highland Civic Association.

July

Atlanta Braves' Game and Fireworks (L8); (404) 249-6400. Almost every Fourth of July, the Braves play in Atlanta. The evening game is followed by fireworks. It's the All-American way to celebrate the Fourth.

Civil War Encampment (B3), Atlanta History Center, 130 West Paces Ferry Rd., NW; (404) 814-4000. Hundreds of costumed interpreters stage a living history of Civil War camp life, Union and Confederate.

Fantastic Fourth Celebration (C6), Stone Mountain Park; (770) 498-5702. Days and evenings of entertainment, gymnastics, dancing, banjo plucking, jazz bands, stage shows, clogging, barbecue, and the Atlanta Symphony family concerts are offered around the key salute to national independence—the incredible fireworks display from the top of Stone Mountain on the Fourth of July.

Peachtree Road Race (B3, C3); (404) 231-9064. Fourth of July. One of the largest foot races in the country moves like a massive snake down Peachtree from Lenox Square to Piedmont Park. The heat and hills challenge the 55,000 runners to their limits. Join the runners or spectators lining Peachtree Street as they cheer friends toward their coveted Peachtree Road Race T-shirts.

Salute to America Parade; (404) 897-7000. Fourth of July. This is the super-parade of Atlanta, sponsored by WSB-TV, with the stars and stripes being marched and played and displayed for miles along Peachtree Street.

Spirit of France Celebration, Chateau Elan Winery, I-85 and exit 126, (800) 233-9463. French independence takes the spotlight as Chateau Elan Winery celebrates Bastille Day in a weekend extravaganza that features concerts, games, and art exhibits.

August

Chateau Elan Vineyard Festival, Chateau Elan Winery, I-85 and Exit 126; (800) 233-9463. In August or September celebrate the vineyard's harvest with grape stomping and watermelon spitting contests, craft exhibits, and country food. Arrive early to beat the crowd.

Falcon Football Home Kickoff (J7); (404) 223-5444. Atlanta's NFL football team starts its season in the Georgia Dome.

Montreux Atlanta International Music Festival; (404) 817-6815. This spectacular 10-day event, sponsored by the Atlanta Bureau of Cultural Affairs, features music from the world over. A combination of paid and free concerts, the festival offers gospel, jazz, blues, country, classical, and contemporary music by local, national, and international artists. Held in Woodruff Park or Centennial Park downtown in late August. Call for more information.

September

American Association of University Women's Book Sale (B3), Lenox Square; (404) 233-6767. During September, this association sponsors a wonderful used-book sale for the amateur or professional collector.

Arts Festival of Atlanta (C3), Centennial Olympic Park and other venues; (404) 589-8777. For two weekends and the week in between, Atlanta celebrates creativity featuring visual art in all media, demonstrations, and many of the city's finest in the performing arts. The festival schedule is filled with events for adults and children during the day and each evening. Marionettes, jugglers, and mimers; jazz, blues, and country music; the symphony, chorales, and visual art from the most sophisticated to the gypsy section—all are part of this great festival of art for the people.

Atlanta Greek Festival (C4), Greek Orthodox Cathedral of the Annunciation, 2500 Clairmont Rd., NE; (404) 633-5870. The Atlanta Greek community has its annual festival complete with Greek dancing, dinners, exhibits, shops, wines, and warm Mediterranean merriment.

Grant Park Festival and Tour of Homes; (404) 624-9553. This two-day event held every year in late September features an arts and crafts show, live music and other entertainment, and a tour of a number of renovated, Victorian homes surrounding Grant Park. The tour is self-guided. The weekend culminates in the Moth Ball, a costumed event in the park pavilion.

Oktoberfest, Alpine Helen, Georgia; (800) 858-8027. A six-week celebration, fashioned after the original Oktoberfest in Germany, the festival lures Atlantans with its blazing autumn spectacle of the North Georgia Mountains and the foods, wine, beer, and entertainment of our little Bavaria.

Powers Ferry Crossroads Country Fair and Arts Festival. Take I-85 south to Newnan exit. Take Georgia Highway 34 through Newnan.

Ten miles beyond see the signs. Annually for 15 years, this festival has displayed the crafts and talents of Southern craftsmen in the country setting of the old Powers plantation, where grist and sorghum mills have been restored under the big oaks of middle Georgia. Expect bluegrass bands and barbecue, clogging and fried chicken, and a fine late summer treat.

Yellow Daisy Festival (C6), Stone Mountain Park; (770) 498-5702. The South's largest arts and crafts show, a flower show, live entertainment, and festive foods celebrate the blooming of the rare Confederate Yellow Daisy in Stone Mountain Park.

October

Atlanta Hawks Basketball Season Starter (J8), Philips Arena; (404) 827-DUNK. The Atlanta Hawks slam dunk for the home crowd in the starter of their October-March season.

Harvest Moon Stroll (C3), Atlanta Botanical Garden; (404) 876-5858. The beauty of nature and the wonder of the moon and stars combine to make this a memorable event with a hint of nostalgia.

Scottish Festival and Highland Games (C6), Stone Mountain Park; (770) 498-5702. Georgia descendants included Scottish stock migrating south from the Appalachians. The third weekend in October the Scottish folk from more than 50 clans, clad in Scottish garb, flock to Stone Mountain to celebrate their heritage. The call of bagpipes, the Scottish sword-dance, the tossing of the caber, and other athletic games are some of the activities of this ethnic festival, which shows all its colors in Sunday's Parade of Tartans.

Tour of Southern Ghosts (C6), Stone Mountain Park; (770) 498-5702. Chilling stories just in time for Halloween.

November

High Museum Antiques Show and Sale; (404) 377-4400. This annual benefit brings together antiques dealers from across the United States to sell their furniture, porcelains, and fine accessories. Activities include lectures in the decorative arts, wine tastings, and galas.

Holiday Celebration at Stone Mountain (C6), Stone Mountain Park; (770) 498-5702. The South's largest "Tree of Lights" crowns parkwide decorations. Horse-drawn carriage rides, yuletide entertainment, traditional decorations in the Antebellum Plantation, Santa and his helpers, and a holiday laser presentation combine to fill the park with holiday cheer.

Lighting of the "Great Tree" (K8), Underground Atlanta. Thanksgiving Day, Atlanta style, has traditionally included the lighting of a magnificent huge evergreen tree at 7 p.m. Originally atop the bridge that connected the two buildings of Rich's downtown department store, the tree now rises proudly from the plaza of Underground Atlanta. Choirs from Atlanta-area schools sing carols and the evening event is a spectacular stirring introduction to the Christmas season. Ride MARTA to the Five Points station.

December

Candelight Tours (B3), Atlanta History Center, 130 West Paces Ferry Rd. Enjoy romantic tours of the festively decorated Swan House, the Tullie Smith Farm and the gardens and nature trails by candlelight.

Christmas at Callanwolde (C4), Callanwolde Fine Arts Center, 980 Briarcliff Rd., NE; (404) 872-5338. The old Candler Mansion is put in the hands of the area's best interior designers for the Christmastide. Period decorations from Christmases of the past renew the holiday spirit of today.

Christmas at the Wren's Nest (D2), 1050 Ralph David Abernathy Blvd., SW; (404) 753-7735. Holiday decorations and celebrations at the historic home of writer Joel Chandler Harris in West End.

Dropping of the Peach (D3), Underground Atlanta; (404) 523-2311. Atlanta's newest New Year's celebration. Our own Southern version of Times Square. A giant peach drops from the tower atop Underground Atlanta to mark the New Year.

Egleston Christmas Parade and Festival of Trees. The parade through downtown Atlanta launches the annual Festival of Trees at the Georgia World Congress Center, an event that has become the cornerstone of Atlanta's festive yule season. Take delight in the varied ornamented trees, more than 200 of them, and help support one of Atlanta's children's hospitals at the same time. A related event, the Festival of Lights, turns Centennial Olympic Park into a sparkling wonderland where school and church choirs offer free concerts.

Lighting of the Chateau, Chateau Elan Winery, I-85 and Exit 126; (800) 233-9463. The Chateau is ablaze with more than 30,000 lights. Santa, holiday music, a gift show, a craft show, festive food, and release of the winery's special holiday vintage label make for festivities that sparkle.

The Nutcracker (I10), Fox Theater; (404) 873-5811. Every year the Atlanta Ballet Company puts on this seasonal favorite. A must for children and adults alike.

Peach Bowl (L8), the Georgia Dome; (404) 894-5447. Atlanta's postseason college football game is usually played on New Year's Eve. A high-kicking, high-spirited parade down Peachtree Street precedes the battle on the football field.

SELF-GUIDED
CITY TOURS

We include two city tours, which you can do on your own, one a walking tour of downtown Atlanta and the second a driving tour of metro Atlanta. If possible take along a reader/navigator for the driving tour; you will both enjoy it more. For walkers, we suggest some comfortable shoes; a companion can make it doubly fun. Allow two to three hours for each tour. In both cases Atlanta awaits your visitation into her throbbing, inner-city core and into the broad sweep of her development north on Peachtree Street.

DOWNTOWN
WALKING TOUR

Introduction

Downtown Atlanta continues to be at an impact stage in its many evolutions as a city. The central focus of the downtown area was redistributed by the mega-complexes of the 1960s and 1970s. The Omni mega-structure anchored the western side of Downtown and Peachtree Center took the top of the hill north of Five Points, which has traditionally been the designated center of Downtown. Meanwhile, the Georgia State University complex expanded to the southeast. The 1980s signaled a time of filling in the stretches between the mega-structures, rejuvenating fine old office buildings in Downtown, and adding a rapid-transit system, city parks, malls, and historic districts to tie the core city together once more.

The 1990s ushered in yet another era, as Atlanta joined Midtown's postmodern building boom with several dramatic new office buildings of its own, including the soaring One Peachtree Center and the twin-towered skyscraper that is 191 Peachtree. And now downtown Atlanta is evolving yet again, spurred by the 1996 Olympics, into an environment

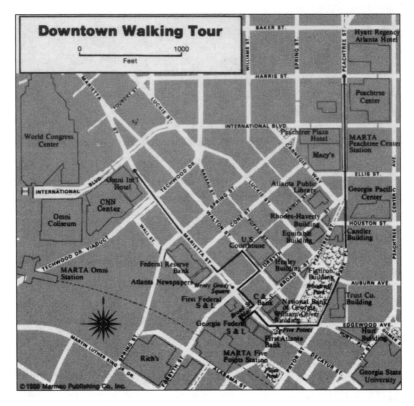

of graceful tree-shaded boulevards and walkways. In-town living, once shunned in favor of the suburbs, has become desirable as new highrise condominiums and apartments join a proliferation of lofts in renovated buildings to lure urbanites.

In a sense Atlanta has been remolded continually over the years and may always be seen in new perspectives. A northern vista appeared, for instance, at Peachtree and Houston streets as the revered Coca-Cola sign was dismantled and the Georgia Pacific Center took its place on the Peachtree corridor. The MARTA land clearance made coming South into town on West Peachtree Street a thrilling sight, and standing at the corner by the public library, the beauty of the Carnegie Building's ornamental upper frieze and triangular shape are silhouetted against the perfect glass cylinder of the Westin Peachtree Plaza Hotel and the multibuilding complex of Peachtree Center.

Atlanta's history, past and in-the-making, is apparent in our downtown tour, and there are many opportunities to stray from this chosen path (some at our suggestion) to enjoy a special lunch and to indulge in random shopping. Allow two hours at an easy pace. We strongly advise a walk-in visit as well as sidewalk view of all the structures and places on this tour. You will then see the city inside out and be in for many pleasant surprises.

The Starting Point ———————————————————

One Peachtree Center is our starting point at **Baker and Peachtree streets.** This dramatic white office tower is the latest in a coordinated cluster of downtown Atlanta buildings by architect/developer John Portman that started an innovative trend in urban development. Facing the Hyatt Regency Atlanta Hotel, the office towers and Peachtree Center's exciting multilevel mall are to your right with shops, restaurants, Hard Rock Cafe, and the Peachtree Center plaza; you will see the entrance to the MARTA station. The western half of Peachtree Center includes the Merchandise Mart, the Apparel Mart, the Gift Mart, and Inforum, the computer mart, the four largest wholesale marts in the Southeast. Moving south on Peachtree, weave through the many large street sculptures. Portman's dramatic Westin Peachtree Plaza Hotel, the site of the first governor's mansion in Atlanta, is on your right and just beyond is Macy's department store with its garlanded arched windows and burgundy convex awnings. Macy's is a proud 1920s landmark on Peachtree Street. Across the street is the delightfully nostalgic 191 Peachtree, one of downtown's most recent office buildings and a distinctive addition to the city's skyline. Next to 191 Peachtree is the Ritz-Carlton Hotel, built by the Atlanta-based company that is also owned by an Atlantan. This small, luxurious hotel, one of two Ritz-Carlton's in the city, is swathed in elegant pink marble and is well worth a trip inside to sit in the lobby, enjoy tea or other refreshments, and relax.

From Macy's ———————————————————

You are beginning your descent down **Peachtree Street toward Woodruff Park and Five Points.** At **Carnegie Way** on your right is the triangular Carnegie Office Building erected in 1926, and on the right corner at **Carnegie Way and Forsyth Street** stands the impressive Atlanta Public Library by international architect Marcel Breuer, dedicated in 1980.

Across from the library on Peachtree Street, the Georgia-Pacific Center and Tower, opened in 1982, dominates the skyline. This was the site of Atlanta's first opera house, the De Give Opera House built in 1893. In 1932 the building was converted into an art deco movie palace, Loew's Grand. Here, the classic movie *Gone with the Wind* premiered in Atlanta a few years later to thousands of Atlantans cheering the arrival of Scarlett O'Hara and Rhett Butler.

Margaret Mitchell Square, dedicated in 1987, is located between the library and Georgia Pacific Center where Peachtree and Forsyth streets converge. The square, on a small triangle of land in the middle of the street, is an excellent pause-and-view point.

From Georgia-Pacific Plaza

On the right side of Peachtree you pass the handsome 1929 Rhodes-Haverty Building. Just beyond is the Equitable Building, a black steel-frame structure covering a full city block. These two buildings, side by side, contrast Atlanta of the 1920s and Atlanta 80 years later.

At 127 Peachtree on your left, the Candler Building, built in 1902, rises 17 stories high, Atlanta's earliest and most elegant skyscraper. Asa Candler, founder of the Coca-Cola Company, built Roman baths in the basement, and covered the surface with white Georgia marble and elaborate sculptures. The ornate frieze above the first story incorporates heroes of the arts and sciences including Shakespeare, Wagner, Michelangelo, and Benjamin Franklin, among others. Inside, on the staircase landing, the sculptured bust of Asa Candler is flanked by low-relief portraits of his mother and father. This prestigious building has been beautifully restored to its original elegance.

At Woodruff Park

Woodruff Park, formerly Central City Park is in full view now. Stop and take a long look at this breathing space in the heart of the central business district. To your right is the tailored Flatiron Building named after its triangular shape, 11 stories high, built exclusively of stone and brick, with a series of stately bay windows and Greek pilasters fronting Peachtree and Broad streets. The Flatiron Building is the oldest tall pre-steel building in the Southeast, designed in 1897 by Bradford Gilbert who later designed New York City's famous Flatiron Building.

Go left on Auburn to begin your **walk around the park.** The land for this Park was given to the city by Atlanta's "anonymous" donor, otherwise known as Robert Woodruff, the philanthropic Coca-Cola heir. At the north end is a combination public amphitheater, fountain, and garden designed for concerts and informal gatherings. The Martin Luther King, Jr. Historic District lies east on Auburn Avenue. For a

"Phoenix Rising" in Woodruff Park symbolizes Atlanta's rise from the ashes of the Civil War to become a world-renowned city.

Courtesy Atlanta Convention and Visitors Bureau

detour here see the SIGHTS chapter. Park Place office building is ahead on your left, home of the First Union Bank.

Turn right on Park Place. SunTrust Bank faces the park on the site of the original Equitable Building, which was Atlanta's first steel-frame structure. The columns and marble sign of this former building, which was designed in 1891 by Chicago architects Burnham and Root, and which the bank later occupied, are set in front as weighty tokens of this past era in Atlanta's history. The secret formula of Coca-Cola, the world's most popular soft drink, is stored in the vaults of this SunTrust Bank.

At the corner of Edgewood look to your left at the Hurt Building. One of Atlanta's first developers, Joel Hurt, built this office in 1913. Notice the curved Corinthian portico and the colorful terra-cotta designs in the upper stories. Hurt also built Atlanta's first garden suburb, Inman Park, and connected the Hurt Building downtown to the residential area with his own streetcar line. Inman Park is now a historic district, alive with Victorian restoration. The lobby of the Hurt Building makes an interesting detour. Directly behind the Hurt Building is the Georgia State University complex, another short detour option.

The Five Points Intersection

Turn right on Edgewood and take a long look back across the park. You are at **Five Points** when you reach the intersection of Decatur/Marietta, Edgewood, and Peachtree. You are in the presence of some of the major financial institutions of the city and the Southeast. On the right look carefully at the William-Oliver Building, built the year of the stock-market crash in 1929, with zigzag and semicircular art deco ornamentation on the exterior and ornate brass grills, elevator doors, lighted brass arrow indicators over the elevators, and a celestial ceiling mural in the interior. If you are interested in preservation efforts, go in and view this lovely lobby.

Promenade on Marietta Street

You are now walking **northwest on Marietta Street** passing the former Citizens and Southern Bank Building on your right at the corner of Broad Street. The exterior classical features are complemented on the inside by a floor copied from the Pantheon in Rome, Italy. The original solid-bronze banking tables and chandeliers, as well as the beautifully proportionate marble interior, were a treat for bankers and visitors. The building was redesigned in this classical fashion in the late 1920s by Atlanta classical architect Phillip Schutze.

Walk left at Broad Street Mall to the wide Broad Street pedestrian mall with its focal sculpture and potted trees leading you to the Five Points MARTA station and beyond to what was for many decades the grand Rich's department store on Alabama Street. Rich's was Atlanta's first department store. Now the building that housed this venerable institution lives on as part of a new federal office building. **Return to Marietta Street** and continue northwest on Marietta to Forsyth.

At the **intersection of Marietta and Forsyth is Henry Grady Square** with the statue of Henry Grady, one of Atlanta's great newspaper editors and promoter of the New South. Grady called Atlanta "a brave and beautiful city," a phrase which characterizes the city even today.

The Fairlie-Poplar Historic District————

Cross Marietta on Forsyth for a short excursion into the Fairlie-Poplar Historic District, which has undergone extensive restoration. On the corner of Forsyth and Walton, to your right, stands the Grant Building, another historic building which has been restored. At 57 Forsyth Street the Healey Building adds a neo-gothic accent to Atlanta's pack of skyscrapers. Built in 1913, the building will surprise you with its refreshing rotunda and courtyard, reminiscent of the medieval cathedral style.

Turn left at Walton Street. The massive low classical structure at the corner is the U.S. Courthouse, formerly the U.S. Post Office and the 1848 site of the First Baptist Church. At the back of the building on Fairlie Street see the original steel loading dock for the postal service. The Walton block gives the tourist an excellent feel for Atlanta circa 1900. Atlanta 2000 looms high above.

From Marietta Street to the CNN Center————

Turn left on Fairlie, return to Marietta, and **cross the street.** Take a **right on Marietta.** On your left, you will pass the Atlanta Newspapers Building, which will host prearranged tours. **Continue on Marietta** until you reach the CNN Center, which connects to Philips Arena via the Hawkwalk. You may want to stop in the CNN Center for a tour of the facility. For a relaxing treat, pick up a lunch or snack from one of the Hawkwalk venders and take it **back across Marietta St.** to Centennial Olympic Park. If you time it right, you can enjoy a 30-min. waterdance show at the Fountain of Rings. Shows begin at 12:30 pm, 3:30 pm, 6:30 pm and 9 pm. Between these shows, you can enjoy water gardens and quilt plazas and the time honored pursuit of people-watching.

Turn right on International Boulevard and return to Peachtree Center, approximately five blocks.

For guided walking tours around preservation interests in old Atlanta in the commercial and residential sections, we highly recommend the Atlanta Preservation Center, located at 537 Peachtree St., NE; (404) 876-2041.

METRO DRIVING TOUR

With two to three hours of driving time, here is your chance to see a big picture of Atlanta, one which includes the downtown arenas of business and finance, the postmodern business and cultural hub of Midtown, and the acclaimed residential sector in the northwest. Our tour will begin at Peachtree Center, proceed north on Peachtree Street, and then return to town via I-75 to complete the downtown survey. You will be following the daily cycle of many Atlantans who live in the immediate suburbs and work in the downtown area.

The Starting Point Peachtree Center ——

We start **north at Peachtree Center.** At the Baker Street intersection, crowned by the massive One Peachtree Center office tower, Peachtree splits into West Peachtree and Peachtree. **Take Peachtree Street on the right.** At the next intersection you will see two large churches: the gray granite First Methodist Church with the red doors on your left, and on Ivy Street and Peachtree to your right, the brownstone Catholic Church of Sacred Heart. Peachtree Street will present the stations of the churches as residential communities developed from Downtown to Buckhead, an exciting series of architectural styles, denominations, and sites.

Driving Up Peachtree ——

After crossing Ralph McGill Boulevard, renamed in the 1970s after the late editor of the *Atlanta Constitution,* you will pass over I-75/I-85. To your left you can see the Peachtree Summit Building and its accompanying MARTA station. On your right look for St. Luke's Episcopal Church. **Continuing on Peachtree** farther on the right is a great little restaurant, the Pleasant Peasant. On your left, at North Avenue, is the magnificent rose granite Bank of America tower and plaza. Look up to the building's stunning see-through cap. You are now entering Midtown, which will extend to Pershing Point. You are riding the Peachtree ridge where the ground falls off on either side.

Entering Midtown ——————————————

At the next traffic light, at Ponce de Leon, you pass the curved facade of the Ponce de Leon Apartments (1913) and the columned Georgian Terrace Hotel (1911). On your left is the Fox Theatre, an intriguing visual counterpoint to the colossal BellSouth tower behind. The Fox's 1920s Moorish onion domes and extravagant trappings are enjoyed as much today as in the heyday of the flappers and their films.

After Ponce de Leon Avenue the streets intersecting Peachtree will begin to be numbered. On your left is the new Midtown Complex. We are following the northern course of the residential development out Peachtree. At 999 Peachtree and 10th, notice the 999 Peachtree Place Building. Virtually across the street is the Margaret Mitchell House, a restored Tudor Revival home.

In the late 1960s and early 1970s, the area from 10th Street to 14th Street was Atlanta's hippie haven, "The Strip." Today the area is evolving into a stunning business environment. At 1000 Peachtree, the new home of the Federal Reserve Bank is only one example of the dramatic Midtown building boom that is taking place. Before the 1960s, the area was a small village with the locus at 10th Street.

Colony Square and Ansley Park ——————————

You have arrived at Midtown's major center, Colony Square at 14th Street. Along with the CNN Center and Peachtree Center, Colony Square was conceived as a multipurpose center in the 1970s. The complex includes the Colony Square Hotel facing 14th Street, two office towers, a skylit retail mall with fine restaurants, and two condominium towers. Also at the corner of Peachtree and 14th is the Campanile Building, a soaring office complex on your right.

Turn left on 14th Street. You will pass the impressive Four Seasons Hotel on your left with its rose granite exterior and multistory entrance arch. This single building, with its many windows, encloses prime office space, apartments, townhomes, and penthouses, as well as the hotel, all created to reflect the ultimate in luxury. You are approaching the IBM Building on your right, one of the latest additions to Atlanta's skyline.

Midtown/ Piedmont Park   *Courtesy Atlanta Convention and Visitors Bureau*

Opened in 1988, the IBM Building is a triumph of architectural design. **Turn right on West Peachtree.** On your right you will see the serene gardens surrounding the IBM Building. **Turn right on 15th Street.** As you approach Peachtree, you will pass the "Castle" on your right, an old, somewhat Gothic Atlanta home which has been restored. Tennessee Williams once stayed there. The American Telephone and Telegraph Building (AT&T) is on your right at the corner of 15th and Peachtree. **Cross Peachtree on 15th and take an immediate left onto Peachtree Circle.**

You have now entered one of Atlanta's finest residential areas, Ansley Park. This turn-of-the-century neighborhood has been restored in recent years and is an excellent view of Atlanta in the early part of the century. **Turn right on Westminster, left on Prado, and left on Peachtree Circle** where Prado dead-ends. **Follow Peachtree Circle** until it joins 15th Street once again. **Turn right on Peachtree Street.** As you do, notice the trylon sculpture fountain by Steffen Thomas on your left which is surrounded by an island of seasonal flowers typical of others in the Ansley Park neighborhood. The domed neoclassical church on your right is the First Church of Christ Scientist.

Back to Peachtree Street and on to Pershing Point

Proceeding north on Peachtree from 15th Street, you'll see the impressive Robert W. Woodruff Arts Center on your left. The center brings together under one roof the cultural powers and performances of major Atlanta arts organizations—the High Museum of Art, which is located next door in its own independent structure, the Atlanta Symphony, the Atlanta School of Art, and the Alliance Theatre. This is the magnetic center of the arts in Atlanta. Just past the center on your right is one of Atlanta's most exquisite restorations, the Reid House Condominiums, built originally by another esteemed Atlanta classicist, Neil Reid.

West Peachtree rejoins Peachtree after a few blocks at Pershing Point, a small triangular park to your left named after Gen. John J. Pershing, its monument listing the names of Atlantans who died in World War I. The Rhodes Memorial Hall, formerly the Rhodes' family residence in 1903, now a branch of the Georgia Trust for Historic Preservation, is on your left at the Peachtree Circle intersection.

Just before Peachtree crosses I-85, look on the right for The Temple, one of Atlanta's oldest Jewish congregations, designed by Phillip Schutze. Immediately after you pass I-85, the small, distinctive Brookwood Station, Atlanta's only surviving passenger railroad station, is on the left, another architectural contribution by Neil Reid.

Brookwood Village

As you approach Brookwood Village (approximately three miles from Pershing Point), you will pass a number of interesting restaurants and shops. Mick's, a terrific restaurant, will be on your left as will Bennett Street Antiques. At Collier Road the numbered streets end. Collier and Peachtree is the village center of the Brookwood Hills neighborhood. The peak of the hill at Piedmont Hospital, one block north on your left, is Atlanta's "heartbreak hill," so named by the Peachtree Road Race runners coming toward Colony Square.

Buckhead's Beautiful Houses

At the bottom of this long hill, about one mile, is Peachtree Battle with the Peachtree Battle Shopping Center to the right. **Turn left on Peachtree Battle** past the neighborhood school. **Take your first right on Habersham, go right on Cherokee** and then **left on Andrews** to the portals of the Atlanta Historical Society on your right. This beautiful Palladian villa by Phillip Schutze is open for tours as is the Tullie Smith House, a simple 1840s Georgia farmhouse that is an excellent example of the architectural style known as "plantation plain." The Swan Coach House is a charming restaurant and gift shop. The Atlanta History Museum always has exhibitions of significance. **Turn left on West Paces Ferry.**

You are now in one of the most beautiful residential areas in the United States. On your right is the Cherokee Town Club, originally a family home, now a private club set far back from the street in the wooded site. Farther on the left will be the Southern Center for International Studies and on the right, past Habersham, the neo-classic, brick Governor's Mansion with its long grassy knolls and spectacular flower gardens is open for tours. With this brief introduction, enjoy your wandering into the residential heart of the north side. Just past the Governor's Mansion, **take a right on Tuxedo,** after half a mile **turn right at the T,** cross over Valley, **left on Blackland, left on Northside, first left on Valley,** cross over Tuxedo, **right on Habersham, right on West Paces Ferry.** West Paces Ferry will take you to I-75. **Take a left at I-75 South.**

The Martin Luther King, Jr.
Historic District

Exit at Courtland Street. Proceed five blocks and turn left on Auburn Avenue. You are now entering the Sweet Auburn Historic District, an area of totally black-owned businesses and part of Atlanta's

Birth Home of Dr. Martin Luther King, Jr.

Courtesy Atlanta Convention and Visitors Bureau

black heritage tour. Herndon Plaza, which houses Atlanta Life Insurance, a black-owned company, will be on your left. On your right is the Auburn Avenue Research Library on African-American Culture and History. Also on your right, at 135 Auburn, is the APEX Museum (African American Panoramic Experience), a museum chronicling the achievements of Auburn Avenue's residents. The Big Bethel AME church (1890s) at 220 Auburn, on your left, with its powerful circular and square towers, is known for an equally powerful choir. After passing under the expressway, you are approaching the Martin Luther King, Jr. Historic District with the offices of the Southern Christian Leadership Conference at 334 Auburn, on your left; the Ebenezer Baptist Church, where Martin Luther King, Jr., preached, on your right; and the Center for Nonviolent Social Change headed by Coretta Scott King, which is the burial site for the slain civil-rights leader, just past the church on your right. Directly across the street is the Martin Luther King, Jr., Community Center. Farther up Auburn at Number 501 is the frame Victorian house where Dr. King was born.

Turn left on Hogue just past Dr. King's home, **left on Irwin, left on Boulevard, right on Auburn,** and **left on Courtland.**

Capitol Hill

You have now entered Atlanta's capital complex of city, county, and state governments. As you proceed down Courtland Street, the Georgia State University buildings will be on your right and left. At Martin Luther King, Jr. Avenue, Courtland Street turns into Washington. Go straight on Washington for a frontal view of the Georgia State Capitol, the bright-domed neo-Renaissance building at the summit of the hill on your left. The dome is gilded with pure gold, mined in the North Georgia hills near Dahlonega; the open rotunda of the Capitol rises 237 feet. The Georgia State Museum of Science and Industry in the Capitol is part of the tour available. Statues of Georgia statesmen, Thomas Watson, Eugene Talmadge, and others form points of political interest among the magnificent manicured gardens on the capitol grounds.

Facing the statehouse is Central Presbyterian Church, a neo-gothic structure built in 1884 on the site of the former church with a congregation that dates to 1860. The two-block capitol area has three major churches of historic significance, another reminder of Atlanta's original residential areas and the characteristic formation of large congregations within the city.

Turn right on Trinity Avenue and then right at Peachtree Center Ave. On your right is Atlanta's City Hall, taking up an entire city block with its neo-gothic structure (1930) and its recent addition. The site has been important in Atlanta's history, first as the headquarters for Gen. William Tecumseh Sherman in 1864, then as the original site of Oglethorpe University in the 1870s, and later as the site of Atlanta's Boys' and Girls' High Schools.

After crossing Mitchell, the State Capitol park and the Shrine of the Immaculate Conception will be on your right. The Shrine stands on the site of the original church, whose pastor, Father Thomas O'Reilly, is credited with influencing Sherman to spare the churches in his burning of Atlanta. A plaque in City Hall commemorates Father O'Reilly.

After passing the Shrine, the entrance to Underground Atlanta, the "city beneath the city," is just to your left. You are on the viaduct crossing the railroad tracks that came through this center of town. Atlanta took its first name after the railroad phrase Terminus, and was the railroad and supply hub of the Confederacy. Underground Atlanta still holds the real key to the city—the zero-mile post, with its historic marker designating the terminus of the Western and Atlantic Railroad and the central point from which the city was measured in all directions.

Proceed on Peachtree Center Ave. to Decatur Street.

The Downtown Business District ————

Before **turning left at Decatur Street,** which changes its name to Marietta Street, look to your right at the second largest complex in the state's university system—Georgia State University, a nonresidential urban-centered academy. Decatur Street takes you to the center of the downtown business district, Five Points. Here Peachtree, Marietta, and Edgewood converge. The downtown offices of several major banks tower over the intersection.

At Five Points, Woodruff Park opens up to your right, a large green space in the heart of the city, donated by Atlanta's "anonymous" donor and Coca-Cola heir, Robert Woodruff. This is a place for pedestrian cross-over, lunch breaks, occasional springtime music presentations, and sitting or stretching out in Atlanta's temperate weather.

Continue on Marietta. Notice the new and old office buildings siding Marietta, a study of contrasts in textures, styles, and shapes. You will pass the *Atlanta Journal-Constitution* Building and the old Federal Reserve Bank of Atlanta on your left.

At Forsyth Street, an island with trees and the statue of Atlanta's "New South" editor, Henry Grady, separates the street. Grady's phrase "Atlanta: a city too busy to hate" spans the post-Civil War and 20th-century credo of the city's movers and shakers.

Continue on Marietta to Spring Street (just past the glass-sheathed skyscraper). **Take a right. Take the next right on Walton Street,** for a short trip back in time. On your right is a whole string of restored buildings from Atlanta circa 1890.

Go right at Forsyth. At this intersection notice the stocky low neoclassical building, the U.S. Courthouse, on your left. The building was previously the U.S. Post Office, and in 1848, the site held the original First Baptist Church.

To the CNN Center

Turn right at Marietta and proceed north on Marietta to the CNN Center, a mighty complex where "CNN News" and "Headline News" shows are produced and broadcast. Continue to the Omni Hotel; the neighboring Georgia World Congress Center, site of trade shows throughout the year; and beyond, the massive Georgia Dome, home of the Atlanta Falcons. **Turn right at International.**

Return to Peachtree Center

Veer right on Carnegie Way (fourth right). The Atlanta Public Library is on your right. **Turn right on Forsyth.** Immediately on the left is Margaret Mitchell Square, dedicated in 1987. Next door is the Rhodes-Haverty Building, an historic office building which has been renovated. **Turn left on Broad Street.** The Flatiron Building, the oldest tall pre-steel building in the Southeast, is on your right as you turn.

Go straight on Peachtree to return to Peachtree Center. You have completed your tour of Atlanta and now it's time for a view from the top and a drink in the revolving Sun Dial Lounge atop the Westin Peachtree Plaza, or maybe lunch at Dailey's, one of the many restaurants. The tour is over; it is time to savor fully your comprehensive introduction to Atlanta.

ONE-DAY EXCURSIONS

It seems that all roads lead to Atlanta, Georgia's great transportation center. We suggest you retrace a selected few of these routes, either spend some delicious crisp time in the North Georgia Mountains or perhaps in the gentle piedmont and fading foothills southwest of the city, returning at the end of the day to Atlanta. Each excursion is a full day and an overnight if you choose.

SOUTH TO WARM SPRINGS, CALLAWAY GARDENS, AND PINE MOUNTAIN
(8 to 10 hours)

You are heading south of Atlanta, edging toward the Alabama border, on this day's excursion. The drive is mostly on the swift and easy interstate. Highlighting the tour are the Little White House, the modest retreat of President Franklin D. Roosevelt, and Callaway Gardens, Georgia's premier resort. If you want to stay overnight in this area, Callaway Gardens is ideal.

First to the Little White House ─────────

Take I-85 south from Atlanta, **exit alternate GA 27 South, to Warm Springs. Take GA 85W south,** to the Little White House.

Franklin D. Roosevelt, four times president of the United States, died here April 12, 1945. Twenty-one years earlier Roosevelt had come south to Warm Springs for the therapeutic warm pools which aided him in his struggle with the paralysis of polio. He helped develop the resort for other polio victims, establishing the Georgia Warm Springs

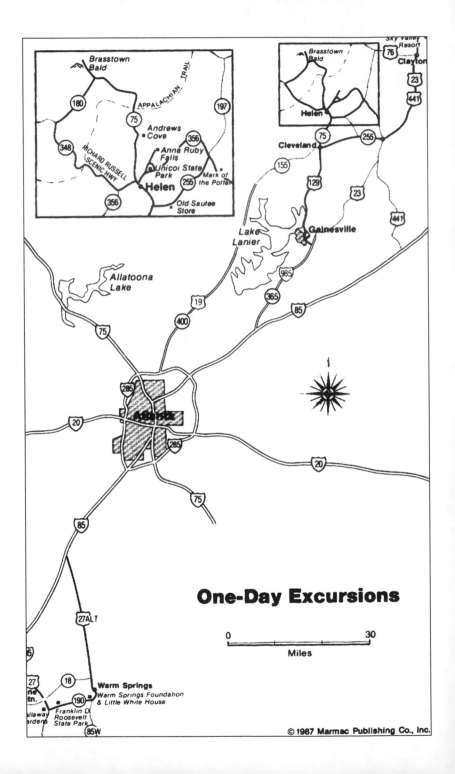

One-Day Excursions

0   30

Miles

© 1987 Marmac Publishing Co., Inc.

Foundation and fostering the subsequent development of health facilities. Before Roosevelt built his house nearby, he had used the site for
picnics. The Little White House was unlike the palatial quarters of his
ancestral home in Hyde Park, New York, and the official White House
in Washington. Roosevelt chose a simple, rustic dwelling for his
Georgia residence, with three bedrooms, an entry, a combination living
and dining room, a kitchen, and a sundeck.

No changes have been made since the president's death—a wheelchair, ship models, his dog Fala's chain, a riding whip in the closet, and
gifts from school children and friends are in the pine-paneled interior.
A taped commentary accompanies your self-guided tour. Outside see
the 1938 Ford Convertible fitted with hand controls, the Guest House
where notables from all over the world stayed, the old Warm Springs
Stagecoach, the memorial fountain, and the walk of states' stones and
flags leading to the Franklin D. Roosevelt Museum. There you'll find
fascinating mementos associated with the president, and a 12-minute
documentary movie is shown free of charge in the museum auditorium.

Visitors are welcome to use the picnic tables on the grounds. A
snack bar and gift shop are located in the Entrance Building. The Little
White House is open daily 9 am-5 pm, open one hour later in June,
July, and August weekends. CH.

On to Callaway Gardens

**From Warm Springs take a right on GA 85W, right on GA 190
west, right on GA 27 north to Callaway Gardens.**

The drive from Warm Springs to Callaway Gardens is exquisite, riding one of the last ridges at the sinking of the Appalachian chain.
Franklin D. Roosevelt State Park is along this route, with more than
100 campsites and 21 cottages. Roosevelt was responsible for the plant-
ing of many of the pine trees within the park area.

Where GA 190 dead-ends in GA 27, don't miss a visit to the
Callaway Gardens' Country Store and the panoramic view of the valley across the highway (a fine place for photos). The country store
smells of assorted good things from the Callaway vegetable gardens,
along with imported deli items. From slab bacon to escargot, from Swiss
chocolates to muscadine preserves and speckled heart grits, this is a
place to food shop with zest and imagination. Have a leisurely lunch in
the Country Kitchen overlooking Pine Mountain valley.

Callaway Gardens is one of America's unique horticultural and
recreational areas. It was founded by Mr. and Mrs. Cason J. Callaway as
a place where all people could find tranquility, natural inspiration, and
wholesome recreation. Admission to the gardens is a modest fee; children

under six, Inn and Cottage guests, and annual pass-holders are free. An in-depth tram tour of the gardens with a staff naturalist is available daily at 1 pm meeting in front of the Inn. There is a small charge for this bus tour; it is well worth your consideration, especially if your time is limited.

Callaway Gardens has 13 miles of scenic drives, nature trails, and bicycle paths winding through 14,000 acres of woodlands, lakes, streams and ponds, wild flowers, and landscaped areas. Callaway Gardens is lush year round; the fall offers beautiful chrysanthemums and brilliant foliage, in the winter there are shiny and berried hollies, the spring has more than 600 varieties of azaleas, and the sunny summer produces a rich green growing season.

The Greenhouse Conservatory Complex displays year-round plants native to their climates. Mr. Cason's Vegetable Garden is 7.5 acres of delicious fruits, berries, and vegetables. The Ida Cason Callaway Memorial Chapel is a gentle place of repose or organ concerts in the woods by the side of a small pond.

The Cecil B. Day Butterfly Center is the first glass butterfly conservatory in North America. Live butterflies and small birds fly free among visitors in this enclosed tropical setting, truly a breathtaking experience to enjoy.

Many sports activities are offered at Callaway Gardens: 63 holes of golf, ten lighted tennis courts, fishing, bicycling on the five-mile bike trail, skeet and trap shooting, and swimming and boating at Robin Lake Beach, the largest inland man-made beach in the world.

Obviously a day trip to Callaway Gardens will leave you with a strong desire for more. The Inn has ample accommodations—345 rooms with convention facilities for 1,000 people. You can also rent a one- or two-bedroom cottage in the woods, one of 50 luxurious villas. See Resorts in the LODGING chapter. Whatever your needs, write to the management at Callaway Gardens, Pine Mountain, GA 31822 or call 1-800-225-5292.

As you leave the gardens, be sure to stop in the small town of Pine Mountain, established in 1882 as a maintenance center for the Columbus and Rome railroad. Antiques shoppers will love **Sweet Home Antiques** at 149 Main St. This shop specializes in antique American furniture, Southern primitives, and Georgia pottery. A few steps away at **Mountain Creek** you'll find recreational gifts and supplies from backpacks to binoculars to picnic baskets.

Chanticleer, 141 Main St., features European home accents, both vintage and new, as well as baby gifts and other treasures. Gardeners will love **Country Gardens,** 155 Main St. Here you'll find native plants, herbs, ornamental iron work, garden gates, and other items to make your garden glow.

Hiking Trails abound at Callaway Gardens

Courtesy Atlanta Convention and Visitors Bureau

Need a pair of good overalls? **Kimbrough Brothers,** an old fashioned general store, has been serving the Pine Mountain area for more than a hundred years. Drop in at **Heart of the South Tea Room,** 129 N. Main St., for a quick pick-me-up or a substantial high tea before heading back to Atlanta.

A Quick Trip Home

Atlanta is not far off; **to return take GA 27 north to I-185** which runs directly into **I-85 to Atlanta.**

NORTH TO THE MOUNTAINS
(8 to 9 hours)

This full day of touring stretches almost to the North Carolina border, introducing you to the unspoiled setting of the Chattahoochee National Forest, Georgia's tallest summit, a myriad of small craft and artisan shops, and Helen, a charming Swiss-style village tucked in the midst of these beautiful foothills. As a bonus you cross the legendary Appalachian Trail, which follows the mountain chain north to the state of Maine.

Alpine Helen

Take I-85 North from Atlanta, left on GA 365 to Gainesville, left on GA 129 to Cleveland, left around the square, right on GA 75 at the light to Helen.

Helen, a small lumber-mill town at the turn of the century, is now a bustling imitation of a Bavarian village, attracting visitors year round with festivals, sporting events, dancing, shopping in the many local mountain craftshops and import shops, restaurants, cafes, and tearooms. There are many fine hotels in the town, and during special festivals the hotels fill up rapidly. We suggest advance reservations. This is your first stopping-off place. Enjoy Alpine architecture and ambience here in Helen with its cool stream running right through town, its cobblestone streets, and Bavarian costume.

October is a special season in the mountains; the fall leaves turn brilliant red, ocher, yellow, and orange, and Helen has its equally colorful, Munich-inspired Oktoberfest. In the early summer Helen hosts the popular Balloon Race to the coast, with a large entry of brilliant patterned balloons lifting from the Helen balloon-port and forming a grand aerial parade to the east. Helen has sports to do as well—trout fishing, horseback riding, canoeing, biking, tennis, golf, and plenty of hiking. Write the Alpine Helen/White County Convention & Visitors Bureau at P. O. Box 730, Helen, GA 30545 or call (706) 878-2274. For information on the Balloon Race, call Head Balloons, (706) 865-3874.

Georgia's Highest Point

From Helen, **proceed on GA 75 north, left on GA 356, right on GA 348**, the Richard Russell Scenic Highway, named after the illustrious late U.S. senator from Georgia. About six miles down the highway, you intersect with the Appalachian Trail at Tessnatee Gap. Park by the roadside, take a 10-minute stroll among the earnest backpackers, and know that you are treading where Native Americans and all generations of settlers after them have made their way from one end of this nation to another.

The Richard Russell Highway is a spectacular drive in North Georgia, the mountains breathlessly beautiful and close. **At GA 180, take a right to Brasstown Bald.** The signs point the way. Brasstown Bald is 4,784 feet above sea level, Georgia's highest point. Take a bus to the top in the summer months. On a clear day you can see four states from this pinnacle: Georgia, North Carolina, Tennessee, and South Carolina. The Visitors Center has an entry fee and is open May 1-October 31.

Unicoi and Waterfalls

From Brasstown Bald **turn left on Ga 180 which becomes GA 66, right on GA 75, and left on GA 356** to Unicoi State Park, one of Georgia's most modern state parks designed for individual and family use, as well as conferences and retreats. Accommodations are moderate to inexpensive, another excellent place for an overnight. The Lodge is contoured into a forested hill above a large recreational lake surrounded by attractive contemporary rental cabins and campgrounds for tents and trailer camping. Unicoi has continuing programs around environmental themes, crafts, folk singing, and water sports. Write Unicoi at P.O. Box 849, Helen, GA 30545 or call (706) 878-2201 for information and reservations.

Just a mile before you reach Unicoi you will see a sign to Anna Ruby Falls and Andrews Cove area, a super side trip to one of the many splendid waterfalls in the Chattahoochee National Forest.

The Mark of the Potter and Old Sautee Store

From Unicoi **continue east on GA 356, right on GA 197, bear left at the fork** to continue **on 197** to Mark of the Potter. This converted old corn mill on the Soque River is now a craft shop brimming with creativity and energy. Here you'll find ceramics, glass, and other works from craft artists in Georgia and the Southeast. The millpond under the upstairs porch is filled with Georgia's finest and fattest trout, who eagerly show their rainbow sides at feeding time. This is a gem of a place.

Go right on GA 197 and left on GA 255 to the Old Sautee Store, with its collection of 18th- and 19th-century memorabilia, farm tools, player piano, posters, and signs, a remarkable museum/store. You can poke around endlessly in the old section and then move into the modern import shop for Icelandic sweaters, Scandinavian wares, and even a steaming cup of glogg during the Christmas season.

Follow GA 17 to GA 75 to Cleveland, to GA 129 to Gainesville, right on GA 365 to I-85 to Atlanta.

A Side Trip to the World of *Deliverance*

From Cleveland take GA 115 east to Clarksville, U.S. 441 north to Clayton. En route you will pass by Tallulah Gorge, where the "Great Wallenda" made his epic tightrope walk in 1970. Stop and see just what a terrifying prospect this must have been despite the stunning beauty around you. Drive on to Clayton, and you will be passing close by the Chattooga River where the movie *Deliverance* was filmed, starring Burt Reynolds and based on the best-selling novel by poet and novelist James Dickey, an Atlanta native. The experienced or the adventurous can raft down the river with a guide. Inquire The Chattooga River Resort at (336) 722-0066.

Clayton is a typical Georgia mountain town. Potters and good country restaurants abound—stop by at the Rabun County Chamber of Commerce Visitors' Center. About 10 miles to the east of Clayton is Sky Valley, near Dillard, a popular year-round resort with the only snow skiing in Georgia. See LODGING chapter under Resorts.

NEW RESIDENTS

Atlanta is your new home. Welcome to this spirited place. You will be busy locating housing, opening bank accounts, moving furniture, and bringing a multitude of items from your life in another city to your new residence. During this transition time you will be establishing your first ring of social and business contacts in Atlanta. We offer a selected group of data and organizations that, together with the rest of this book, will get you off to a fresh and efficient start.

Welcome Services

Welcome Wagon; (770) 955-8770. This nationally recognized organization will assist you in settling in and introduce you to merchants and products in your new location.

AN INTRODUCTION TO ATLANTA LIVING

Atlanta is synonymous with growth. The city continues an unabated course of development as a key business and commercial center. At the same time the quality of life in Atlanta receives national acclaim—the city consistently comes out on or near the top when pollsters ask executives their favorite destinations for corporate relocations.

Atlanta is the 10th largest city in the country and the greater 15-county area has 83 incorporated towns and cities with more than 3 million people. Wherever you live—in town, within the perimeter or beyond the perimeter—you will join in the experience of creating Atlanta's identity.

Atlanta has always been seen by Georgians in other cities, especially the older towns such as Savannah, Columbus, and Augusta, as the "New South." And that term does fit this marvelous city, host to people from all parts of the South. Its magnetism has equally drawn people from throughout the country and now is attracting an international population. The mix seems to be the making of Atlanta.

Atlantans' love of outdoor living and entertaining in their homes has extended to the availability of outdoor cafes, well suited to the moderate climate. People enjoy picnicking in the city parks and at the surrounding lakes on the weekends. Sports activities of all kinds keep Atlantans on the run and fit and trim. A cultural surge is taking off in the visual and performing arts. Theater "districts" have emerged, the Atlanta Symphony Orchestra is receiving national recognition, along with multiple Grammy awards, the High Museum of Art occupies its landmark building, and galleries proliferate. Tens of thousands of newcomers make their homes in Atlanta each year. Rings of residential and commercial development ripple out again and again from the city, and the "New South" town wears yet another necklace of enchantment.

GEOGRAPHICAL PROFILE

Atlanta is situated in the foothills of the southern Appalachian mountains in north central Georgia, more than 1,000 feet above sea level. To see how far inland Atlanta is located from the Atlantic Ocean, Chattanooga, Tennessee is due north, about an hour-and-a-half drive. The ocean is more than a five-hour drive to Savannah, the Golden Isles of St. Simons, Jekyll, Sea Island, or Hilton Head, South Carolina, the closest and favorite seaside resorts.

To reach the Gulf of Mexico, also allow at least five hours of driving from Atlanta to points south such as Panama City and Destin, Florida. The interstate system makes the trips possible in this period of driving time.

To the north the mountains provide a haven for refreshment within one or two driving hours. The Chattahoochee National Forest and small northern Georgia towns and inns are frequented by Atlantans throughout the year; Southern ski resorts are active in cold winters, the autumn festivals are as colorful as the changing leaves, and spring and summer are always a refuge for the naturalist and mountain lover.

Nearby man-made Lake Lanier, Lake Allatoona, and Lake Oconee are within an hour's drive. Within two hours is West Point Lake to the southwest on the Alabama border; Lake Jackson to the southeast; Lake Hartwell to the northeast on the South Carolina border; and to the north the multiple lakes in the Chattahoochee National Forest, Blue Ridge, Nottely, Chatuge, Burton, and Rabun. Due west is Birmingham, Alabama, a three-hour drive through the beautiful rolling piedmont.

ATLANTA INSIGHT

Autos

Auto Insurance

Georgia law requires that drivers of automobiles carry no-fault insurance, and you must have a Georgia Insurance Identification Card in your possession at all times while driving. These cards are issued at the time of purchase of insurance. Check with your insurance agent.

Auto Registration

You must buy your Georgia license tag within 30 days of establishing residency. When you purchase your tag, you must have proof of insurance and proof of ownership of your vehicle; plus, you must pay your vehicle's ad valorem tax (personal property tax) at this time. Call tag offices in your county:

```
Clayton . . . . . . . . . . . . . . . . . . . . . (770) 477-3331
Cobb . . . . . . . . . . . . . . . . . . . . . . . (770) 528-4020
DeKalb . . . . . . . . . . . . . . . . . . . . . (404) 298-4000
Douglas . . . . . . . . . . . . . . . . . . . . . (770) 949-2309
Fulton . . . . . . . . . . . . . . . . . . . . . . (404) 730-6100
Gwinnett . . . . . . . . . . . . . . . . . . . . (770) 822-8801
Fayette . . . . . . . . . . . . . . . . . . . . . . (770) 461-3611
Forsyth . . . . . . . . . . . . . . . . . . . . . . (770) 781-2112
Henry . . . . . . . . . . . . . . . . . . . . . . . (770) 954-2471
Paulding . . . . . . . . . . . . . . . . . . . . . (770) 443-7584
Rockdale . . . . . . . . . . . . . . . . . . . . . (770) 929-4097
```

Driver's Licenses

Out-of-state drivers are given 30 days to obtain a Georgia driver's license. Minimum age for a license is 16 years. A learner's license may be obtained at 15 years of age. If you have an out-of-state license, you're not required to take a Georgia road test, but you must take an eye test and a written exam. A four-year license for driving a passenger car costs $15. A learner's permit costs $10.

It's helpful if you take your out-of-state license, your fee, and your social security card with you when you apply for a Georgia's driver's license. To find the licensing station nearest you, call the Driver's License Bureau (404) 657-9300.

Emission Control Inspection

Georgia's motor vehicle laws currently require that all gas-burning vehicles less than 12 years old in Cobb, DeKalb, and Fulton counties be checked for emission standards every year. The inspection costs $25. It can be done at any of the state-designated inspection stations. Non-gas-burning vehicles, such as diesel cars and trucks, and motorcycles, are exempt from the inspection. To find the inspection station nearest you, call (800) 449-2471.

Reporting of Auto Accidents

In an accident on a **public** street call the police immediately at the emergency number 9-1-1. If outside Atlanta city limits, call (404) 658-6666. If location of the cars is essential in determining fault leave the cars in the position at the time of accident and be sure traffic can proceed around them. If the cars are blocking traffic, or causing danger, pull cars over to side of the street.

Have your car registration, insurance cards, and driver's license available.

Police will handle situations where drivers are intoxicated or drugged or where persons need emergency assistance because of bodily injury.

In an accident on a **private** street call police immediately. You will have to fill out an SR-B form within 10 days of the accident to submit to your insurance company. These forms are available at Police Headquarters and precincts.

Banking ———————————————

Atlanta is a powerful banking center in the Southeast. The city is the headquarters of the Sixth Federal Reserve District.

With the flexibility of current banking laws, banks and savings and loan associations are offering diversified banking services and financial investments. This competitive situation means that interest rates, service charges, down payments, time-limited programs, and special premiums are communicated directly to the consumer.

Call the **Georgia Bankers Association,** (404) 522-1501, for further information about banks in Atlanta and the South.

Chambers of Commerce ———————

For newcomers, prospective home buyers, and businesses the Chambers of Commerce are helpful in securing information and seeking business contacts. Also, foreign countries are establishing branches of their chambers in Atlanta.

The following is a list of chambers in Metro Atlanta.

Metro Atlanta C of C .... (404) 880-9000
Chamber of Commerce
  of the United States .... (770) 393-0140
Cherokee C of C .... (770) 345-0400
Clayton C of C .... (404) 608-2770
Cobb County C of C .... (770) 980-2000
Conyers-Rockdale County
  C of C .... (770) 483-7049
DeKalb C of C .... (404) 378-8000
Fayette County C of C .... (770) 461-9983
Gwinnett County C of C .... (770) 513-3000
Henry County C of C .... (770) 957-5786
Greater North Fulton C of C .... (770) 993-8806
South Fulton C of C .... (770) 964-1984

Churches, Synagogues, and Temples ——

Atlanta, Georgia, is in an area generally referred to as the Bible Belt, with more than 2,000 metro churches and with a predominance of Baptist and Methodist churches in a matrix of more than 70 denominations (Christian and others), more than 25 synagogues, and numerous religious organizations. As residential growth continues, new churches are established to meet the needs of the new congregations.

Notice that Peachtree Street from the Capitol downtown to Lenox Square is a seven-mile Church Row with bold ecclesiastical structures facing this main artery through the city. These churches and synagogues are landmarks in the historical development of Atlanta.

Churches in Atlanta and in the South are important meeting places for social fellowship and church programs such as day-care, as well as worship. Members also provide an array of urban outreach programs such as food banks, shelter programs, literacy training, counseling services, child care, immigrant work, etc.

Among the major denominational and ecumenical organizations are:

A.M.E. 6th District Church Headquarters, 208 Auburn Ave., NE; (404) 524-8279.

Atlanta Baptist Association, 2930 Flowers Rd., Chamblee; (770) 455-4870.

Atlanta Jewish Community Center, 5342 Tilly Mill Rd., Dunwoody; (770) 396-3250.

Jewish Federation of Greater Atlanta, 1440 Spring St., NW; (404) 873-1661.

C.M.E. Church Headquarters, 2001 Martin Luther King, Jr. Dr., SW; (404) 752-7800.

Catholic Archdiocese of Atlanta, 680 W. Peachtree, NW; (404) 888-7801.

Christian Council of Metropolitan Atlanta, Inc., 465 Boulevard, SE; (404) 622-2235.

Church of God State Offices, 7200 Buford Hwy., Doraville; (770) 448-9300.

Episcopal Diocese of Atlanta, 2744 Peachtree Rd., NW; (404) 365-1010.

First Christian Church of Atlanta, 4532 Lavista Rd., Tucker; (770) 939-4358.

First Church of Christ, Scientist, 3579 McEver Rd.; (770) 535-2741.

Georgia Baptist Convention, 2930 Flowers Rd.; (770) 455-0404.

Greek Orthodox Diocese of Atlanta, 2480 Clairmont Rd., NE; (404) 634-9345.

Lutheran Ministries of Georgia, 756 W. Peachtree St.; (404) 607-7126.

Presbyterian Church in America, 1852 Century Pl., NE; (404) 320-3366.

Presbytery of Greater Atlanta, 1026 Ponce de Leon Ave.; (404) 898-0711.

Southeast Conference of the United Church of Christ, 756 W. Peachtree St., NW; (404) 607-1993.

Southern Union Conference of Seventh-Day Adventists, 3978 Memorial Dr., Decatur; (404) 299-1832.

Unitarian Universalist Congregation of Atlanta, 1911 Cliff Valley Way, NE; (404) 634-5134.

United Methodist Center, 159 Ralph McGill Blvd., NE; (404) 659-0996.

Clubs and Associations

Private clubs are plentiful in Atlanta, many associated with neighborhood recreational facilities or apartment and condominium complexes.

Other private city clubs and country clubs require sponsorship or the courtesy of transfer membership from an affiliate club.

Business associations include the Chambers of Commerce listed previously in this chapter, as well as the following, many of which have chapters throughout the Metro Area.

Atlanta Women's Network .... (404) 256-8787
Atlanta Jaycees .... (404) 881-1676
Kiwanis Club of Atlanta .... (404) 521-1443
Rotary Club of Atlanta .... (404) 522-2767
Women's Commerce Club .... (770) 395-1582

Join the civic association in your neighborhood immediately. These are vibrant groups in Atlanta—a perfect "starter" for newcomers, politically and socially.

For the sports enthusiast, there are many organizations that provide field trips, clinics, sports and exercise programs, good times, and camaraderie. See the SPORTS chapter for contacts for a particular sport. The **YWCA, YMCA,** and **Jewish Community Center** provide excellent facilities and curricula. Groups such as the **Atlanta Ski Club,** the **Georgia Canoeing Association,** the **Sierra Club,** and many others have a minimal membership fee and offer many opportunities for making new sporting friends. See SPORTS chapter.

Interested in cultural associations? Try Young Careers or the Junior Committee or other programs at the **High Museum of Art,** the **Symphony,** or **Ballet;** adopt an animal at **Zoo Atlanta;** attend seminars at the **Atlanta Botanical Garden;** take an historic tour with the **Georgia Society for Historic Preservation;** or play in a community orchestra. These are just starters; attach yourself to any cultural organization in the city as patron or participant. See the VISUAL ARTS chapter and PERFORMING ARTS chapter for referrals.

Education ————————————————————————————

Public Schools, Primary and Secondary

Metro Atlanta has 20 county and 5 city school systems, all on the quarter plan. Ask your real estate agent about the school system in your area and call the **Georgia Department of Education** at (404) 656-2446 to obtain specific data: scores on the state tests for reading and math for your school, the teacher-student ratios, teacher salaries, number of students graduating, and college-bound students. Then set an appointment with the school principal to inspect the school and talk about the curriculum and special courses for the gifted and for special students.

Georgia has public school kindergarten available to five-year-olds. Children entering the first grade must be at least six years old before September 1 of the entering year. School generally opens in mid to late August. Enrollment requires the child's birth certificate, proof of residency, immunization documents, and the latest report card for a transfer student.

Call your local school board for full details concerning county or municipality educational programs.

Atlanta .... (404) 827-8000
Cobb County .... (770) 426-3300
DeKalb County .... (404) 297-1200
Fayette County .... (770) 460-3535
Forsyth County .... (770) 887-2461
Fulton County .... (404) 768-3600
Gwinnett County .... (770) 963-8651
Buford .... (770) 945-5035
Clayton County .... (770) 473-2700
Decatur .... (404) 370-4400
Douglas County .... (770) 920-4000
Marietta .... (770) 422-3500
Rockdale County .... (770) 483-4713

Private Schools

Metro Atlanta has scores of private schools, many with church affiliations. Accreditation is through the **Southern Association of Colleges and Schools,** a good source to check for a prospective student application. Call the Association at (404) 679-4500. The **Southern Association of Independent Schools** will provide a complete listing, which is available through any one of the independent schools. A joint-testing admission program is administered by the Association. For information call the Association at (404) 633-2203.

For Catholic parochial schools call the **Atlanta Archdiocese** at (404) 888-7833. For other church schools, call your local church office.

The **Jewish Educational Services Agency** can be reached at (770) 677-9480.

Colleges and Universities

Major Atlanta colleges and universities are listed under the SPECIAL PEOPLE chapter.

Government ─────────────────

City Government

Atlanta is governed by a mayor and an 18-member City Council presided over by a President of Council elected city-wide. Twelve council members are elected from single-member districts; six are elected city-wide from paired council districts. Elections for mayor and council are held every four years.

County Government

Counties are governed by Boards of Commissioners comprising four to six elected commissioners with one serving as chairman.

Congressional Districts

The seven-county area of Fulton, Cobb, DeKalb, Clayton, Rockdale, Douglas, and Gwinnett counties is included in the five U.S. Congressional districts in metro Atlanta.

A political directory for Atlanta and Fulton County is published by the League of Women Voters. Call (404) 874-8683 to purchase a copy.

Health Care

Health care is readily available in Atlanta in private and government medical institutions and hospitals. The 15-county area has more than 60 licensed hospitals and a combined bed capacity of around 15,000. The **Emory Medical School** is well known throughout the South for its medical research and training for doctors and nurses. The **Morehouse School of Medicine** is making an impressive name for itself as part of the predominantly black **Atlanta University Center.** The **Centers for Disease Control** (CDC) of the U.S. Public Health Service is the nation's number-one research center for tracking communicable diseases. And Atlanta has recently become the headquarters for the **American Cancer Society.**

Many of the following Atlanta hospitals have 24-hour emergency care. We list them by area:

Downtown

Crawford Long Hospital of Emory University, 550 Peachtree St., NE; (404) 686-4411.

Atlanta Medical Center, 303 Parkway Dr., NE; (404) 265-4000.

Grady Memorial Hospital, 80 Butler St., SE; (404) 616-4307.

Midtown

Piedmont Hospital, 1968 Peachtree Rd., NW; (404) 605-5000.

North

North Fulton Regional, 3000 Hospital Blvd., Roswell; (770) 751-2500.

Northside Hospital, 1000 Johnson Ferry Rd., NE; (404) 851-8000.
Saint Joseph's Hospital, 5665 Peachtree-Dunwoody Rd., NE; (404) 851-7001.
West Paces Ferry Medical Center, 3200 Howell Mill Rd., NW; (404) 351-0351.

East

Decatur Hospital, 450 N. Candler St., Decatur; (404) 501-6700.
DeKalb Medical Center, 2701 N. Decatur Rd.; (404) 501-1000.
Emory Hospital, 1364 Clifton Rd.; (404) 712-7021.
Rockdale County Hospital, 1412 Milstead Ave., NE, Conyers; (770) 918-3000.

West

Cobb Hospital and Medical Center, 3950 Austell Rd., SW, Austell; (770) 732-4000.

Northeast

Emory Dunwoody Medical Center, 4575 N. Shallowford Rd., Dunwoody; (770) 454-2000.
Gwinnett Medical Center, 1000 Medical Center Blvd., NW, Lawrenceville; (678) 442-4321.
Northlake Regional Medical Center, 1455 Montreal Rd., Tucker; (770) 270-3000.

Northwest

Kennestone Hospital, 677 Church St., Marietta; (770) 793-5000.

South

Henry Medical Center, 1133 Eagle's Landing Pkwy.; (770) 389-2200.
South Fulton Medical Center, 1170 Cleveland Ave., East Point; (404) 305-3500.
Southern Regional Medical Center, 11 Upper Riverdale Rd., SW, Riverdale; (770) 991-8000.
Southwest Hospital & Medical Center, 501 Fairburn Rd., SW; (404) 699-1111.

Medical Facilities for Specialized Treatment and Aid:

Alcoholics Anonymous Referral Service . . . . (800) 711-6375

Children's Hospitals

Henrietta-Egleston Hospital for Children . . . . (404) 325-6000
Scottish Rite Children's Hospital . . . . (404) 256-5252

Emergency Mental Health by County

Fulton . . . .(404) 730-1600
Cobb . . . .(770) 422-0202
Fayette . . . .(770) 229-3003
DeKalb . . . .(404) 892-4646
Clayton . . . .(770) 996-4357
Gwinnett, Rockdale, and Newton . . . .(770) 985-2494
Paulding . . . .(770) 443-7823
Metropolitan Atlanta Council
  on Alcohol and Drugs . . . .(404) 351-1800
Poison Control Center . . . .(404) 616-9000
Rape/Abuse Hotline/Helpline . . . .(404) 616-4861
Shepherd Spinal Center . . . .(404) 352-2020

Referral Associations

Medical Association of Atlanta . . . .(404) 881-1714
Northern District Dental Society . . . .(770) 270-1635
Planned Parenthood . . . .(404) 688-9300
DeKalb Medical Society . . . .(770) 270-1733
Medical Association of Georgia . . . .(404) 876-7535

Home Decorating

Rich's, Macy's, Home Depot, and most major furniture companies have staff designers, whose services may be complimentary.

Atlanta Decorative Arts Center (C3), 351 Peachtree Hills Ave., NE; (404) 231-1720. Nicknamed ADAC, this center is a major regional hub for wholesale antiques and complete decorator products. You will need your designer or architect for admission, but it's well worth the venture into this great consortium of design houses. If you do not have a designer, they can recommend some to you.

Home Expo (A4), 1201 Hammond Dr., NE; (770) 913-0111. This Home Depot "superstore" is the place to come if you're building or renovating a home. Experts help you choose bath fixtures, kitchen cabinets, doors, windows, wall and floor coverings, and other interior finishes—all at no charge. Home Expo carries top-name brands to choose from, all at great prices. If you're after specific advice, such as help in designing your kitchen, we suggest you call before you visit to see if you need an appointment. Home Expo can get crowded and its experts pressed for time.

Jury Duty

Jurors are called from the registered voter lists of persons 18 and older. There is no residency requirement for jury duty, and there are no exclusions except for convicted felons who have not had their civil rights restored. Doctors, lawyers, teachers, and those with physical handicaps may ask for exemptions in writing.

There are two levels of court service in the state courts. Jurors are called from the county in which they reside to serve either on the State or Superior trial court in their county for both civil and criminal cases. Jurors are called from the multiple counties of the North Georgia district to serve on the U.S. District Court in Atlanta.

Legal Services

For references call the Atlanta Bar Association's **Lawyer Referral Service** at (404) 521-0777.

Libraries

The **Atlanta-Fulton Public Library System** (404) 730-1700 has a central downtown library (One Margaret Mitchell Square) and 35 branches in the city and Fulton County. See the SIGHTS chapter. Services are free to residents of Atlanta and Fulton County.

Major county libraries providing community library services are listed below. Call for the branch nearest you for information.

Cherokee County .... (770) 479-3090
Clayton County .... (770) 473-3850
Cobb County .... (770) 528-2320
DeKalb County .... (404) 370-3070
Fayette County .... (770) 461-6841
Forsyth County .... (770) 781-9840
Fulton County .... (404) 730-1700
Gwinnett County .... (770) 978-5154
Paulding .... (770) 445-5680
Rockdale County .... (770) 388-5040

Local Laws

Liquor Laws

State laws require that you must be 21 to buy alcohol. Liquor, wine, and beer are sold in package stores from 7 or 8 am to midnight, Mon-Sat, with no sales on Sun. Grocery and convenience stores sell beer and wine also, Mon-Sat.

Bars, restaurants, sports arenas, and other entertainment areas serve liquor, beer, and wine seven days. Alcoholic beverages are sold after 12:30 pm on Sunday. Some restaurants have a license limited to beer and wine, but allow liquor to be brought by the customer in a "brown bag." Surrounding counties have varying liquor laws.

Property Laws

Atlanta has established firm zoning laws that require certain procedures for changes in residential structures from one classification to another, such as condominium conversion. Variances or minor changes of a structure within the same zoning classification require obtaining a work permit from the city.

Historic districts have special zoning restrictions. Contact your neighborhood civic association before applying for a work permit to be sure your changes are in compliance or to seek the support of your civic association for the variance or zoning change.

Medical —————————————————————————

See Health Care above.

Newspapers and Periodicals ——————————

The major newspaper is *The Atlanta Journal-Constitution* (404) 526-5151. The **Atlanta Daily World** is the nation's oldest black-owned newspaper, (404) 659-1110. Other daily or five-days-a-week newspapers published in the metro area include the **News Daily,** (770) 478-5753; **Douglas County Sentinel,** (770) 942-6571; **Fulton County Daily Report** (for Atlanta's legal, business, and political communities), (404) 521-1227; **Gwinnett Daily Post,** (770) 963-9205; **Marietta Daily Journal,** (770) 795-3000; **Rockdale Citizen,** (770) 483-7108.

Popular neighborhood papers include *The Community Review,* (404) 371-8878 and the many weekly **Neighbor** newspapers, covering the metro area, (770) 795-3000.

Two popular weekly newspapers are **Creative Loafing,** (404) 688-5623 and **Atlanta Press,** (404) 614-1259, and the city magazine is *Atlanta* Magazine, (404) 872-3100. For foreign publications in Atlanta see the SPECIAL PEOPLE chapter.

Business news is focused on in the newspaper *The Atlanta Business Chronicle* (404) 249-1000; and the magazine *Georgia Trend* (770) 931-9410.

Pets

Laws require annual rabies vaccination for pets by a licensed veterinarian. Pets must be confined to owner's property except when on a leash. Dogs running at large will be picked up by the Animal Control Unit, and the owner fined.

Public Services

City of Atlanta Public Services are supplied by the following:

Electric: Georgia Power Co.; (888) 660-5890.
Natural Gas: Several companies provide natural gas. Call the Public Service Commission at (404) 656-4501 for a list.
Telephone: Bell South Telephone Co.; (404) 780-2355.
Water: United Water Services; (404) 658-6500.
Garbage Collection: City of Atlanta Solid Waste Services; (404) 330-6250. Free curbside garbage pickup is once a week. The City will provide each residence with a free "Herbie Curbie" container on wheels.

Metro Public Services. If you are relocating outside the city limits of Atlanta, check with the specific county or municipality to establish the essential services.

Cherokee County	(770) 479-1953
Clayton County	(770) 473-3900
Cobb County	(770) 423-1000
DeKalb County	(404) 371-2000
Fayette County	(770) 460-5730
Forsyth County	(770) 781-2160
Fulton County	(404) 730-4000
Gwinnett County	(770) 822-8000
Rockdale County	(770) 929-4000

Often your real estate company or apartment manager will have this information for you.

Taxes

Individual Income Tax

Georgia requires a tax on all sources of income unless they are exempt by statute. Employers are required to withhold state income tax for both resident and nonresident employees.

Property Tax

Property taxes in metro Atlanta vary by county and municipality. There are various homestead exemptions in different areas. Call your local tax commissioners.

Atlanta . . . . (404) 730-6100
Fulton . . . . (404) 730-6100
Clayton . . . . (770) 477-3311
Cobb . . . . (770) 528-8600
DeKalb . . . . (404) 298-4000
Gwinnett . . . . (770) 822-8800
Fayette . . . . (770) 461-3611
Forsyth . . . . (770) 781-2110
Henry . . . . (770) 954-2470
Paulding . . . . (770) 443-7581
Rockdale . . . . (770) 929-4025

Sales and Use Tax

A state and county sales and use tax is added to all retail purchases, rentals, uses, and consumption of tangible goods, personal property, and special services. This tax throughout most of metro Atlanta is either 6 or 7 percent.

TV and Radio

Atlanta is the headquarters of a national broadcasting company, Turner Broadcasting System and its Cable News Network. See MATTERS OF FACT chapter for complete TV and radio listings.

Volunteering

People who wish to volunteer their time and talents should call **United Way Volunteer Center,** 100 Edgewood Ave., NE; (404) 614-1000 or simply dial 211. Many arts organizations also need volunteers. Call the group of your choice.

Voting

Voter Registration

To vote in city, county, state, and federal elections, you must be a U.S. citizen, be at least 18 years old (17 1/2 to register), be mentally sound, and not be under conviction of a felony. You must be a legal resident of the state and county.

Voter registration forms are available at libraries, city halls, and county courthouses. You may also register when getting your driver's license, applying for Medicaid, and in other locations. Deadline for registration is the 5th Monday before a general primary, general election or presidential preference primary. Dates will vary for special elections.

To transfer your registration from another county in Georgia, apply to the local Voter Registrar's office.

To keep your registration current, you must vote at least once every three years in a primary or in a general election. However, if your registration is canceled, you will be given an opportunity to reregister.

For information about local elections, call your city or county government in your new area. The League of Women Voters is also helpful; (404) 874-7352. For your convenience we list the following political party headquarters in Atlanta.

Democratic Party of Georgia, 1100 Spring St., NW, Suite 710, Atlanta 30309; (404) 885-1998.

Republican Party of Georgia, 5600 Roswell Rd., NE, East Bldg., Suite 200, Atlanta 30342; (404) 257-5559.

ATLANTA REAL ESTATE

An Overview

Atlanta has been on a continuous residential building program with new subdivisions rising among the pine-covered hills and hardwood forests of the surrounding counties. The Metropolitan Statistical Area (MSA) of Atlanta defined by the U.S. Office of Management and Budget now includes a 20-county complex influenced by and relying upon the Central City that is its economic base.

This MSA total population grew nearly 32 percent between 1990 and 2000 for a total of more than 3.8 million people. In the same period, the outlying counties of Fayette, Gwinnett, and Cherokee increased by roughly 56%, 62%, and 53% respectively. The Home Builders Association of Atlanta reports a more than 150% increase in residential construction permits in the past decade. Multi-family construction jumped 85% between 1998 and 1999 alone. Per capita personal income has also grown—more than 60% since 1990. Employment increased nearly 40%, and nearly 600,000 new jobs were created during the ten years. Obviously, Metro Atlanta continues to thrive

Multiple forms of housing are available, from executive-style dwellings on estate-size lots to modest starter homes, cluster homes, town homes, high-rise condominiums, and high-rise and garden apartments. There are places to live in every price range and in every location—intown, midtown, uptown, and in every quadrant of the metro area.

The suburban spread has reached as far as Peachtree City in Fayette County to the shores of Lake Lanier in Forsyth County, from Crabapple in the north end of Fulton County to beyond Stone Mountain in DeKalb County. Development has followed GA 400 and I-575 north of Atlanta into Forsyth and Cherokee counties and beyond. And the expressway convenience of GA 316 has created a building boom in Lawrenceville and the far reaches of Gwinnett County.

The older City of Atlanta has spruced up its intown neighborhoods, adding to the National Register of Historic Districts the areas of Druid Hills, Inman Park, Ansley Park, Grant Park, and others.

Styles of housing are mixed with a recent revival of Williamsburg and Victorian traditions in both cluster developments and single homes.

Information and Referrals

The **Boards of Realtors** have information about residential property and realtors in the metro area.

Atlanta	(404) 250-0051
Clayton	(770) 477-7579
Cobb	(770) 422-3900
DeKalb	(770) 493-6100
Fayette	(770) 461-2401
Gwinnett	(770) 963-3253
Rockdale	(770) 922-3039

Other sources include the **Home Builders Association, Inc.-Greater Atlanta,** (770) 938-9900, and the **Georgia Association of Realtors,** (770) 451-1831.

Buying and Renting ─────────────────

Consider the many variables that confront you whether you are seeking a home purchase or a rental unit. The proximity of your housing to your place of employment is important. Since Atlanta is still a "car" town, in spite of its excellent rapid rail and bus mass transit system, the school district, the location of private schools, and cultural and recreational facilities figure in as well. Look at the financial considerations such as tax structure (remember that metro Atlanta is made up of a number of small counties, each with its own tax structure; be aware in your house hunting when you cross county lines), cost of improvements and utilities, and insurance rates. And finally, feel comfortable in the neighborhood of your choice.

Regional and Neighborhood Profiles ──────

The following is an analysis of some of Atlanta's most recognized neighborhoods to facilitate your choice and introduce you to the many possibilities for settling in. Most civic associations have newsletters; ask your real estate agent to make these available to you. You can sense the spirit of the neighborhoods from these publications along with your inspection of houses, condominiums, and apartments.

MARTA public transportation is available to all parts of the city within the perimeter, and beyond to Dunwoody, Sandy Springs, Roswell, Alpharetta, Chamblee, Tucker, Stone Mountain, Fairburn, and the Six Flags area. Cobb County is served by Cobb Community Transit buses, which link up with the MARTA rail system at the Arts Center station. Presently, Gwinnett County is not served by public transportation. Check with MARTA route and schedule information, (404) 848-4711; or Cobb Community Transit (CCT), (770) 427-4444.

Intown Neighborhoods ─────────────────

The following are renovated neighborhoods less than 20 minutes from Downtown in rush hour.

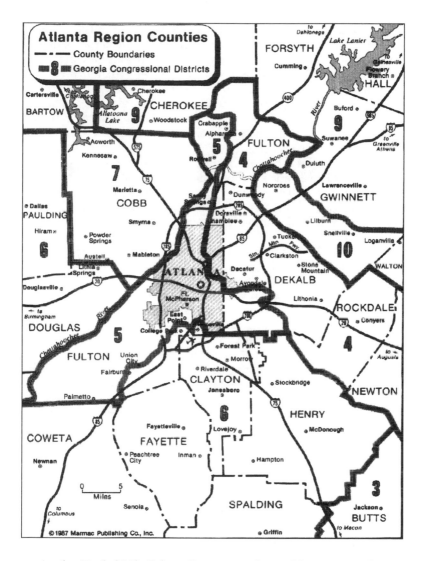

Ansley Park (C3), Fulton County, is a beautiful intown professional neighborhood of restored homes dating from the early 1900s and four interior parks, one with tennis courts. Ansley Park is now on the National Register of Historic Districts and has a very active and influential civic association. The public gardens of Ansley Park have received national awards.

Cascade Heights (D3), Fulton County. Cascade Heights has been a favorite residential area for prominent members of the black community. Luxury homes are featured on ample lots and the area is convenient to the Atlanta University complex and downtown Atlanta.

Grant Park (D3), Fulton County, was named an Historic District by the City of Atlanta in April 2000. Many of its frame Victorian homes have been restored. The Atlanta zoo and the Cyclorama are centered in Grant Park itself, and the neighborhood is a mix of young professionals and old-time residents.

Inman Park (D4), Fulton County, showcases Atlanta's Victorian homes, the original residences of some of the city's prominent early families. Inman Park was Atlanta's first suburb, attached by streetcar to downtown Atlanta. This historic district takes great pride in its neighborhood festivals and continuing restoration. Take Edgewood Avenue east from Downtown.

Midtown (C3), Fulton County, is an area of arbored streets, large, small, and multiple family homes and apartments. Midtown is bounded by Ponce de Leon on the south, 10th Street on the north, Peachtree on the west, and Monroe Drive on the east. Numerous new "old-style" condominiums and town houses stand beside original homes from the turn of the century.

Morningside (C4), Fulton County, is an area of homes from the 1920s, ranging in size from bungalows to large mock-Tudor residences. There are interior parks with playgrounds and tennis courts. The Morningside-Lenox Park Association is active in grounds beautification and neighborhood political and social life.

Virginia-Highland (C4), Fulton County. The bungalow-style home from the early 20th century is still alive and well in this neighborhood. The intersection of its two namesakes, Virginia and Highland Avenues, has become one of the most popular places for small restaurant dining in the city. It's a low-key area of artists, professional folks, and entrepreneurs who understand the beauty of village-living in a city.

West End (D3), Fulton County, is an old Atlanta neighborhood in a predominantly black community. Restoration of homes is well under way, rendering the community a model of revived Victorian charm. MARTA trains service the area into Downtown.

Buckhead Neighborhoods

Brookwood Hills (C3), Fulton County. Brookwood Hills is a small residential area of fine older homes in a beautiful rolling, wooded section. The neighborhood has its own pool and tennis courts and has walking access to the galleries, eateries, and service stores in Brookwood Village on Peachtree Street.

Collier Hills (C3), Fulton County, is built around the famous Memorial Park at Peachtree Battle Creek. The houses are small, gracefully sited on the hills and in the dells. This is a community where young professionals make their first house purchase and where others return in later life because of the intown convenience and lower maintenance of small residences.

Garden Hills (B3), Fulton County. Homes are generally small and charming, nestled in the wooded terrain of the area. Garden Hills is bounded by Lindberg Drive on the south and Pharr Road on the north, Piedmont on the east, and Peachtree on the west.

Peachtree Battle to Northside (C3-B2), Fulton County. From Peachtree Battle extending west and northwest to the Chattahoochee River is one of Atlanta's most celebrated residential areas. Large estate homes, including the Georgia Governor's Mansion, rest on imposing properties with long lawns and immaculate landscaping. Northside is the high school. The Bobby Jones public golf course and the Bitsy Grant tennis center afford excellent recreational opportunities.

Peachtree Hills (C3), Fulton County. This cozy neighborhood of small houses and apartments has the advantage of the Peachtree Battle Shopping Center on the west with its neighborhood eateries, boutiques, and shops. The city has a recreation center with multiple tennis courts in Peachtree Hills across from the Atlanta Decorative Arts Center's massive complex on the east side. The Lindberg MARTA station serves the area.

Cobb County Communities

Marietta (A1), East Cobb County, is a thriving area with fine condominiums and apartments and new exquisite home communities. Simultaneously, the restored town square in Marietta is a hub of civic and business activity. Dobbins Air Force Base and Lockheed are two large employers in the area. Marietta continues to grow, boosted by I-575 and Town Center Mall to the north and a strong development push into once-rural West Cobb.

Powder Springs, western Cobb County, is a fast-growing community that was not long ago a sleepy country town. The area has become a magnet for new residents who enjoy the convenience of I-20 into Atlanta and easy access to Atlanta Airport. A wide variety of new homes is available, yet Powder Springs itself keeps its small-town charm.

Vinings (B2), East Cobb County, has been discovered by more and more folks in East Cobb. This tiny crossroads of antique shops, an inn, and a convenience store is now growing up. Beautiful tracts have residential development down to the river and attractive cluster homes, condos and apartments appeal to singles and couples. Nearby Cumberland Mall and the Galleria provide exceptional shopping.

North Fulton, Cherokee County Communities ─────────

Alpharetta, North Fulton County. A fast-developing rural community, convenient to U.S. 400 and the Perimeter complexes. Windward, a vast, award-winning development of attractive homes, offices and retail businesses, golf, tennis, and a lake, has spurred rapid growth in this beautiful area.

Crabapple, North Fulton County. In rolling hills and spacious pastures, fine old houses and picturesque horse farms are interspersed with new subdivisions. Built around a few stores and antique shops, this is the center of metro Atlanta's "horse country."

Roswell, North Fulton County, is another antebellum town, which used to be considered outside of Atlanta's sphere of influence. No longer. Roswell's town space offers fine shopping and dining, and urbanites have found the charm of restoring frame houses, while developers have prospered with swim-and-tennis residential subdivisions and townhome communities.

Sandy Springs (A3), North Fulton County, is the oldest and most established perimeter community, spreading from both sides of Roswell Road into forested areas of single-family homes, apartments, and town houses. Sandy Springs is the suburbs at its best, with the convenience of shopping at nearby Perimeter Mall and Park Place. In the posh Mt. Paran Road area, homes often sell in the multi-millions.

Woodstock, Cherokee County, has exploded into a full-fledged suburban community in only the past few years. Towne Lake, a massive subdivision on the Cobb-Cherokee line, is responsible for much of the growth.

DeKalb County Communities ─────────

Decatur (C4), DeKalb County, is an incorporated city whose history predates Atlanta. The MARTA East Line ends in adjacent Avondale Estates, which makes the six- to eight-mile commute ideal. Lovely homes, town houses, and apartments are available for a relaxed small town life-style, only a stone's throw from Atlanta. Decatur has seen dramatic growth in downtown business development since 1995 but has done a remarkable job of preserving its small-town ambience. Agnes Scott College is a central part of the Decatur scene.

Druid Hills (C4), DeKalb County, is the neighborhood of Emory University professionals and students, a lush district originally designed by Frederick Law Olmstead at the turn of the century and popularized as the setting of the play and movie *Driving Miss Daisy*. This historic district has handsome English Tudor architecture. A prime example is the Candler mansion, now the Callanwolde Arts Center, a focal point of cultural events in the neighborhood and the city.

Dunwoody (A4), North DeKalb County, a favorite residential area for corporate moves, has the Williamsburg look, with even the Dunwoody Village à la Williamsburg. Dunwoody's prominence nationwide was saluted by the Rand McNally rating as the number-one suburb in the United States. The luxury homes are spacious, the natural landscape is respected and enhanced by plantings, with many elegant communities fronting the river. Perimeter Mall and the office complexes nearby make this an ideal area for corporate executives.

Lithonia, DeKalb County, was not long ago a small town far from Atlanta's influence. Lately the area has enjoyed new growth and popularity as a community chosen by many young, black, professional families.

Stone Mountain (C6), DeKalb County, is beyond the perimeter to the east of Atlanta. This older community has taken on the restored loveliness of the original village. With the impressive form of Stone Mountain as backdrop, the village affords comfortable living in the frame houses and apartments with full amenities.

Tucker (B5), DeKalb County, is an established community of homes in the medium price range, served by convenient shopping centers that include popular Northlake Mall. Main Street in Tucker is a charming restored center, and the convenience of MARTA bus service also attracts residents.

South Metro Atlanta Communities ———

East Point, College Park, Hapeville (E2), South Fulton and Clayton counties. These are three longtime Atlanta communities located in the Atlanta airport area, catering to airport personnel and business. First-time home buyers are beginning to gravitate to the modest but solid homes, which are more affordable than in many areas north of Atlanta and offer a reasonable commuting time.

Peachtree City, Fayette County. Peachtree City is an award-winning planned community south of Atlanta at Georgia Highways 74 and 54. The condominiums and single-family homes are designed around five villages, all connected by paths for the golf carts that are residents' main mode of transportation within Peachtree City. Full recreational amenities and a school system through high school serve some 33,500 residents. Built with private funds, Peachtree City has been recognized by the *Ladies' Home Journal* as one of the finest planned communities in the United States.

Gwinnett County, Forsyth County and Lake Lanier Communities

Duluth, Norcross, Gwinnett County, represent posh suburbia and are growing fast. Close to GA 400, their rolling hills are green with country club golf courses. Homes are gracefully traditional. Norcross has attracted many of Atlanta's high-tech industries to its well-planned business and office parks.

Lawrenceville, Gwinnett County, was recently a bustling town outside Atlanta's sphere. The county seat of Gwinnett, Lawrenceville is now sprouting subdivisions faster than daisies in the field. GA 316 links the community to I-85 and puts residents just a few minutes from Atlanta's northern perimeter.

Lilburn, Gwinnett County, is just over the DeKalb-Gwinnett county line. Its moderately priced homes combine convenience with suburban amenities.

Snellville, Gwinnett County, is another little town turned suburb. Snellville enjoys good schools and is flanked by two attractive country clubs. It consistently ranks as one of the safest communities in which to live.

Lake Lanier area, Gwinnett, Forsyth, Hall counties. Since the early 1960s this man-made lake with more than 500 miles of shoreline has always been popular as a second-home area and is now a thriving primary living area, with route 400 and I-85 making commuting easy into north Atlanta. The country living and accessibility to lake recreation are great drawing cards to the communities of Buford and Cumming. Many lakefront homes are the latest in luxury.

Counties Beyond

Paulding, Douglas, Henry, Butts, Rockdale, Pickens and **Newton** counties are now part of the MSA of Atlanta, which has grown to 20 counties from its original five—Fulton, DeKalb, Cobb, Gwinnett, and Clayton. These outlying counties are actually close in for commuters to jobs along Atlanta's I-285 perimeter or beyond.

In conclusion, living and working in metro Atlanta can occur with commuting in either direction or living near one's place of work. Take your pick.

HOME AND GARDEN SHOPPING NEEDS

These author's choices will get you started. Many of these listings have several locations.

Air Conditioning Repairs—Estes Heating and Air Conditioning; (404) 366-9620.

Appliance Repairs—City Used Appliances; (404) 659-1403.

Auto Repairs—Jordan's Garage; (404) 688-3491. Or see your car dealer.

Blinds and Shades—American Sun Control; (770) 476-8600.

Building Materials—Home Depot; (404) 231-1411.

Carpet and Rug Cleaning—Sharian; (404) 373-2274.

Doors—Peachtree Doors; (770) 497-2000.

Electrical Repairs—Benedict Electric Co.; (404) 292-4113.

Furniture Rentals—Aaron Rental Purchase; (404) 289-8900.

Furniture Repairs and Upholstery—Trinity Furniture Shops; (770) 482-1133.

Glass (Auto and Home—Mirrors)—Automobile Glass Co.; (404) 881-0443.

Home Accessories—See "Home Interiors" under SHOPPING.

Landscaping Nursery—Pike Family Nurseries, (404) 634-8604; Hastings Nature & Garden Center, (404)869-7447; The Urban Gardener, (404) 529-9980.

Leather Cleaning—Ram Leather & Fur Care; (770) 483-3454.

Locks—Bullards Lockmaster and Safe Co.; (404) 876-1267.

Painting, Residential—Your Personal Painter William, (404) 346-9413; Crouch Painting, (404) 634-0642.

Paintings Restored—Reinike Gallery; (404) 364-0490.

Pest Control—York Pest Control; (770) 875-7137.

Picture Frames—House of Frames, (770) 422-5225; O'Karma Jones, (404) 874-9461.

Plaster Moldings and Character Items—House Parts; (404) 577-5584.

Plumbing—M. Cary & Daughters Plumbing Contractors; (404) 622-6192.

Pool Services—Atlas Pools & Spas; (770) 451-3700.

Remodeling—Sawhorse, Inc.; (404) 256-2567.

Rentals (tools, machines, clearing equipment)—Northside Tool Rental; (404) 233-6722.

Silver Repair (also brass, gold)—Estes-Simmons Silverplating; (404) 875-9581.

Stained Glass—Jennifer's Glassworks; (404) 355-3080.

LET'S HAVE A PARTY

You're here, you're settled, you want to celebrate your good fortune at having shed your "newcomer" status and having become simply an Atlantan. Why not try something different for that special occasion? Whether you're on a shoestring budget or have the champagne corks popping, why not try something typically "Atlanta"? Let us make a few wild and wonderful suggestions. Or if you want to hire some creative talent to organize your party, call in a professional party planner, like **Fun Services,** at (404) 321-0293.

Buy the Bus

Ever wanted to just get on a bus and ask your friends to go along for the ride? **MARTA** will do it for a price. You bring the drinks and goodies and plan the route. See you at the bus stop. MARTA Customer Services; (404) 848-4800.

Caterers

With the city's temperate year-round climate, Atlantans are devotees of picnics and outdoor suppers with musical entertainment. Even in bad weather, party-givers like to put out special spreads of foods and wines. A number of catering firms around the metro area prepare picnic baskets for concerts in Chastain Park, and complete luncheons and suppers for your own dinner table at home. These may range from a traditional Southern picnic with fried chicken and potato salad, to Mediterranean hummus and tabbouli; French and Italian cheeses and seafood salads to London broil, rice pilaf, and chocolate mousse. Call or drop by one of these Atlanta firms.

Affairs to Remember (H12), 680 Ponce de Leon Ave., NE; (404) 872-7859.

Basket Bakery at the Village Corner (C6), 6655 Memorial Dr., Stone Mountain; (770) 498-0329.

Collard Green Cafe (C4), 2746 Clairmont Rd., NE; (404) 634-3440.
EatZi's (B3), 3221 Peachtree Rd.; (404) 237-8646.
Food Among the Flowers (C3), 869 Greenwood Ave., Virginia-Highland; (404) 881-0372.
Margie's Pantry (C4), 653 East Lake Dr., Decatur; (404) 377-3818.
Tuohy's Catering (C3), 442 Armour Circle, NE; (404) 875-3885.
Palace Catering (C4), 2881 N. Druid Hills Rd., NE; (404) 315-9017.
Proof of the Pudding by MGR (C3), 2033 Monroe Dr. NE; (404) 892-2359.
Ya Ya's Cajun Cuisine (C4), (404) 373-9292.

A Christmas Cutting

Have a family party or put together your favorite families to cut your own Christmas tree. The *Atlanta Journal-Constitution* publishes a list in late November or early December of Christmas tree farms within an hour's drive of metro Atlanta. So does the **Georgia Farmers and Consumers Market Bulletin**, available free from the Georgia Department of Agriculture; (404) 656-3722. Choose your tree farm, pack some hot drinks and sandwiches or stop over at a restaurant on the way, and toast bringing home the tree.

Fox Holes

For all you big spenders, contemplate a takeover of the **Fox Theatre.** Maybe the Egyptian Ballroom or the Moorish Grand Salon. Bring in your caterers, bring in your guests, and fill up the holes with a giant party to end all parties. The Fox Theatre; (404) 881-2100.

A Garden for All Seasons

The **Atlanta Botanical Garden** is the perfect setting for your next garden party outdoors. Expand your guest list, hire a caterer, and schedule your time to expose your guests to one of the most beautiful nature spots right in the heart of the city. Atlanta Botanical Garden; (404) 876-5858.

Kids' Time Out

For something different, try pony rides either at your home or at the

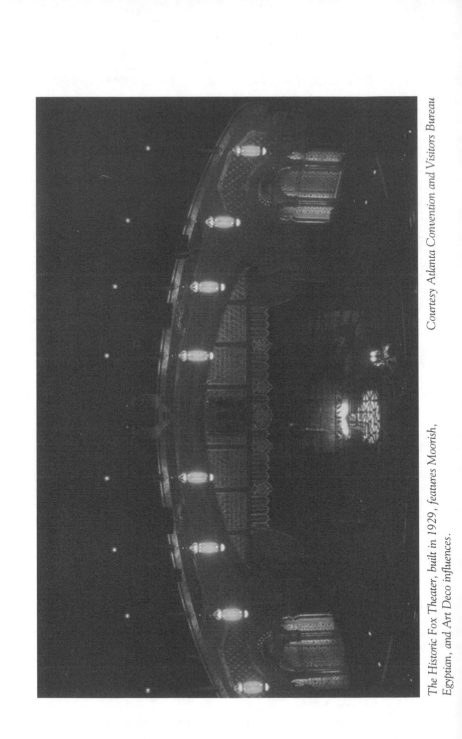

The Historic Fox Theater, built in 1929, features Moorish, Egyptian, and Art Deco influences.

Courtesy Atlanta Convention and Visitors Bureau

stables. Four ponies and two stable hands will be provided by **Briarcliff Stables & Pony Parties**; (770) 475-4761.

Mind Your Manors ────────────

The fine English Tudor manor house built in the roaring twenties by Charles Howard Candler will host a music concert, a festive ball, or catered dinner in one of the many rooms available. **Callanwolde Fine Arts Center**; (404) 872-5338.

Or rent the **Howard School** mansion, a turn-of-the-century classic design by Neil Reid on Ponce de Leon Avenue. The Howard School; (404) 377-7436.

Or rent the **Druid Hills Golf Club,** built just after the turn of the century for the recreational enjoyment of then-suburban Atlanta; (404) 377-1766.

Paddleboat Party ────────────

Stone Mountain Park has the boat on the water—all aboard for a **Henry W. Grady Riverboat** ride and a meal catered by the Stone Mountain Inn. What a great party for 150 or a cruise for 300 guests. Stone Mountain Park; (770) 498-5600.

SPECIAL PEOPLE

THE INTERNATIONAL VISITOR

International visitors from all the continents of the world arrive daily in Atlanta, the historic gateway to the southern United States. The city has transformed herself into an international center. The Atlanta Hartsfield International Airport welcomes the foreign traveler in its separate international concourse with full immigration and customs facilities.

Consulates and ethnic societies in Atlanta have multiplied rapidly during the last decade as global economics, politics, and cultural exchange have interlaced the peoples of the world. We list aids and resources for international visitors and new residents in Atlanta, beginning with the consulates, trade offices, and ethnic societies.

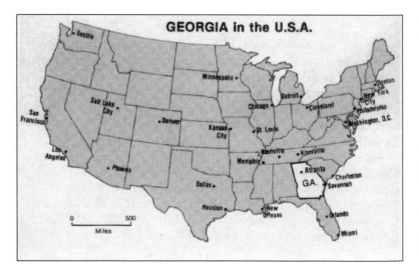

Georgia Council for International Visitors (H11), 34 Peachtree St., NE, Suite 1200, Atlanta 30303; (404) 832-5560. This fine group will help you secure translators from their language bank of more than 50 languages, introduce you to ethnic groups in the city, exchange and be an overall resource center for professional and emergency services. The council is responsible for the programming of official international visitors to the city. Mon-Fri from 9 am-5 pm; after-hours callers can leave messages.

Atlanta International Hostel (H11), 229 Ponce de Leon Ave., NE; (404) 875-2882. Atlanta member of the International Youth Hostel Federation, the Atlanta International Youth Hostel has about 90 beds at hostel rates for college-age international travelers.

Woodruff Bed and Breakfast Inn (I11), 223 Ponce de Leon Ave., NE; (404) 875-9449. This bed and breakfast inn, next door to and affiliated with the Atlanta International Hostel, provides lodging for adult international visitors.

Villa International. See STUDENTS section.

Consulates, Trade and Tourism Offices —

For additional information on consulates and foreign trade and tourism offices in Atlanta, call the Georgia Department of Industry, Trade and Tourism, (404) 656-3571, or the Atlanta Chamber of Commerce, (404) 880-9000.

Argentina, Consulate General of Argentina, 245 Peachtree Center Ave., (404) 880-0805.

Australia, Consulate General of Australia, 3060 Peachtree Rd., NW; (404) 760-3402.

Austria, Consulate of Austria, 4200 Northside Parkway, NW; (404) 264-9858.

Austria, The Austrian Trade Commission, 4200 Northside Parkway, NW; (404) 995-9347.

Belgium, Consulate General of Belgium, 235 Peachtree St., NE; (404) 659-2150.

Belgium, The Flemish Foreign Trade Board, 235 Peachtree St., NE; (404) 659-9611.

Belgium, Walloon Foreign Trade Board, 235 Peachtree St., NE; (404) 584-2002.

Bolivia, Consulate of Bolivia, 1401 Peachtree St., (404) 522-0777.

Canada, Canadian Consulate General, 1175 Peachtree St., NE; (404) 532-2000.

Chile, Consulate of Chile, 2876 Sequoyah Dr., NW; (404) 355-7923.

Colombia, Consulate of Colombia, 5780 Peachtree Dunwoody Rd., (404) 237-1045.

Costa Rica, Consulate General of Costa Rica, 1870 The Exchange, Ste. 100, (770) 951-7025.

Cyprus, Republic of, Consulate of the Republic of Cyprus, 895 Somerset Drive, (770) 941-3764.

Czech Republic, Consulate of the Czech Republic, 2110 Powers Ferry Rd., Ste. 220, (770) 859-9402.

Denmark, Consulate of Denmark, 1100 Spring St., NW; (404) 876-5511.

Denmark, Danish Trade Commission, 285 Peachtree Center Ave., (404) 588-1588.

Dominican Republic, Consulate of the Dominican Republic, 191 Peachtree St., 46th Floor, (404) 572-4814.

Finland, Honorary Consulate of Finland, 1230 Peachtree Rd., NE; (404) 815-3682.

France, Consulate General of France, 285 Peachtree Center Ave., NE; (404) 522-4226.

France, French Trade Commission, 285 Peachtree Center Ave., NE; (404) 522-4843.

Germany, Federal Republic of, Consulate General of the Federal Republic of Germany, 285 Peachtree Center Ave., NE; (404) 659-4760.

United Kingdom of Great Britain & Northern Ireland, British Consulate General, 245 Peachtree Center Ave., NE; (404) 524-5856.

Greece, Consulate of Greece, 3340 Peachtree Rd., NE; (404) 261-3313.

Guatemala, Consulate of Guatemala, 4772 East Conway Dr., NW; (404) 255-7019.

Honduras, Consulate of Honduras, 3091 Chaparral Pl., (770) 482-1332.

Iceland, Consulate of Iceland, 20 Executive Park West, (404) 321-0777.

Ireland, Consulate of Ireland, 3200 Arden Road, NW; (404) 332-6401.

Israel, Consulate General of Israel, 1100 Spring St., NW; (404) 487-6500.

Israel Economic Mission, 1100 Spring St., NW, (404) 724-0830.

Italy, Consulate of Italy, 755 Mount Vernon Hwy., (404) 303-0503.

Italy, Italian Trade Commission, 233 Peachtree St., NE; (404) 525-0660.

Jamaica, Consulate of Jamaica, 950 E. Paces Ferry Rd., Ste. 1900, (404) 398-6168.

Japan, Consulate General of Japan, 100 Colony Square, Ste. 2000, (404) 892-2700.

Korea, Republic of, Consulate General of the Republic of Korea, 229 Peachtree St., NE; (404) 522-1611.

Liberia, Consulate General of Liberia, 2265 Cascade Rd., SW; (404) 753-4753.

Luxembourg, Grand Duchy of, Consulate of Luxembourg, 1230 Peachtree Rd., (404) 815-3762.

Mexico, Consulate General of Mexico, 2600 Apple Valley Rd., (404) 266-2233.

Mexico, Trade Commission of Mexico, 229 Peachtree St., NE; (404) 522-5373.

The Netherlands, Consulate of the Netherlands, 2015 South Park Place, (770) 937-7123.

New Zealand, Honorary Consulate of New Zealand, 75 14th St., Ste. 3000, (404) 888-5123.

Nicaragua, Consulate of the Republic of Nicaragua, 3161 Lemons Ridge, (770) 319-1673.

Nigeria, Consulate General of Nigeria, 4488 Shallowford Rd., (770) 821-5362.

Norway, Royal Norwegian Consulate, 3715 Northside Pkwy., (404) 239-0885.

Panama Consulate General of Panama, 229 Peachtree St., NE; (404) 522-4114.

Peru, Consulate of Peru, P.O. Box 831231, Stone Mountain, GA 30083; (404) 299-8234.

Philippines, Consulate of the Philippines, 950 East Paces Ferry Rd., (404) 233-9916.

Romania, Consulate of Romania, 3481 Washington Way, (770) 634-4814.

Sao Tome and Principe, Republic of, Consulate of Sao Tome & Principe, 512 Means St., Ste. 305, (404) 221-0203.

Senegal, Consulate of Senegal, 830 Westview Dr., SW; (404) 614-6040.

Sierra Leone, Republic of, Consulate of Sierra Leone, P.O. Box 831981, Stone Mountain, GA 30083; (404) 292-2009.

Slovenia, Republic of, Honorary Consulate of Slovenia, 55 South Prado, NE; (404) 815-1068.

Spain, Consulate of Spain, 1010 Huntcliff, Ste. 2315, (770) 518-2406.

Sri Lanka, Honorary Consulate of Sri Lanka, One Atlantic Center, (404) 881-7164.

Sweden, Royal Swedish Consulate, 2500 Cumberland Pkwy, Ste. 210, (770) 431-3300.

Switzerland, Consulate General of Switzerland, 1275 Peachtree St., NE; (404) 870-2000.

Taiwan, Republic of China Coordination Council, 233 Peachtree St., NE; (404) 522-0481.

Thailand, Royal Thai Consulate Office, 3333 Cumberland Cir., Ste. 400, (770) 988-3304.

Turkey, Consulate General of Turkey, 7155 Brandon Mill Rd., (770) 913-0900.

United States of America, Atlanta Consular Corps, 229 Peachtree St., NE; (404) 659-7560.

Ethnic Societies

Many of these societies or groups are run by individuals from their homes, so keep calling if there is no answer.

China: World Journal Chinese Bookstore, (770) 451-4628.
Finland: Atlanta Suomi-Finland Society, (404) 231-5160.
France: Alliance Française d'Atlanta, (404) 875-1211.
Germany: Goethe Institute of Atlanta, (404) 892-2388.
Greece: Greek Orthodox Cathedral of the Annunciation, (404) 633-5870.
India: India Cultural and Religious Center, (770) 436-3719.

Japan: Japan-America Society of Georgia, (404) 524-7399.
Korea: Korean Association of Greater Atlanta, (770) 263-1888.
Latin-American Countries: Latin American Association, (404) 638-1800; (770) 420-6556.
Liberia: Liberian Community Association, (404) 292-9361; (770) 908-3978.
Norway: VASA Order of America, Nordic Lodge, (770) 977-7629.
Philippines: Filipino-American Association of Greater Atlanta, (770) 279-4969.
Scotland: Burns Club of Atlanta, (404) 627-2941.
Sweden: VASA Order of America, Nordic Lodge, (404) 633-7733.
United Kingdom: Daughters of the British Empire, (770) 541-1959.
Vietnam: Our Lady of Vietnam Catholic Church, (770) 471-8453.

Many other groups help international newcomers to Atlanta, often providing language classes, computer classes, job placement, help with Social Security, and other transition assistance. Some are listed here:

Bridging the Gap Project, (404) 872-9400.
Christian Council of Metro Atlanta, (404) 622-2235.
Georgia Mutual Assistance Association, (404) 296-5400.
International Rescue Committee, (404) 292-7731.
Newcomers Network, (404) 299-6265; (404) 299-6217.

Bank Hours

Atlanta's banking hours are generally weekdays from 9 am to 4 pm, although some banks' branch locations are open on Saturday mornings as well. Some of the grocery chains have bank branches inside their larger stores, for example Publix has SunTrust and Kroger's has Bank of America. Many of these branches are open until 8 pm on weekdays and 6 pm on Sat.

Currency Exchange and International Banking

Always try to exchange foreign currency in a bank, which will offer you the most competitive rate. However, after hours the cashier in the major hotels will be able to change money.

International banking services available in Atlanta include, as well as purchase and sale of foreign currencies and foreign travelers' checks, cable transfers, foreign drafts on overseas banks, foreign collections, import/export financing, acceptance financing, and issue of commercial letters of credit. The following banks are at your service; all have numerous other locations.

Bank of America (I10), Bank of America Plaza, 600 Peachtree St., NW; (404) 607-4850.

Bank South (K9), International Banking Dept., 55 Marietta St., 12th Floor; (404) 529-4817.

First Union (J9), 55 Park Place; (404) 865-3410.

SouthTrust Bank (J9), 230 Peachtree St., NW; (404) 222-6920.

SunTrust Bank (J9), International Division, 1 Park Place, 10th Floor; (404) 586-6405.

Wachovia (K8), International Banking Division, Main Banking Floor, 2 Peachtree St., NE; (404) 865-4000.

These international banks have offices in Atlanta: Bank Austria Credit Anstalt, the Bank of Nova Scotia, the Bank of Tokyo-Mitsubishi, Ltd., Canadian Imperial Bank, Commerzbank (German), Credit Lyonnais (French), Credit Suisse First Boston(Swiss), Industrial Bank of Japan, Ltd., Sakura Bank, Societe Generale (French), Summit National Bank (Japanese owned).

Customs Allowances

You are allowed to bring into the United States from overseas the following purchases duty free:

One liter of alcoholic beverages; 100 cigars; 200 cigarettes. Be aware, however, that state liquor laws supersede the national regulations.

There is a personal exemption of $400 for returning U.S. residents, $100 for visitors; over this amount the next $1,000 in goods is charged at a flat rate of 10%.

Gifts that are mailed to the U.S. under the value of $100 are duty free; over that amount the recipient will be charged duty.

Driving

Driving in the United States is in the right lane. An international driver's license should be secured through your local automobile association before you leave home. U.S. gallons of gasoline are one-fifth smaller than the United Kingdom's imperial gallon. Gasoline stations along the highways are generally open on weekends or in the evenings, and some remain open 24 hours—watch for signs.

The 55 m.p.h. speed limit is observed and enforced by the use of police radar observation. In some sections of the interstate system, you are allowed to drive 65 m.p.h. Watch for signs. In Georgia you are allowed to turn right, after stopping, at a red traffic light except where posted. The law dictates that you must turn your headlights on when it is raining and call the police immediately when you have an accident. Seat belts must be worn and children under four must be in authorized car seats at all times.

Electricity

110 volts 60 cycles AC. Bring an adapter for your razor or hair dryer.

International Publications and Newspapers

The stores listed are in the downtown area. If you are staying near an ethnic neighborhood, local stores may have foreign newspapers published in the U.S. in a foreign language.

Atlanta-Fulton Public Library (J9), 1 Margaret Mitchell Square, corner Forsyth and Carnegie Way; (404) 730-1700. Newspapers and magazines from most countries. Books: fiction, nonfiction, and dictionaries in most languages.

Eastern Newsstand (J9), Peachtree Center Shopping Gallery, 1st floor, 231 Peachtree St.; (404) 659-5670. Open Mon-Sat. Newspapers: German. Magazines: French, German, Italian.

Georgia State University Library (K9), Washington and Gilmer Sts., accessible from Washington St. into university courtyard; (404) 651-2199. Open to guests. Most foreign newspapers and magazines are available at Georgia State. A list is on the wall as you enter.

International newspapers and magazines in Atlanta include:
Atlanta Chinese News, (770) 455-0880
Korea Times, (770) 458-5060
Korean Southeast News, (770) 454-9655
Mundo Hispanico, (404) 881-0441
Omdoa Tribune, (404) 325-9200
Rang Dong Magazine, (770) 454-6346

Russia House Newspaper, (404) 250-9422
World Journal Chinese Daily News, (770) 451-4509

Medical Insurance

Medical insurance should be secured prior to arrival. There is no national health service.

Money

The U.S. dollar ($) is divided into 100 cents (¢). The coins are the penny worth 1¢ (copper-colored), nickel 5¢, dime 10¢, quarter 25¢, half-dollar 50¢ (all silver colored), and occasionally a silver dollar coin. The bills or notes are all one color—green—and are in denominations of one dollar, five dollars, ten dollars, twenty dollars, fifty dollars, one hundred dollars, and one thousand dollars.

Postage

Mail service is generally good, and letters can cross the country in one to three days. Zip codes must be used for guaranteed delivery. Express Mail is available. Check with the nearest post office for information on rates.

Public Holidays

The following holidays are considered legal holidays in most businesses, including government offices. Banks and businesses will not operate on these days. Some holidays are celebrated on the closest Monday to the holiday in order to give working people a long weekend. This is indicated in the listing.

January 1, New Year's Day.
January 15, Martin Luther King, Jr.'s Birthday, celebrated on closest Monday.
February 22, George Washington's Birthday, celebrated on closest Monday.
May 31, Memorial Day, celebrated on closest Monday.
July 4, Independence Day.

September, Labor Day, first Monday after first Tuesday.
October 12, Christopher Columbus Day, celebrated on closest Monday.
November 11, Veterans Day.
November, Thanksgiving Day, fourth Thursday.
December 25, Christmas.

Telephone and Telegrams

Most public pay phones require a 35¢ coin deposit, but read the instructions before inserting your coin. When calling long-distance, dial 1, the area code, then the number. Telephone numbers preceded by (800), (877), or (888) are toll-free in the United States.

To send a mailgram (guaranteed next-day delivery by mail and less expensive than a telegram), telegram, international message, or charge-card money order, call Western Union, (800) 325-6000.

Tipping and Taxes

Tipping is your way of rating and rewarding service. These general guidelines will help you adjust the size of the tip you wish to give. A 15% tip is customarily considered for restaurant service, hotel laundry and valet service, room service, bar bills, and taxi fares. Bellhops and porters generally receive $1 per bag. Atlanta counties have a 6% to 7% sales tax on merchandise and 3% on food. In addition to sales tax, there is a 7% occupancy tax on hotel and motel rooms in Atlanta and surrounding counties.

Tour Companies, Foreign Language

Atlanta Arrangements Inc., (404) 262-7660, specializes in group tours with multilingual guides.

Translators

Catholic Social Services, (404) 881-6571, provides assistance for Spanish-speaking visitors, Mon-Fri 9 am-5 pm.

Georgia State University Language Acquisition and Resource Center, (404) 651-2283. Professionals are available in German, French, Italian, and Spanish, Mon-Fri 9 am-5 pm.

Language Services, 400 Perimeter Center Terrace; (770) 939-6400. Professional translation, interpreters, foreign language instruction, and city tours are all available at Language Services.

TV Channels and Radio Stations
Broadcasting in Foreign Language ——————

Univision (cable channel 49 in Atlanta, Fulton County and DeKalb County) broadcasts entirely in Spanish. In Atlanta the language broadcast other than English will generally be Spanish because of the large and varied Hispanic population in the city. However, Access Channels 6, 9, 11 and 12 sometimes broadcast Asian shows after midnight. Various radio stations also have Spanish, or other, broadcasts. See Radio Stations under MATTERS OF FACT.

METRIC CONVERSIONS

Length

1 millimeter = .039 inch (in.)	1 inch = 2.54 cm.
1 centimeter = .39 in.	1 foot = 0.30 m.
1 meter = 3.28 feet (ft.)	1 yard = .91 m.
1 kilometer = .62 mile (mi.)	1 mile = 1.61 km.

To convert miles to kilometers, multiply the number of miles by 8 and divide by 5.

Weight	1 oz. = 28.35 g.
1 gram = .04 ounce (oz.)	1 lb. = .45 kg.
1 kilogram = 2.2 pounds (lbs.)	1 ton = .91 metric ton

Liquid

	2.11 pints (pt.)	1 pt. = .47 liter
1 liter =	1.06 quarts (qt.)	1 qt. = .95 liter
	.26 gallon (gal.)	1 gal. = 3.79 liters

Temperature

To convert Fahrenheit temperatures to Centigrade (Celsius): Take the Fahrenheit temperature, minus 32 and divide by 1.8.

CONVERSION CHARTS FOR CLOTHING

Dresses, coats, suits and blouses (Women)

British	10	12	14	16	18	20
American	8	10	12	14	16	18
Continental	40	42	44	46	48	50

Suits and overcoats (Men)

American/British	34	36	38	40	42	44
Continental	44	46	48	50	52	54

Shirts (Men)

American/British	14	14½	15	15½	16	16½	17	17½
Continental	36	37	38	39	40	41	42	43

Shoes (Men) for ½ sizes add ½ to preceding number

British	6	7	8	9	10	11
American	7	8	9	10	11	12
Continental	39½	40½	41½	42½	43½	44½

Shoes (Women) for ½ sizes add ½ to preceding number

British	3	4	5	6	7	8	9
American	4½	5½	6½	7½	8½	9½	10½
Continental	35	36	37	38	39	40	41

STUDENTS

Students visiting Atlanta will find camaraderie at the many colleges and universities in the area. Your most important document as a traveling student is your student identification card, which certifies your student status and helps stretch the travel budget. Always ask if a student discount is applicable for accommodations or transportation systems, at restaurants, theaters, cultural programs, museums, and places of entertainment. Be aware of the "Happy Hour" at bars and restaurants, when drinks are offered at half-price or discount price. Drinking age in Georgia is 21.

Lodging

Lodging in Atlanta is available for your specific travel needs. A good place to start your search is a call to the **American Youth Hostels/Georgia Council,** 223 Ponce de Leon Ave., NE, Atlanta 30308; (404) 872-8844. They provide student lodging at hostel rates. We also suggest the following accommodations for students.

Bed and Breakfast (see LODGING chapter). This gives you the opportunity to stay with a family in their home.

Cheshire Motor Inn (C4), 1865 Cheshire Bridge Rd., NE; (404) 872-9628. Moderate rates, modest and clean accommodations, and a convenient location between Midtown and Buckhead make this a good choice for students. The Colonnade restaurant next door serves plenty of good American fare. A number of fast-food places are within a block or two.

Days Inns of America (see LODGING chapter). Days Inns are on the expressway on the outskirts of the city and are reliable, clean accommodations, well-suited for individuals or a group.

Villa International, 1749 Clifton Rd., NE; (404) 633-6783. The Villa, supported by the Christian community, welcomes people from all religions, races, and political persuasions. Inexpensive rates for private room with bath; community kitchen. It's a 5-minute walk to the CDC and about 12 minutes on foot to the Emory campus. On a MARTA bus line. Since 1972 the Villa has served more than 17,000 guests from 140 different countries.

The universities have variable policies concerning short-term room rental to students. If you are interested in applying to an Atlanta area college, the admissions office will see that you are lodged on campus during your visit. Also, film, art, music, reading and lecture programs, social gatherings, and special campus events are worth checking by phone or on the bulletin boards at the student centers and administration offices. Excellent free or $1 films are shown each weekend as a starter. Student cafeterias are always a good place to meet other students over an inexpensive lunch.

Metro Colleges and Universities ————

Agnes Scott College, (C5), College Ave. at McDonough St., Decatur; (404) 371-6285, Ext. 230. Agnes Scott is a women's college, founded in 1889, with an outstanding annual series "The Arts at Agnes Scott," special festivals and symposiums, a student theater, and art exhibits and film series.

Atlanta University Center, (D3), 111 James P. Brawley Dr., SW; (404) 522-8980. A.U. is the oldest and largest consortium of black colleges in the country, and offers a wide variety of lectures, exhibits, and programs.

Clark Atlanta University, (D3), James P. Brawley Dr., SW, and Fair St.; (404) 880-8000. One of the Atlanta University Center colleges, Clark Atlanta is known particularly for its communications program and its sponsorship of WCLK, Atlanta's premiere jazz radio station.

Columbia Theological Seminary, (D5), 701 Columbia Dr., Decatur; (404) 378-8821. Founded in 1828 and affiliated with the Presbyterian Church (USA), Columbia offers basic and advanced degrees to train persons for leadership in the church.

Emory University, (C4), 1380 S. Oxford Rd., NE; (404) 727-6123. Emory is located near Decatur, has a Methodist affiliation, funding from the Coca-Cola company, and an excellent reputation for all its art, film, music, and cultural programs.

Georgia Institute of Technology, (H9), 225 North Ave., NW; (404) 894-2000. This renowned technical school in downtown Atlanta offers exciting college football; a superb student-run radio station, WREK-FM; and a mixture of public programs in the sciences, arts, and film.

Georgia State University, (K9), 129 Sparks Hall, University Plaza, SE; (404) 651-2000. Georgia State is Atlanta's large public university in the heart of Downtown, with a continuous schedule of film series, art exhibits of national caliber, musical programs, readings, and lectures.

Interdenominational Theological Seminary, (D3), 700 Martin Luther King Jr. Dr., SW; (404) 527-7700. This respected seminary, one of the learning institutions that make up Atlanta University Center, attracts an international roster of students to its religious programs.

Morehouse College, (D3), 830 Westview Dr., SW; (404) 681-2800. Often called the "black Harvard," this Atlanta University Center college has a list of prestigious graduates that includes the late Dr. Martin Luther King, Jr., as well as movie maker Spike Lee. There is great pride associated with being a Morehouse man.

Morehouse School of Medicine, (D3), 720 Westview Dr., SW; (404) 752-1500. Although quite young as medical schools go—it was begun in the mid 1980s—Morehouse Medical School enjoys a considerable reputation and regard. Its first president, Dr. Louis Sullivan, was named President George Bush's Secretary of Health. This is the most recent addition to the Atlanta University Center's higher learning institutions.

Morris Brown College, (D3), 643 Martin Luther King, Jr. Dr., NW; (404) 220-0270. Morris Brown, another of the Atlanta University schools, is known especially for its hospitality/hotel management program.

Oglethorpe University, (B4), 4484 Peachtree Rd., NW; (404) 261-1441. North of the city in Chamblee, this small liberal-arts college hosts the Georgia Shakespeare Festival each summer. The school's University College allows working students to pursue their degree via evening classes.

Spelman College, (D3), 350 Spelman Lane, SW; (404) 681-3643. If Morehouse College is a "black Harvard," then surely Spelman is a black Radcliffe. This fine institution has been educating black women since the 1880s. Recently, it has received substantial endowments from the family of actor/comedian Bill Cosby. The college draws top black female high school graduates from all over the country.

CHILDREN

Visiting children will enjoy the many sights described in this guide. Places children enjoy without question are the Fernbank Science Center, Six Flags over Georgia, the Wren's Nest, the Zoo and Cyclorama, the High Museum's children's exhibit, Stone Mountain, the captivating Children's Garden at the Atlanta Botanical Garden, and the Center for Puppetry Arts. You can't go wrong with these kid-pleasing winners. See the SIGHTS chapter for details.

During the year Atlanta has special treats for young people. **Children's Theater** at the Alliance Theatre has a wonderful production. The Atlanta Symphony orchestra performs several young-people's concerts during the year, and the summer outdoor pops series at the Chastain Park amphitheater is a charmer. During the Christmas season, the Atlanta Ballet presents *The Nutcracker* each year.

The public library downtown has a special reading room for children, with soft-sculpture chairs and a carpeted conversation pit for "down-to-earth" storytime. The High Museum of Art has a standing children's exhibit to heighten their visual awareness of the world around them. And playgrounds are available through the Atlanta Parks Department or the recreation departments of suburban counties.

Children can also have a fine time just seeing the city from different perspectives, from the MARTA train as it passes over the downtown cityscape, from the outside elevators zooming up the Westin Peachtree Plaza Hotel, and from the interior bubble elevators of the Hyatt Regency Hotel.

SENIOR CITIZENS

The older traveler is recognized as an integral part of the large traveling population in the United States and abroad. Travel agencies nationwide focus many of their travel promotions and group trips on

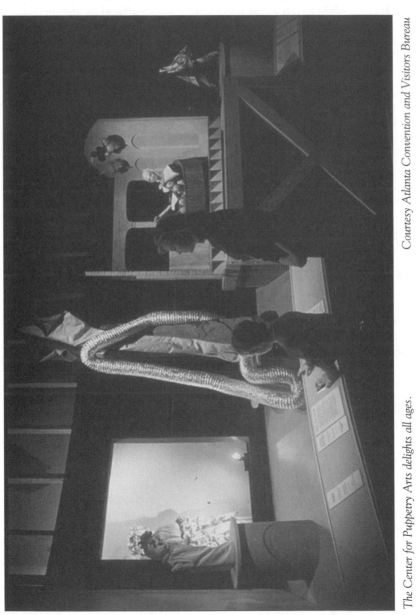

The Center for Puppetry Arts delights all ages.

Courtesy Atlanta Convention and Visitors Bureau

the interests of the mature traveler, interests that range from fixed-income capabilities to comfortable transportation and accommodations, from available medical facilities to theme tours and social life. These are the same concerns of the older person who is visiting Atlanta.

Discounts for Travel, Events, and Lodging

Most major airlines in Atlanta offer special rates for senior citizens, with discounts as high as one-third of the regular rate. AMTRAK allows 15% off its regular fares for senior citizens, and Greyhound bus service is discounted 10% for bus-traveling senior citizens who join their Seniors Club for $5 a year. Public transportation within the city on MARTA is half-fare.

Special discounts for senior citizens are available frequently for sports events, concerts, tours of homes, theaters, and other attractions. Ask the box office about senior citizen rates or call Atlanta's central ticketing organization, Ticketmaster, (404) 249-8300.

Also check the public libraries and arts centers of Atlanta for ongoing cultural programs for older persons.

Many restaurants, cafeterias and fast-food outlets offer senior citizen discounts on meals. Some hotels and motels offer a lower rate for senior citizens, so inquiries should always be made at the reservations office. A recommended accommodation in Atlanta for older travelers is the Bed-and-Breakfast program listed in LODGING. Staying with an Atlanta family can create a comfortably paced visit and a personable introduction to this energetic city.

Special Organizations

Two organizations in Atlanta are helpful to the older person as expansive referral sources. The **American Association of Retired Persons** is a nongovernmental, nonpartisan, and nonprofit national organization for men and women 55 years of age or older, whether employed or not employed. The nominal annual membership fee entitles AARP members to numerous benefits, which include 10-25% discount rates at participating hotels and motels and discounts at several car rental agencies. For more information on the AARP and its 25 chapters in metro Atlanta call (404) 888-0077 or write AARP, 999 Peachtree St., Suite 1650, Atlanta 30309.

The second organization which offers 11 operational components is the **Senior Citizen Services of Metropolitan Atlanta,** a private non-profit agency and member of the United Way. Although this agency is primarily designed for the needs of older Atlanta residents and new-comers, it serves as an invaluable information pool for older travelers in Atlanta. The Senior Center (H11) is located at 1705 Commerce Dr., NW, Atlanta, GA 30309. Call them at (404) 351-3889.

DISABLED PERSONS

More and more disabled persons are on the move for both business and pleasure. The wheelchair, the laser cane and sonic glasses for the blind, and the network of dialysis centers, combined with public sup-port and awareness and accommodations mandated through the Americans with Disabilities Act (ADA) 1990, have opened new path-ways of travel and visitation for the disabled.

Accessibility and Discounts ─────────────

The key advice to the disabled person is always call ahead to check accessibility at your place of destination. Be specific about your needs. This will reassure you of the features of each particular hotel, restau-rant, center, theater, or other establishment.

The Atlanta airport was designed for complete accessibility with ramps, special elevators, rest rooms, and parking lots clearly marked with the international logo for the disabled person. The city bus and rapid transit system is also designed for wheelchair riders. "Lift" buses that assist wheelchair riders to and from work are on fixed routes and on fixed schedules. A minimum of four riders is required by MARTA to establish a fixed route. Call MARTA at (404) 848-5389 for detailed information. MARTA trains have wheelchair parking, and ticket gates at all MARTA rail stations have wheelchair accessibility. MARTA fares are reduced 50% for the handicapped.

Lodging for the disabled traveler continues to improve. The down-town Atlanta Hilton has 144 guest rooms fully equipped for the handi-capped, and it has easy front entry and a ramped coffee shop. Some of the other hotels and motels providing facilities include Days Inns, Holiday Inns, Ramada Inns, the Marriotts, Sheraton Hotels, Terrace Garden Inns, Omni, and Hyatt Regency. See the LODGING chapter and again, call ahead about your specific requirements. Days Inns and Holiday Inns, with handicap-coded guidebooks to all their inns, are setting an excellent precedent for all hotel and motel chains. These guidebooks are valuable references especially to the disabled person who travels frequently.

When attending a concert or theater function at the Robert W. Woodruff Arts Center, the Fox Theatre, Civic Center, Philips Arena, or Turner Field, call ahead for arrangements. Special rows are available for wheelchairs. Stone Mountain is accessible including a refreshing steamboat ride on the lake. Six Flags provides assistants for wheelchairs. For special admission rates for the disabled call Special Audiences at (404) 221-2537 and Ticketmaster at (404) 249-8300.

Services for the Visually Impaired ────────

The **Center for the Visually Impaired** (H11), 763 Peachtree St., NE; (404) 875-9011, has extensive information for the visually impaired traveler or newcomer to Atlanta. At the same location is a museum of touch. The High Museum and Fernbank Science Center also offer touch programs. Another helpful agency for the visually impaired is the **American Foundation for the Blind** (404) 525-2303. Call your restaurant for the availability of braille menus. Atlanta law allows you to take your seeing-eye dog into restaurants and food establishments.

The **Georgia Radio Reading Service** (C3), 260 14th Street, NW, (404) 685-2820, consists of reading current newspapers, periodicals, and best-sellers to the blind through a special receiver and cable TV. Some hospitals also have receivers. There are nearly 100 such reading services nationwide. Applications for the receiver can be made at the Library for the Blind, (404) 756-4619.

The **Georgia Library for the Blind and Physically Handicapped** (D3), 1150 Murphy Ave., SW, (404) 756-4619, has 13 subregional free-lending libraries. Cassette players, tapes, talking-book machines, books-on-records from the Library of Congress, magazines-on-records, and cassettes, excerpts from the daily *New York Times*, and *Atlanta Magazine*, as well as large-print books are all available free of charge to certified applicants.

Dialysis Centers ────────────────────

Atlanta has a number of dialysis centers in the metro area. Travelers who need dialysis while in the city must contact their home nurse or social worker to plan their Atlanta itinerary and dialysis schedule before arrival.

State Park ──────────────────────────

For a day's excursion from Atlanta or for an overnight stay in a natural area, fully equipped for the disabled person, visit **Fort Yargo State**

Park, Winder, GA 30680. The Will-away Recreational Center within the park offers picnic tables, two beaches, boat rentals, fishing, and cottage accommodations. The park is about an hour from Atlanta, northeast on I-85 to Hwy 316 into Winder. Turn left onto Hwy 81 and go 3 miles to the park. Call (770) 867-6123. This is a beautiful and comfortable site.

Lastly we recommend the **Easter Seals of North Georgia** office as a central clearinghouse for information concerning any disabled person. Call (404) 633-9609.

For wheelchair repairs consult the following:

Georgia Wheelchairs (C4), 1754 Tullie Circle; (404) 350-0265. Call to schedule an appointment.

Atlanta Orthotics, Inc. (I10), 1789 Peachtree St.; (404) 876-5832.

BITS AND PIECES

Atlanta has its legends that emerge out of oral history, storytelling, and an enthusiasm for a living tradition. Atlanta's own 19th-century author, Joel Chandler Harris, produced the Uncle Remus tales that were told to him by America's first Africans, enriching man's brotherly bond with the animal world. Remember Brer Fox and Brer Rabbit? But Atlanta continues to evolve.

Did you know that. . . .

—Atlanta is 1,010 feet (308 meters) above sea level, the highest elevation of any U.S. city east of the Mississippi River.

—Atlanta is the capital of Georgia, one of the 13 original colonies, and the sixth largest state in the nation.

—"The City of Trees" is a description often applied to Atlanta, which was once designated a "city in a forest" by the U.S. Forestry Service.

—Georgia is the Peach State officially, and beautiful young women are called Georgia Peaches, although Georgia's major agricultural crop is peanuts.

—The Cherokee rose is Georgia's state flower, a pale, flat climbing rose named after one of the large Indian nations from North Georgia.

—Georgia is a leader in the production of honeybees. The South Georgia land near the Okefenokee Swamp is a natural breeding ground for the bees, which are exported all over, from Florida to Minnesota, for pollinating flowering trees and plants.

—The fashionable north side of Buckhead took its name from a tavern where a buck's head was mounted, a vestige of wildlife since departed to the Chattahoochee National Forest.

—The Chattahoochee River in metro Atlanta means "flowering stone" in the Creek language, an apt description for nearby Atlanta, a blooming, durable civilization.

—The oldest building in Atlanta is the Freight Depot, built in 1869, which is located in Underground Atlanta.

—Atlanta's Grant Park was not named for Ulysses S. Grant, but for a Confederate colonel Lemuel P. Grant. Colonel Grant designed the fortifications for the city during the Battle of Atlanta and gave the land to the city.

—The Carillon at Stone Mountain Park is the largest electronic carillon in the world. The original carillon, a gift from the Coca-Cola Company after the 1964 World's Fair, had 610 bells. Stone Mountain has added 122 bells to make the carillon the largest of its kind with 732 bells.

—None of the famous movie *Gone with the Wind* was filmed in Georgia, so a local historian took two bushels of Georgia red clay to the Hollywood studio to sprinkle over the set, and so made it authentic.

—They say that Coca-Cola has made a thousand millionaires in Atlanta. The world-renowned beverage was invented by Atlanta druggist John Pemberton as a headache cure and first dispensed in 1886 in a downtown Atlanta drugstore.

—The CNN Center was the first land development project of its kind because no land changed hands: The CNN Center City Corporation has a 99-year-lease of the *air* over the railroad bed owned by Southern Railway.

—All the trees in the CNN Center and the Georgia World Congress Center are planted in artificial soil because real soil weighed too much to be supported on the steel-enforced concrete pillars on which the two complexes are built.

—Atlanta University was first housed in a railroad car.

—The Fox Theatre was originally built as a Shriners' temple, but when the Depression hit they were unable to finish it, so it was sold to William Fox, the movie mogul, who turned it into a theater.

—The Centers for Disease Control (CDC) has been located in Atlanta since its conception during World War II. Many experiments were conducted in the Georgia swamplands because their topography and climate were similar to the Pacific Islands, and so the laboratories were located in Atlanta.

—Visitors flying in and out of Atlanta's busy airport for years have complained that, "Whether you go to Heaven or Hell when you die, you will have to change planes in Atlanta."

—Emory University is often referred to as "Coca-Cola U" because of the generosity of the Candler and Woodruff families, closely identified with Coca-Cola.

—The *Atlanta Daily World* is the oldest black-owned newspaper in the United States.

—The highest ground in Atlanta is at the Piedmont Plateau in front of downtown Macy's on famous Peachtree Street between Ellis and International Boulevard. This point is a signal watershed where the water runs west toward the Pacific and east to the Atlantic Ocean.

—Atlanta is the Dogwood City, where a snowstorm of white and pink dogwood blossoms festoons streets and lawns during springtime. There is also a special legend of the dogwood. The dogwood was the tree whose wood was chosen for the cross of Christ. The tree was so distressed that this was to be its appointed mission, that Christ promised that never again should a dogwood tree grow large enough to produce a cross. It would be slender and gnarled, and its blossoms form a cross, with two long and two short petals. At the outer edge of each petal would be nail prints, stained rust brown and red for Christ's blood, and in the center of the flower a crown of thorns.

—And, of course, Atlanta's main street is named after a tree and honors a fruit tree with its Peachtree Street. There are more than 30 variants and versions of Peachtree—Peachtree Road, Peachtree Street, Peachtree Industrial Boulevard, Peachtree Circle, West Peachtree, Peachtree Crossing, Peachtree Lane, and others. The name first came from the Indian village Standing Peachtree and later was transferred to the government's Fort Standing Peachtree. Why the peach tree? One folktale suggests a huge peach tree on the site. Another suggests a misinterpretation of the Creek word for "pitch." This later interpretation states that a huge pine tree on the site was blazed by the Indians for the pine resin which was used in waterproofing their canoes. In either case, Atlanta is webbed with the many strands of Peachtree streets.

"We've raised a brave and beautiful city."
Henry Grady

INDEX

A

AAA, 27
Academic Life, 22
Aircraft Rental and
    Charter, 33
Airlines, 32
Airport, 31
Ambulance Service, 27
Antiques, 131
Area Codes, 27
Art Supplies, 135
Associations, 212
Atlanta Past, 15
Atlanta Today, 19
Atlantans, 25
Auburn Avenue, 194
Auto Insurance, 209
Auto Registration, 209
Auto Rental, 34

B

Babysitters, 27
Bakeries, 144
Bank Hours, 240
Banking, 210

Battle of Atlanta, 16
Bicycling, 160
Books, 135
Bowling, 161
Brunch, 87
Buckhead Neighborhoods,
    226
Bus, 34

C

Calendar of Events, 27
Caterers, 232
CD's, 136
Centennial Olympic Park,
    107, 189
Chambers of Commerce,
    210
Cherokee County
    Communities, 228
Children, 249
Children's Clothing
    Outlets, 142
Churches, 211
City Streets, 35
Civil War, 16
Climate, 25, 27

Clothing, 137, 138, 139, 141, 142
Clubs, 212
Cobb Community Transit, 36
Cobb County Communities, 227
Coffee or tea, 89
Coins and Stamps, 139
College Football, 157
Colleges and Universities, 247
Congressional Districts, 215
Consulates, 237
Conversion Charts For Clothing, 246
Crafts, 140
Cultural Clusters, 24
Currency Exchange, 240
Customs Allowances, 241

D

Dance, 92
DeKalb County Communities, 228
Dentist, 27
Dialysis Centers, 253
Disabilities, 252
Disabled Persons, 252
Discount Stores, 141
Doctor, 27
Driver's Licenses, 209
Driving In The United States, 241

E

Education, 213
Electricity, 242
Emergency Rooms, 27
Emission Control Inspection, 210
Ethnic Societies, 239
Excursions, 199

F

Fabrics, 143
Factory Outlets, 141
Film, 103
Fire, 27
Flea Markets, 143
Florists, 144
Food, 144
Foreign Auto Service, 28
Forsyth County, 230
Furniture Makers, 148

G

Ga, 400, 33
Galleries, 122
Geographical Profile, 208
Gift Shops, 149
Golf, 159, 161
Gone With The Wind, 114, 116, 256
Gourmet Foods, 146
Government, 22, 214, 215
Gwinnett, 230

H

Health Care, 215
Health Clubs, 162
Health Food Stores, 145
Hiking, 163
Holidays, 243
Home and Garden
  Shopping Needs, 231
Home Decorating, 217
Home Interiors, 150
Horseback Riding, 164
Hospitals, 28

I

Ice Skating, 164
International Banking, 240
International Visitors, 236
Interstate Highways, 33
Intown Neighborhoods,
  224

J

Jewelry, 152
Jury Duty, 218

K

Krispy Kreme, 90

L

Lake Lanier Communities,
  230

Laws, 28, 218
Leather, 153
Legal Aid, 28
Legal Services, 218
Libraries, 28, 107, 218
Linens, 143

M

Major Leagues, 159
Margaret Mitchell House,
  114
Markets, 147
MARTA, 25, 36
MARTA Bus and Rail, 28,
  33
Martin Luther King, Jr.
  Historic District, 114,
  194, 196
Medical Insurance, 243
Mental Health Services,
  27
Metric Conversions, 245
Money, 243
Motor Racing, 159
Museums, 120
Music, 93

N

Native American origins,
  15
Neighborhood Profiles,
  224
New Residents, 207

New South, 17
Newspapers, 28, 219, 242
Nightlife, 99
North Fulton County,
    228

O

Office Supplies, 153

P

Pandas, 119
Party, 232
Peachtree Road Race,
    178
Peachtree Street, 257
Performing Arts, 92
Periodicals, 219
Pets, 28
Pharmacy, 24-Hour, 28
Photographic Supplies,
    153
Planetarium, 110
Poison Control, 28
Police, 28
Polo, 171
Population, 28
Post office, 28
Postage, 243
Private Schools, 214
Public Schools, 213
Public Services, 220
Public Transportation, 36

R

Racquetball, 165
Radio Stations, 28
Real Estate, 222
Restaurants, 63
Rifle Ranges, 165
Roller-Skating, 165
Rugby, 172
Running, 165

S

Senior Citizen Discounts,
    251
Senior Citizens, 30, 249,
    252
Shoes, 142, 154
Shopping Districts, 127
Sights, 105
Skiing, 171
Skin Care, 155
Soccer, 172
Social Services, 30
Softball, 172
South Metro Atlanta
    Communities, 229
Special Events, 174
Sports Car Rallies, 172
Sports Equipment, 155
Sports To Do, 160
Sports To See, 157
State Park, 253
State Patrol, 30
Stone Mountain, 111

Students, 246
Studios, 126
Synagogues, 211

T

Tapes, 136
Taxes, 221
Taxicabs, 38
Team Sports, 171
Telegrams, 244
Telephone, 244
Temples, 211
Tennis, 160, 166
Theater, 95
Tickets, 30
Time, 30
Tipping, 244
Tour Companies, Foreign
  Language, 244
Tourist Information, 30
Tours, 39, 183, 190
Toys, 156
Trade and Tourism offices,
  237
Train, 34

Translators, 244
Transportation, 31
Traveler's Aid, 30
TV, 30
TV Channels, 245

V

Visual Arts, 120
Visually Impaired, 253
Volunteering, 221
Voter Registration, 222

W

Walking, 39, 163
Water Sports, 167
Weather, 30
Welcome Services, 207
Wheelchair Accessibility,
  252

Z

Zoo Atlanta, 119